19/09/2016 | EAS

D1357369

C016166108

THE SCAPEGOAT

THE SCAPEGOAT

The life and tragedy of a fighting admiral and Churchill's role in his death

Steve R. Dunn

Book Guild Publishing
Sussex, England

First published in Great Britain in 2014 by
The Book Guild Ltd
The Werks
45 Church Road
Hove BN3 2BE

Copyright © Steve R. Dunn 2014

The right of Steve R. Dunn to be identified as the author of
this work has been asserted by him in accordance with the
Copyright, Designs and Patents Act 1988.

All rights reserved. No part of this publication may be reproduced, transmitted, or stored in a
retrieval system, in any form or by any means, without permission in writing from the publisher,
nor be otherwise circulated in any form of binding or cover other than that in which it is published
and without a similar condition being imposed on the subsequent purchaser.

Typesetting in Garamond by
YHT Ltd, London

Printed and bound in Great Britain by
CPI Group (UK) Ltd, Croydon, CR0 4YY

A catalogue record for this book is available from
The British Library.

ISBN 978 1 84624 971 6

This book is dedicated to Vivienne and Emily, without whom it would not have come to fruition.

Nec Temere, Nec Timide
(Neither rash nor timid)
Cradock family motto

He [the hero] must be, to use a rather weathered phrase, a man of honour – by instinct, by inevitability, without thought of it, and certainly without saying it. He must be the best man in the world and a good enough man for any world. I do not care much about his private life; he is neither a eunuch nor a satyr; I think he might seduce a duchess and I am quite sure he would not spoil a virgin; if he is a man of honour in one thing he is that in all things

(Raymond Chandler, *The Simple Art of Murder*,
originally written 1944; published Hamish Hamilton 1950)

Contents

Preface

On 1 November 1914 one man condemned 1660 other men, and himself, to death. He chose to fight an unwinnable battle against overwhelming odds. His name was Christopher Cradock and he was a Rear Admiral in the British navy. His defeat was the worst British naval loss in a century.

It is not unusual for generals to send men to certain death – in the First World War this was almost an act of policy; but the red tabbed generals did it from safely behind the front, sitting in luxurious chateaux and sipping tea or wine. Comparatively few two- or three-star generals were killed in that war. Cradock sailed and fought with the men he condemned and died with them. What is more, I believe that he knew the cause was hopeless and he would perish in the attempt; but still he acted. With a scrapyard fleet, against a superior enemy and with no apparent hope of relief, he went to war.

His final battle – the Battle of Coronel – is well known to anyone with an interest in naval history and is covered in all the standard texts, but the emphasis is always placed on the retribution wrought by a second, avenging British fleet, rather than Cradock's lonely death in the darkness of a South American evening. This embarrassing loss is quickly dealt with, to get to the greater glory of victory, and Cradock is a fleeting, silent figure in the archives – little seems to be known of him and the impulse that drove him to that tumult in the ocean.

I first met Kit Cradock in a second-hand bookshop in Cambridge in around 1990. I was going through my second divorce, seeking solace in a good book and an equally good claret. Kit was lying in wait for me, hiding in Geoffrey Bennett's *Naval Battles of the First World War*. This book is as good a review of the war at sea as you will find today, despite being of 1968 vintage, and Bennett's descriptions of Cradock's travails in this and his *Coronel and the Falklands* of 1962 remain the definitive accounts of the battle. But Kit is an elusive figure in these books; there is no attempt to describe or define the man who could act so boldly, or stupidly, and why. He began to intrigue me. I wanted to understand him.

As I pursued Cradock through the records I found a fascination for the Victorian and Edwardian navies growing in me. Today the world is united in the belief that strategy and tactics, leadership and decision making, are critical, but these qualities seemed to be sadly lacking in the military (and political) leadership of those times. Particularly at sea, the public's expectations for some new Trafalgar were repeatedly dashed as the German commanders realised the value of a 'fleet in being' to tie up enemy resources, rather than seeking a definitive battle that they could well lose, as did the Italian admirals later, in the second global conflict.

On land and at sea the First World War was fought with recognisably modern weapons, often unchanged in all but trivial details from then till now. But the quality of strategic thinking was lamentable and the politicians were lost in the mayhem they had unleashed. The leaders had all grown up in the Victorian world – a world of Empire and economic hegemony – and they could not help being the products of that age with its arrogance and rigidity of thought. I came to appreciate the difficulties such a system and such technological advances created for commanders.

Guns now fired at ranges beyond the ability of the eye to see. The 12-inch guns of HMS *Inflexible*, to be met later in this book, ranged 16,400 yards (9.3 miles). The 15-inch guns of the Queen Elizabeth fast battleships that would feature at Jutland ranged over 13 miles. That's the distance from Heathrow to Kensington (or for any American readers who have wandered in, from Central Park South to La Guardia). And yet radar was non-existent (it wouldn't be invented until 1937). Gunnery sighting and aiming technology was at best primitive and had been resisted until around 1910. Director firing (all guns controlled from a central location) was in its infancy at the start of the war. Radio was primitive and prone to failure – it also gave away one's position to the enemy. The human eyeball and the ability to out-think an opponent were the main tactical tools.

Consider Jellicoe at Jutland in May 1916. Standing on the deck of HMS *Iron Duke* he had to decide how to deploy his main battle fleet; get it wrong and he could lose the war for Britain. He alone had to take the decision – that was the form. He had no sophisticated technology to help him. In essence he had the same tools as Nelson had, except that Nelson closed the enemy at about 3–5 knots. The British and German main battle fleets were converging at a combined speed of 40 knots, and Jellicoe needed to deploy from cruising formation to a line of battle and cross the enemies 'T' – pouring his full gun power into the van of the enemy. A wrong decision would put his fleet on the receiving end instead. He had been given no useful (indeed erroneous) information by Beatty, commanding his battlecruisers; his cruisers, the eyes of his fleet had let him down; the Admiralty had not been able to provide any meaningful assistance; he was on his own. Eventually he gave the order 'equal speed Charlie London' and the fleet deployed. He didn't smash the enemy, but he called the order correctly, for the other options open to him proved in retrospect to have been less good or positively bad.

As with Jellicoe, so with Cradock. Alone with his small squadron in the wastes of the Pacific and Atlantic oceans, he had only his experience, his background and learning, and his instincts to go on. As with Jellicoe the Admiralty proved a positive nuisance. In every book that has covered the Cradock's battle the accounts have never changed. Most are based on Bennett's analysis, none brings new insights. Cradock remains silent and shadowy, condemned (as by Churchill) or lauded (as in propaganda) but never understood.

Eventually everything comes down to the man on the spot, the man in the ring. Today we push buttons, tap keys, run algorithms and the answer is presented to us. The characters in this book did not have that option. They summoned up their experiences, beliefs and inner codes, and acted as they saw fit. Cradock was one such man and this book is an attempt to understand him better. I have tried to right the wrong and give Cradock, and the 1660 men who died with him, a better memorial. I am not a naval officer or a professional historian, but I have spent a lifetime involved in leadership and strategy and their consequences – it is this that led to my fascination with this one dreadful battle.

This is not a naval history. It is not a dry and exact recitation of dates and events; but it is the story of a time, an ethos, a mind-set and a group of human beings thrown into circumstances they could not fully understand or control. Cradock left little in the way of autobiographical material. Unlike his contemporaries – Jellicoe, Beatty, Keyes, for example – he did not leave voluminous files of papers and letters for scholars to pore over. His time was cut short before he had the chance to write his *Apologia Pro Vita Sua*. The biographer is forced to uncover previously unexamined texts, and to rely to an extent on secondary sources, oral tradition and the newspapers and magazines of the period. The British Library, Houses of Parliament Archives and National Archives hold whispers of the man, as do the descendants of his sister. And, of course, the age and navy in which he lived and served were important influences on him, his character and his behaviour. In understanding the mores and culture of the time we can go a long way to understanding Cradock. Occasionally I have had to include speculation, but the story is mostly based on facts and their interpretation.

Some Dramatis Personae and their Posts, 1 September 1914

William Allardyce; Governor of the Falkland Islands
H.H. Asquith; Prime Minister of the United Kingdom
A.J. Balfour; Conservative MP and ex-Prime Minister
Prince Louis von Battenberg; First Sea Lord
Vice Admiral David Beatty; commanding battlecruiser squadron
Lord Charles Beresford; retired Admiral and MP (Charlie B)
Admiral Archibald Berkley-Milne; commanding Mediterranean fleet
Captain Frank Brandt; Captain HMS *Monmouth*
Admiral Sir Francis Bridgeman; retired First Sea Lord
Rt. Hon. Winston Churchill; First Lord of the Admiralty
Rear Admiral Sir Christopher Cradock; commanding 4th Cruiser Squadron
Major Sheldon Cradock; brother of Christopher Cradock
Lt Colonel Montagu Cradock; brother of Christopher Cradock
Admiral of the Fleet Lord John Fisher; retired First Sea Lord
William Charles de Meuron Wentworth Fitzwilliam, 7th Earl Fitzwilliam (Billy Fitzbilly)
Captain Phillip Francklin; Captain HMS *Good Hope*
Captain Heathcote Salusbury Grant; Captain HMS *Canopus*
Admiral Sir John Jellicoe; commanding British Grand Fleet
Vice Admiral Martin Jerram; commanding China station
Commodore Roger Keyes; commanding Harwich force
Captain John Luce; Captain HMS *Glasgow*
Admiral Hedworth Meux; Commander in Chief, Portsmouth
Rear Admiral Sir George Edwin Patey; commanding Australia station
Vice Admiral Maximilian Graf von Spee; commanding German East Asiatic Squadron
Rear Admiral A.P. Stoddart; commanding 5th Cruiser Squadron
Vice Admiral Doveton Sturdee; Chief of Staff, Admiralty
Rear Admiral Ernest Troubridge; commanding 1st cruiser squadron, Mediterranean fleet
Vice Admiral Sir George Warrender; commanding 2nd Battle Squadron, Grand Fleet

1

Armageddon: HMS Glasgow, *1 November 1914, 1950 hrs*

The column of flame rose over 200 feet into the night sky. It was a bright-yellow, sulphurous flame thick with dark smoke. A roaring, explosive noise followed, sweeping over the exposed decks of the *Glasgow*. From the bridge Captain John Luce, far from his home in Halcombe St Mary, saw the funnels of the old cruiser fly up into the air. A shell had clearly penetrated her magazine. He knew that the ship was finished; such a blow was mortal. As his vision regained its hold on the night Luce realised that HMS *Good Hope*, the flagship of Rear Admiral Sir Christopher Cradock, KCVO, CB, and of the squadron in which Luce was sailing, was destroyed.

In fact, in the 20 minutes since action had been joined, the flagship had been hit by at least 35 shells from SMS *Scharnhorst*, mostly of 21-cm (8.2-inch) calibre and each containing over 380 pounds of explosive. J.D. Stephenson, a sick berth steward on the *Glasgow* thought that 'firing at her [the *Good Hope*] was merely target practice' and could see the ship being struck by 'shell after shell whilst only firing one or two guns in return'.[1]

The three-ship British squadron was now down to two and its second most powerful vessel, HMS *Monmouth*, was in obvious trouble. Already holed, down by the head and with a fire in the forecastle, she was now taking the full weight of the two German heavy ships' fire whilst the smaller ships on the German side were left to engage *Glasgow*. A heavy sea was running and *Monmouth* told Luce she was taking water forward and was trying to turn her stern

1

to the tide. Luce signalled her captain asking could she steer a course away and that the enemy were astern of him, but he received no further response.

By this time, *Monmouth* was in a sinking condition, her engines largely disabled. Captain Frank Brandt, Indian born and lifelong navy man, a torpedo and submarine specialist, was making one last attempt to get into a torpedo firing position before his ship died. Drifting and powerless, at 2120 she was attacked by SMS *Nurnberg*, newly arrived on the scene, and hit by no fewer than seventy-five 10.5-cm (4.1-inch) shells at close range. She sank – a blasted, fiery carcass.

Luce was in serious trouble. Although he had landed a 6-inch shell on the *Gneisenau*, he was now engaged with all three enemy vessels. His ship was holed in the side and part of the deck was collapsing, held up by a damage control party with props. A shell exploded in his cabin, destroying it; another just missed an engine room steam pipe. Two shells landed in the coal bunkers, but as these were full did little harm, and another had hit the number two funnel.[2] Furthermore, his ship was not designed for line of battle engagement; its planned role was scouting, protection of trade and showing the flag in far stations, and his crew, like the rest of the British navy (and unlike the Germans), was not trained in night gunnery. Under a rising moon Luce turned away and made full speed on a course for safety.

As the smoke of sea war cleared, the moon revealed an empty ocean, defaced only by the debris and human flotsam of sunken ships. The two largest Allied units in the southern Pacific and Antarctic oceans had been sunk. Vice Admiral Maximilian Graf von Spee, in command of the German squadron, was the undisputed master of the waves under which Rear Admiral Sir Christopher Cradock and 1660 British officers and men now lay.

Luce lived to tell the tale. *Glasgow* had been hit five times, three of which were duds. She suffered no casualties but did lose the majority of the fifty parrots, pets of the crew, which had been released prior to the battle but refused to leave the ship.

In his report to the Admiralty Luce commended the spirit of his men and their discipline under fire, and expressed their unanimous wish to meet the enemy again. Both he and the *Glasgow* survived the war and he achieved flag rank. His son, also John David, became the first submariner to be appointed First Sea Lord in 1963. Luce lived out his final days in Wiltshire and is commemorated by a memorial in Malmesbury Abbey; but he never forgot the slaughter off the coast of Coronel.

2

Yorkshire, 1720–1874

Christopher George Francis Maurice (Kit) Cradock was born at
Hartforth Hall (near Richmond) in Yorkshire on 2 July 1862. The
American civil war was raging. The first battle between ironclad
warships took place. Lord Palmerston was British prime minister.
Queen Victoria had been on the throne for 25 years and would
continue to reign for 39 more.

Kit Cradock's mother, Georgina Jane Abercromby Duff, was the
daughter of a soldier, Major Gordon Duff of the 92nd Highlanders.
His father, also Christopher, was a member of the minor gentry, a
landowner with tenants and a home farm on which were bred short-
horn cattle, one of the 7000 or so aristocrats or landed gentry who
owned eighty per cent of the British Isles. Generations of Cradocks
had farmed the Hartforth estate since 1720 when Kit's great-great-
great grandfather, William Cradock, purchased it from the local
Wharton family for £1200. William was descended from a lineage
which could trace its origins back to Kirby Stephen, now in Cum-
bria, at the time of Edward I. He was a direct descendant of John
Cradock, Chancellor to the Bishop of Durham, who died in 1627, is
buried in Durham cathedral and was reputedly poisoned by his wife.
John had been Vicar of Gainford, some 11 miles from Hartforth,
and built Gainford Hall as his home.

The purchase of Hartforth included the pre-existing house, and
William lived there with his wife Mary (nee Sheldon) until his death
in 1726. Sheldon, his eldest son, inherited the estate but after he
married Elizabeth in 1739 fire destroyed the property. He immediately set about building a new one in the fashionable Palladian

style, assisted by an architect called Garrett, and it must have been finished around 1744 as there is a lead gutter-head with that date still extant. In the meantime Sheldon had remarried, to Sarah, after the death of his first wife in 1742 and the name of Sheldon became a Cradock baptismal name for five generations.

In 1792 Kit's great-grandfather, another Sheldon, called in the well-known architect John Carr of York to extend the hall and redecorate the rooms, installing ornate plaster friezes and a lush black and gold colour scheme to some of the principal chambers. Carr had been working on nearby Aske Hall, seat of the Marquess of Zetland, Lawrence Dundas, since 1783. Subsequently Kit's father built a water tower and an orangery in 1850 (both very *à la mode* for the time) and an aesthetically disastrous portico was added in 1900 by Kit's brother Sheldon.

Hartforth Hall still exists. It is a large, plain, Georgian box with little ornamentation bar some roof finials and a pediment to the garden front, sitting in the river valley. Its large plate windows stare out over uninterrupted views of fields and trees, the little river Gilling running through the grounds. Even today it is quiet, peaceful, calm, and timeless.

The Cradock fortune reached its apogee with Kit's grandfather, another Sheldon (1777–1852). Educated at Manchester Grammar School and Trinity College Cambridge, he inherited Hartforth and his mother's estates at Thorpe-on-Tees in 1814. A wealthy man, he never married but lived with his mistress, Jane Wilson, by whom he had eight children. He served in the North Yorkshire militia, rising to the rank of colonel by 1820, and in 1822 was returned to the rotten borough of Camelford in Cornwall as one of three constituency MPs. The nomination was in the hands of his neighbour, the 3rd Earl of Darlington. In his manifesto he declared himself 'a supporter of constitutional principles, an enemy to all encroachments on public liberty, an advocate for economy and just retrenchment ... and a friend to the agricultural interest'. Unsurprisingly he was a Whig, the party of the big landowners. He retired from parliament on the abolition of rotten boroughs in 1832.[1]

On his death Sheldon left property at Marske (near Richmond) to Jane and his six daughters, more property at Stapleton, near Darlington, to his younger illegitimate sons Richard and Henry, and the main family estates to Christopher, his eldest son and Kit's father. In his will Sheldon also recognised the children as his, and Christopher senior later obtained the formal right ('royal licence and authority') from the Queen to use the Cradock name and title. Like his father, Christopher attended Trinity College, Cambridge. He became a JP and a deputy lieutenant of Yorkshire, was an enthusiastic follower of the Turf, kept hounds and helped maintain the Raby and Zetland hunts, being Master of the Raby for 10 seasons between 1866 and 1876.

All this time Cradocks had farmed the land, their wealth resting on wheat and cattle, as reflected in their coat of arms (heraldically, *argent, on a chevron azure, three garbs* [wheatsheafs] *or, a bordeure wavy of the second*). When Kit was born, it was into a family which had 140 years of roots sunk deep into the rich Yorkshire soil – 140 years of tradition as landed gentry, hunting, farming and following the sporting enjoyments of their class.

Kit's parents were married in 1855 at the local parish church of Saint Agatha, West Gilling. The officiating priest was Georgina's uncle, James Alexander Barnes, Rector of Gilling. It might have been James who had first brought them together. The Barnes connection would be important to Kit in his later life, but Reverend James would not be part of it as he was committed to a lunatic asylum five years after Kit was born.

Christopher senior and Georgina were to produce a total of seven children within as many years, two of whom – Sheldon and Marmaduke – were to die in infancy aged one and two-and-a-half respectively. The surviving children were all born within five years of each other: four boys – Sheldon William Keith (1858), Montagu (1859), Charles Frederick William (1861), Kit (1862) – and a girl, Gwendoline (1863).

The four boys were separated in age only by four years, with Kit the youngest. Their life revolved around horses, dogs, hunting, fishing, shooting. It was a rumbustious, romantic childhood, aping their father's interests and enjoying the Hall and its environment; the river running through the grounds, the ruined gatehouse bestriding the drive, the bustle and activity of the home farm.

In a break with family tradition all the boys were educated locally, in Richmond. Unlike their father and grandfather they did not go to college, and in this may be seen the first evidence that the family's wealth was not as it had been; Christopher senior's inheritance sundered by the many offspring of his father, and the returns from the estate perhaps under pressure since the Repeal of the Corn Laws in 1846 had reduced the profit from growing wheat.

But this idyllic lifestyle was fated not to last. In 1865 Kit's mother, Georgina, died aged only 35. Christopher senior's surviving correspondence indicates that the marriage was a love match and he was devastated. He wrote, 'I don't know how I am going to look after the family' but was comforted that his wife was 'able to pray to the end' and that 'God has forgiven her her sins'.[2] He never remarried, and erected a magnificent memorial to his wife in the guise of a stained glass window in the east wall of the north chapel at St Agatha's church. It dominates the church, glowing red and purple in the morning sunlight.

The care of the children was now his concern but as a typical Victorian *pater familias* he relied on servants and female kin to undertake most parental duties. Servants and governesses were employed at the Hall (some twelve in total) but Kit was also cared for by his grandmother Janet Duff (nee Barnes) who was living in Cheltenham. Certainly Kit was staying with her in 1871 as the census reveals. Cradock senior's interests were hunting, riding and his local legal duties. The raising of an unruly brood of young boys would not be high on his priority list. He needed to find ways of getting them off his hands and into an occupation suitable for their class. Sheldon and Montagu were to join the army; but Kit, at the age of twelve years and six months, was sent away to sea. He was packed off to HMS *Britannia*, the Royal Navy's officer training ship at Dartmouth.

3

Cadet, Midshipman, Lieutenant, 1874–1883

Kit arrived at *Britannia* in 1874. In later life he was to refer to it as the year he was 'harpooned'.[1]

It was not unusual for the younger sons of gentry to join the navy. The general rule was that the eldest joined the army and then ran the family estates on the parents' demise, whilst the youngest joined the church or the navy (this was indeed the case with Kit, his eldest brother Sheldon William Keith taking over the estate on his father's death in 1896). The navy was cheaper than being in a top regiment, and younger sons needed to seek their fortune as they would not inherit much from the family. Primogeniture was the order of the day.

Entry into *Britannia* required a nomination, which was not easy unless one had connections. Every captain had a right of nomination on hoisting his pennant for the first time and the rest were under the personal control of the First Lord of the Admiralty. In this way the gene pool of the navy was kept pure. Candidates then had to take an entrance examination and a medical. There were specialist 'crammers' to get entrants up to the required level to pass the oral and written exams. The exam required candidates to amass a total of 720 points from a possible 1200. Subjects covered included 'arithmetic, as far as proportion and vulgar and decimal fractions', elementary algebra, 'up to easy fractions and simple equations', elementary geometry, Latin parsing and translation, French oral and translation and 'Scripture History'.

Kit would have been sponsored by someone with a naval connection who was known to him but there are no records of who that was. However, one of Kit's grandfather Sheldon's executors was a Captain John Prince RN, who had married Sheldon's sister Isabella. Perhaps that was the connection. The cost of tuition was £35 a term, payable in advance, with a discount to £20 for deserving sons of RN officers (this was more than the average annual wage for a miner or agricultural labourer).

Britannia was the fifth ship of that name, launched in 1860 as a screw ship of 131 guns. Two terms of cadets joined every year and each term spent two years on board. It was a tough and monastic life, exclusively male, with a regime of hard discipline and exercise. Kit's routine was dull – prayers, inspection, classes, meals, boat work, exercise. After school there would be field sports. Punishments for infractions included bread and water diets; it was a Spartan environment and an enclosed world with its own rules and culture, introspective, insular, self-absorbed. Cadets were not allowed to open accounts with 'tradesmen' or to have their own money over and above an allowance paid from their account by the Paymaster. Like all the cadets, Kit had to provide his own clothing at his family's cost (see Appendix 1 for details). On the positive side the ship had its own hunting pack and cadets were allowed to hunt at weekends.

Britannia was a sailing ship and Kit had to master yards and stays, sails and masts, climbing and rigging. His natural athleticism, honed in his Yorkshire Eden, stood him in good stead.

The navy was locked in a backward-looking mind-set that refused to consider a changing world and looked to the past for its inspiration and training. The spirit of Nelson still loomed large. Even when steam power was demonstrably proven to be superior to sail the Admiralty hung onto masts and spars, and strange hybrid warships of sail and steam were built. As late as 1889 the Admiralty was building a sail training ship (HMS *Martin*). Such training continued until the end of 1899 when the remaining four sail training ships were decommissioned to release men for the Boer War, otherwise it could well have continued into the twentieth century. Admiral Gerard Noel, CinC Home Fleet in 1903, lecturing to the

United Services Institute, deplored the passing of sail and masts and said that the new generation were no longer seamen.

The year that Kit joined *Britannia*, Captain Philip Colomb proved mathematically that carrying masts and sails round the world cost more coal than it saved, but old beliefs died hard. As did the adherence to old training regimes. As late as 1892 a Captain John-stone presented a paper, which received wide support, in which he affirmed that 'I am certain that the only way of training sailors and men to be sailors is in masted ships, making them work the ships under sail, working the masts and yards, and entirely depending upon masts and sails'. This was only five years before the battleship HMS *Canopus*, which we shall meet as part of Kit's battle, was launched. The navy's officer class was the inheritor, not the maker of tactical thought; thinking was ossified in the time of Trafalgar and seniority knew everything.

The curriculum that Kit studied reflected these attitudes. It was divided into three parts – seamanship, study and out-study. While seamanship aimed to cover practical sailing sea lore and signalling, study gave the young cadets the chance to learn mathematics and navigation, with out-study focused on French and drawing (both very practical: France was our oldest enemy and an ability to draw maps and visualisations was of practical use).

Interestingly, naval history was studied at Oxford and Cambridge but not at *Britannia*. Much emphasis was placed on sports – especially sailing and boxing – and the ability to shin up and down masts and dress yards was much prized. These physical attributes were the more likely to gain a cadet respect while doing too well in the mathematical subjects could be injurious to one's reputation. It's easy to imagine that Kit, with his childhood background, enjoyed these outdoor activities best. Indeed it could be positively deleterious to one's standing to perform too well in a scholastic manner. It was not necessary, or even desirable, to be academically gifted in order to progress in the Victorian navy. A 'three-oner' – a man who obtained first-class passes at his Seamanship Board, Royal Naval College and Excellent (for gunnery) – was suspect and 'three-oners' were held in contempt by many in the navy as being 'too clever by half', as were officers who pursued outside interests. Fitting in socially and coming from the 'right' background was much more important.

Kit did not disappoint when measured against these criteria. In December 1876 he passed out of *Britannia* with third-class passes. He was marked lower in seamanship than in 'general conduct' and his report card was endorsed 'can draw fairly'. He was deemed deserving of advancement. Posted first to HMS *Alexandra*, Kit was quickly re-assigned to HMS *Pallas*, a wooden hulled ironclad whose principal weapon was the ram, based in the Mediterranean and thus giving Kit his first experience of Malta, an island he grew to enjoy. Promotion to midshipman came the following year, Kit having achieved at least 600 out of a possible 1,000 marks available in topics such as the ability to work a 'day's work' by tables as well as by projection; to find the latitude by observation of the Meridian Altitude of the Sun, Moon and Stars; longitude by chronometer, and to work an amplitude.

If anything, life as a midshipman was even tougher. He would have been living in the gun room with his peers, responsible for the ship's boats, still supposed to study – a hard and energetic life as a 'snotty' which had to be endured for five years until a panel of four captains deemed him fit to progress to sub-lieutenant. The gun room was a tough place, bullying was frequent, as were 'gun room evolutions' – roughhouse games, fighting and pranks – all ruled over by a sub-lieutenant or senior midshipman. Kit would learn to use his fists and handle himself, as well as determining how to survive in a male environment very similar to the public schools exemplified in novels such as *Tom Brown's Schooldays*. Kit clearly dealt with this and other temptations well enough, for his 'report cards' for the period stress his temperate nature (drunkenness was rife in the Victorian navy), his good physique and his zealousness, but note that he was subject to occasional attacks of nausea. For example, 1877 on the *Alexandra*: 'conducted himself with sobriety and to my satisfaction'. Same year on the *Pallas*: 'sobriety and attention to detail'. In 1879 as a midshipman: 'sobriety and great attention to detail. Promising'.[2]

Kit's first brush with Imperial glory came in 1878 when, as a result of the Cyprus convention between Britain and Turkey, Britain took over the administrative responsibility for the country in line with the strategic requirement to secure a base in the eastern Mediterranean. The *Pallas* was present at the British occupation of Cyprus and Kit participated in the hoisting of the Union flag at Paphos and Limassol.

Whilst Kit was in the Med there were changes happening at Hartforth Hall. The four brothers became three in 1879 when Charles Frederick William, in search of a different life, emigrated to Colorado, USA aged 18. He had 'impaired health' and the mountain air was thought to be beneficial to him. He ranched (on a farm purchased by his father it would appear) raising cattle, cereal and chickens, and married, dying in 1925. There is, however, a family tradition that it might not have been his health that was the over-riding factor; there were whispers of girl problems; a black sheep perhaps.

In 1880 Kit returned to England and as an 18-year-old mid-shipman was appointed to HMS *Cleopatra*, a 14-gun screw corvette (powered by sail but with a steam engine too), destined for the China station. He joined her on 24 August but with time to kill before she sailed he went out walking and visited the theatre, seeing one play several times. Eventually, on 1 October, *Cleopatra* sailed off to her station as part of a 'flying squadron', a voyage that would cover 36,270 nautical miles, last for 276 days and see Kit make landfall in South America, the Antarctic, South Africa, Australia, Japan and China. Kit's account of the voyage makes dull reading, reflecting a monotonous daily routine of watches and cleaning ship, but whenever possible there was sport, especially cricket, rowing matches and shooting. His 'bag' included wallabies and opossums. A fellow midshipman on the voyage was Dudley de Chair, a future friend, Admiral and Governor of New South Wales. During the cruise, in December 1881, Kit was promoted to Acting Sub-Lieutenant, the first step on the long ladder to his own command.[3]

Finally returning to England in March 1882, he was assigned to

HMS *Excellent* to sit his lieutenant's exams and a year later suc-cessfully passed them. That he obtained a third-class award shows he was not at risk of being classified as one of the navy's 'brains' and remained true to the gentleman's code. Kit was now a ranking sub-lieutenant, a rank he would hold for nearly three-and-a-half years during which he served mainly in shore based berths as he took gunnery and pilot's (navigator's) courses, apart from a brief sojourn in the Mediterranean fleet with the *Alexandra* and the *Superb*.

4

Egypt, the Sudan and Promotion, 1884–1893

In the latter half of the nineteenth century the 'pax Britannica' meant that there were limited opportunities for naval officers to demonstrate their prowess and bravery at sea, but imperial ambition brought with it many such opportunities on land, and naval brigades were despatched to them with regularity. Ambitious officers sought such duties and Kit Cradock was no exception. He participated in four wars in his forty-year naval career, excluding the one in which he met his death. In each he fought on land rather than at sea, and all had their proximate causes in the quest for, or defence of, Empire. Twice in Egypt and the Sudan, once in China and once in Latin America, imperial ambition and a lack of military preparedness called Kit to the colours as a land fighting man.

The Mediterranean, Egypt and the Sudan occupied much government attention during the latter part of the nineteenth century, especially because of the Mahdist Wars. The wars in Sudan, generally categorised as the Mahdist Wars, lasted intermittently from 1881 to 1899. Kit was involved twice, in 1884 and again in 1891–3. At their heart was an Islamic fundamentalist – the Mahdi – who ascribed to himself mystic powers, promised his followers that bullets could not harm them and desired an independent Sudan, free from control by Egypt (which was itself under the de facto control of Britain). Initially fought between the followers of the Mahdi – also known as dervishes – and the Egyptian army, it eventually became an Anglo–Sudanese conflict in which the British army swept away the Mahdi's powerbase at the Battle of Omdurman.

British imperial interest in Egypt was a result of the need to

15

protect the Suez Canal, the vital link to India, the jewel in the crown of the Empire. To allow any other country to gain control of it – especially the French, who had built it – would be a strategic disaster and Britain was therefore committed to maintaining a friendly regime in Egypt at any price, even if it meant supporting some pretty unimpressive rulers. In 1881, for example, General Wolseley had been sent to restore the Khedive to power and remove the pretender Colonel Arabi, who was preaching anti-British sentiment. When the Mahdists gave the Egyptian army a severe beating at the Battle of El Obied in 1883 things came to a head. Britain was increasingly taking control of Egyptian governance in order to ensure that the interest on the huge national debt would be repaid (to Britain amongst others) and that the country remained out of foreign influence, especially French. The British financial advisors decided that it would be better to let the Sudan go, and General Gordon was sent to Khartoum in 1884 to arrange an orderly retreat of the Egyptian armies currently in the country. Instead he managed to get himself besieged and cut off, partly due to his conviction that the Mahdi would be a destabilising influence on Egypt if allowed unfettered control in the Sudan and partly because he wanted to give all the garrisons the very best opportunity to make their getaway.

Strong pressure from the British public forced Prime Minister Gladstone to send Wolseley with a relief expedition, but it was too late to save Gordon. Britain withdrew from the Sudan and in 1885 the Mahdi died. However, the Egyptian people and rulers continued to believe that they had a legitimate claim to the Sudan and its loss rankled. Likewise, as Gordon had predicted, the Mahdists continued to make border raids and incursions into Egypt. Finally from around 1896 and at the behest of Salisbury (Prime Minister) and Joseph Chamberlain, British troops took part in the reconquest of the Sudan, in Egypt's name, concluding full acquisition in 1899.

By way of passage on the *Himalaya* (a troopship) Kit was to gain his first experiences of warfare in 1884 as part of the forces sent to Upper Egypt during the Mahdist Wars, where he served as a sub-lieutenant in the Naval Brigade on garrison duties. This campaign included the second Battle of El Teb, when forces under Sir Gerald Graham defeated the Mahdists and redeemed the earlier defeat of Baker Pasha (and where Naval Captain Arthur Wilson, a future First Sea Lord, won the Victoria Cross for his conduct during the fighting, holding off a Mahdist attack while his ratings brought their Gardiner Gun, a heavy machine gun, into action). Kit's conduct during the campaign can have done him no harm for on his return to England he received two pieces of good news. First he was given four months' paid leave – the first leave granted since 1874 and the first opportunity for him to return to his family – and in June 1885 he was promoted to full lieutenant.

Kit was now to serve on HMS *Linnet* for three years as First Lieutenant. She was a 756-ton composite screw gunvessel, built in 1880. Lightly armed and possessing both sails and a small steam engine, *Linnet* was of a class of ships already obsolete in their reluctance to abandon masts and rigging, and designed to 'show the flag' and patrol and police the rivers, deltas and coastline of the far-flung Empire. Kit's navy record is silent on her activities but it is entirely likely that she served on the China station.

The year 1889 brought Kit bad news. On 9 May he was officially placed on half pay. Half pay was the navy's way of reducing costs and manpower when it had surplus officers. Kit was not wanted and there was no post available for him; not good news for a young and ambitious officer. He had to hold himself available for duty but would be paid only half of his salary – not helpful for career or for pocket. Fortunately salvation was at hand. In July 1889 he joined the brand new battleship HMS *Howe* for three months as part of her shakedown cruise and during the Spithead review. The ship's commander was Francis Bridgeman, a fellow Yorkshireman who will play an important role later in this story. The future King George V, then Prince George, was an honorary member of the ship's wardroom. Neither of these contacts would do Kit any harm at all in later life.

Service on the *Volage* for 12 months followed. This was not a prestigious appointment. *Volage* was an iron screw corvette built in

1869 and again a mixture of sail and steam, existing anachronistically alongside a modern warship like the *Howe*. During Kit's service on board she was assigned to the Training Squadron, based at Portsmouth and Chatham and under the overall command of Commodore Second Class Albert H. Markham whose example was to play an unwitting part in Kit's later life and death. Markham was a poor officer and a stickler for protocol.

Kit must have made use of the time on half pay and in the Training Squadron, and his experiences on the China station, for in 1890 he became a published author. *Sporting Notes from the East* was the first of three books he was to write about his naval life. It details the sort of game shooting available in the Far East and the success or otherwise that he had. The Victorian obsession with listing their huge bags of avian and other prey is manifest in it.

Again Kit's luck was to change, for on 6 September 1890 he was made First Lieutenant of HMS *Dolphin* and found himself in the middle of a lovely war. *Dolphin* sailed for the Red Sea and once again Kit found himself fighting on land in the Near East. He had two opportunities to make his name generally known and he seized them both

At the beginning of 1891 he contrived to be part of the Eastern Sudan Field Force at the capture of Tokar, and then obtained the post of Aide de Camp (ADC) to Colonel Holled-Smith (commander of the Suakin garrison who had been sent to secure Tokar). Kit took an active part in the fighting for which he was later decorated with the quixotically named 'Insignia of the Order of the Medjiidieh of the Fourth Class'. He was also awarded the Khedive's bronze star and clasp. He writes of how, on HMS *Dolphin* where he was Lieutenant and second in command, they took a whole 'Soudanese' battalion, 900 strong, from Suakim to Trinkikat (actually this would have been the three battalions that Holled-Smith took with him, 900 men in total), and his naval record states that he 'displayed great tact and resource, especially during the battle of 19 February'.[1] He had begun to establish the reputation for courage which would become the defining part of his reputation.

This reputation would be further burnished in 1893. Back serving as First Lieutenant on the *Dolphin*, Kit led the rescue of the Brazilian corvette *Almirante Barossa* which had run ashore in the Red Sea at Ras Dib under an Arab pilot. There was a heavy sea and wind running but Kit was able to rescue 400 officers and men who had been on the beach for two days and were in a distressed state (he writes, 'it was blowing far too hard with a very heavy sea running ... we anchored to windward and veered our boats astern and rescued the whole lot'). They were apparently very dehydrated and he set up a grog tub full of drinking water on the deck – as each man came over the side he drank his fill.[2] As a gesture of gratitude her commander, Captain Joaquim Marques Basista de Leao, gave Kit the corvette's brass boat's badge (which is still in the possession of Kit's sister's descendants).

In over four years on the *Dolphin* Kit had at last started to establish his name and career. The next six years would see it inked in for good. But first he had a month on half pay and a three-month gunnery course at HMS *Excellent* – in which he surprised himself by obtaining a first-class certificate.

5

Following Orders, 1893

Whilst Kit was saving lives in the Red Sea the navy suffered a completely avoidable disaster in the Mediterranean. It is important to an understanding of Kit and his peers to grasp the culture of respect for authority, seniority and orders which was implicit in the 'Vicwardian' navy, and was so cruelly revealed in the incident of the *Victoria* and the *Camperdown*.

An unquestioning adherence to orders, respect for the chain of command and deference to superiors were essential requirements for success in the Victorian and Edwardian navies. Father knew best, and admirals and captains especially expected slavish obedience to their commands. This could even extend to religion – Admiral Sir Algernon Charles Fiesche 'Pompo' Heneage refused to wear uniform for the service of prayers, saying that 'no Royal Navy officer could be seen kneeling to a higher deity'.[1] To question an instruction from a senior officer was an act of rebellion. This was the navy Kit grew up in, and such a philosophy was ingrained in his soul. It would have been his everyday experience of life in the service.

On 22 June 1893 Vice-Admiral Sir George Tyron was exercising the Mediterranean fleet. A big man with a big personality, Tyron was known as a man with revolutionary theories regarding ship handling and manoeuvres. He saw himself as trying to break up the fusty traditionalism of the navy and was known for expressing extravagant theories and issuing outrageous orders just to get a reaction. In particular he loved to plot and execute unusual ship evolutions. The handling of a fleet at sea, in unison with all captains following a pattern laid down by their admiral, was seen as the defining feature of seamanship at the time, and Tyron seen as one of its most able executioners. He flew his flag in HMS *Victoria*, one of the worst warships ever built, with two huge 16.5-inch guns in a single turret on her foredeck which, because of its low freeboard, was often under water. The guns were seldom fired for fear of damaging the ship.

As his second in command Tyron had Rear Admiral Albert Markham, last met in command of the Training Squadron. They were complete opposites. Markham was not a man to inspire, tetchy with subordinates and fawning with his superiors, ten years younger than his admiral, a man who had reached the flag rank through the actions of time and connections rather than ability. His brother, Clements, was to be the sponsor of Captain Robert Falcon Scott to lead the *Discovery* polar expedition of 1901–04. Tyron thought little of him. Markham flew his flag in HMS *Camperdown*, built in 1885 and, amazingly, fitted with a piece of technology taken from the early Phoenicians and Greeks who had plied the Med 2000 years before – a ram. This archaic armament had been briefly fashionable after the success of the Confederate rams in the American civil war but was truly an evolutionary dead end in modern warfare.

Sailing to Tripoli from Beirut, Tyron had set an interesting manoeuvre leaving the port and was determining to set an even more testing one for entering harbour. Summoning his staff to his cabin, he laid out a plan for the evolution to his flag captain and staff commander – the former, the Honourable Maurice Bourke, a dashing and well-connected man, young for his rank, with an eye on a promising future; the latter, Hawkins-Smith, an old grizzled pro, passed over for promotion to captain. The plan involved the fleet forming into two columns six cables apart and then manoeuvring into a single column by turning inwards. Hawkins-Smith immediately objected that eight cables would be required, but when Tyron called for his flag lieutenant to issue the order he once again specified six cables. With the signal at the masthead, Staff Commander Hawkins-Smith was puzzled and asked for Flag Lieutenant Lord Gillford to have it reconfirmed. This was an uncomfortable mission and Tyron dismissed him brusquely, repeating 'six cables'. The real point here is that everyone knew this distance would result in a collision, but no one was willing to challenge it. Captains on all of the ships expressed their puzzlement, but were so used to Tyron's brilliant plans that they just accepted that the admiral knew best. As the order to execute the turn was made, Lord Gillford again tried, without success, to draw Tyron's attention to the distance between the ships, but was ignored.

Victoria was at the head of her line, *Camperdown* at the head of hers. After an initial hesitation, Markham made no objection to the order and as the two great ships began to turn it became clear on both bridges that a collision was inevitable. Bourke pleaded with Tyron to be allowed to go astern; eventually Tyron relented but by then it was too late. The *Camperdown* smashed into the side of *Victoria*, her ram doing terrible damage. Markham then made matters worse by going astern and allowing water to flood in through the gash in *Victoria*'s side. She began to sink. As a result, 358 officers and men died, including Admiral Tyron. Amongst those who escaped was Commander John Jellicoe, ill with Malta fever in the sick bay but surviving to lead the Grand Fleet in 1914. Neither captain thought to close watertight doors or hatches, but waited instead for orders from their respective admirals.

Bourke and Markham were court martialled. After a long trial, Bourke was acquitted and the court recorded its opinion that 'the discipline and order maintained on board the *Victoria* to the last ... was in the highest degree creditable to all concerned'.[2]

As for Markham, 'the court feels strongly that, although it is much to be regretted that Rear Admiral Albert Hastings Markham did not carry out his intention to (communicate) to the Commander in Chief his doubts as to the signal, it would be fatal to the best interests of the service to say that he was to blame for carrying out the directions of his Commander in Chief, present in person'.

In other words, it was better to carry out a patently deadly instruction than to question the chain of command.

6

Royalty and Back to School, 1894–1899

On 31 August 1894 Kit was appointed to the Royal Yacht *Victoria and Albert*, a posting he was to hold for two years. A posting to a royal yacht was either an appointment of patronage or a reward for an exceptional officer, but mainly the former. William Goodenough (to become an admiral and command a cruiser squadron at Jutland and a future President of the Royal Society) recalled being posted to the *Victoria and Albert*: 'I had just time to buy the gold laced trousers and laced mess jacket that traditions enjoined … It was, of course, an appointment of patronage. I went as my father's son [he was also Queen Victoria's godchild]. There was some tradition … to give early promotion to someone who had done good service … but I don't know how far this was observed in reality'.[1]

The reality of life on board the royal yacht was that it was dominated by spit and polish, ceremony and punctilious adherence to protocol and orders. The ship, the second of her name and built in 1855, was a steam driven paddle steamer with a crew of 240. There was a strong royal interest in the navy and there was much resentment over the role of the royal court in the promotional prospects of officers. Both the future George V and his elder brother Albert Victor ('Eddy', who died before he could inherit the throne) served as midshipmen on *Britannia*. Edward VII, both as King and as Prince of Wales, and George V took an active interest in matters naval and had many friends and connections in the service. By way of example we can examine the careers of several such officers whose royal connections carried them beyond their abilities

– service on the royal yacht or as an ADC was a proven route to promotion, as was having served with royalty.

Evan-Thomas, a friend of George V from *Britannia* days, served with a great lack of initiative as an admiral in Beatty's command at Jutland. Battenberg (a German Prince married to Queen Victoria's granddaughter) rose to be an ineffective first sea lord. The admirals in charge of the *Aboukir*, *Hogue* and *Cressy* debacle (see Chapter 18) – Christian (captain of Osborne College when the royal cadets were there) and Campbell ('minder' to George V when a prince in India and First Governor to his son and, according to First Sea Lord Jackie Fisher, 'a dammed sneak') – were royal favourites. So was the Second Sea Lord at the outbreak of war, responsible for personnel and training, Vice Admiral Sir Frederick Hamilton, a lazy and incompetent officer who owed his position in part to his court entrée gained through his sister, who was married to Vice Admiral Colin Keppel, in charge of the royal yachts before the war.

Sir Archibald Berkley Milne was another such 'Royal'. After service in the Zulu War as an ADC to Lord Chelmsford, and escaping the massacre at Isandlwana, he rose to the rank of captain in the navy before accepting the post of Captain of HM Yacht *Osborne*, a post usually held by a commander, reasoning that exposure to royalty offered him better hopes of promotion. Such posts were often seen as mixed blessings for they lacked warlike qualities, but Milne loved the ceremony and obsessive spit and polish of service in the Royal Squadron and went on to command the royal yachts from 1903 to 1905. He became good friends with King Edward VII and, especially, Queen Alexandra who nicknamed him 'Arky-Barky'– an appellation which soon got round the fleet, to risible effect. A fellow officer asserted that Milne's hobbies were collecting rare orchids and entertaining royal ladies. Never an intellect (he is recorded as saying 'they don't pay me to think, they pay me to be an admiral'[2]) and lacking any martial experience, he was nonetheless promoted through royal influence to flag rank. In 1912 Winston Churchill, First Lord of the Admiralty, and under pressure from George V, made him Admiral commanding the

Mediterranean fleet (raising his flag in HMS *Good Hope*), causing ex-First Sea Lord Fisher to write to Churchill that he had 'betrayed the Navy'.[3] We will meet Milne again later in this book, presiding over the escape of the *Goeben*, hence bringing Turkey into the war on the German side. Fisher continued to excoriate Churchill for allowing the appointment and insisted on calling Milne 'Sir Berkley-Goeben' after the event.

Kit's time on the *Victoria and Albert* seems to have been uneventful but he no doubt made royal connections that would be valuable in later life, as will be seen. On 5 February 1896 he acted as a pallbearer at the funeral of Prince Henry of Battenberg, husband of Queen Victoria's fifth daughter Princess Beatrice, who had died off the coast of West Africa of malaria whilst on active service in the Ashanti War, for which service Cradock was honoured by the Queen.

Death struck the Cradock family too that year as Kit's father, Christopher senior, died. Sheldon William Keith, Kit's eldest brother, inherited the estate and its management, returning from the army to do so. The family, later to be so prolific with their own memorial monuments, did not raise one for their father.

Then on 31 August of the same year Kit was promoted to the rank of commander and assigned to HMS *Britannia* as second in command of the navy's cadet school, the same school that he himself had attended in 1874. It is interesting to note that Kit's last three appointments – a training squadron, the Royal Yacht and *Britannia* – all called for a combination of instructional and diplomatic skills. His didactic qualities are certainly borne out by his writings, for in 1894 he had published *Wrinkles in Seamanship or help to a Salt Horse*, a book of tips and lessons for aspiring and junior officers. It should be noted that they emphasise the old navy of masts and sails, stays and ropes.

Kit seems to have enjoyed his time at *Britannia*. He could indulge his passion for hunting using the ship's own pack, the Britannia Beagles. In a book printed in 1899, *An Old Raby Hunt Club Album*, Kit and his brothers are depicted in caricature by the artist George

A. Fothergill. Montagu and Sheldon, drawn in 1898, are shown in full hunt rig, scarlet cut-away coats, jodhpurs, top hats, whips and riding boots. They are both moustached, Montagu rather more fiercely. Kit, depicted in 1899 possibly when he was home on half pay towards the year end, is shown in the uniform of his beloved Britannia Beagles. He wears a bluish Norfolk jacket with 'BB' emblazoned on the breast pocket, jodhpurs and a flat hat, and behind him there is the faint outline of sailing ships.

It was at *Britannia* that Kit met the man who would become his best friend in the service and companion in arms at the dawn of the new century, Roger Keyes (later Admiral of the Fleet Sir Roger Keyes). Keyes first met Kit when the latter was Commander at *Britannia* and Keyes a newly appointed lieutenant and commanding officer of HMS *Opossum*, a small (260 tons) destroyer based at nearby Devonport. They became firm friends despite a rank and ten-year age difference, and Kit invited Keyes over for hunting with the Britannia Beagles on a regular basis in the winter of 1898, making him an honorary member of *Britannia*'s wardroom. Keyes said of Cradock that 'he was a gallant sportsman and a good friend and it was the beginning of a friendship which I would always treasure'.[4] They fought together in China, shared a common personal indifference to danger, and corresponded all their lives. Their personalities were similar and this might have cemented their friendship. Marder, for example, described Keyes as one whose 'judgement ... was often overruled by their fiery temperament and he never looked much further than the launching of an operation'.[5]

Five letters from this correspondence, all from Cradock to Keyes, have survived in the Keyes papers at the British Library and they provide a revealing and candid insight into Kit's personality. He signs them as from 'Kit' or 'Christopher' and addresses Keyes as 'My Dear Old Roger'. These are letters between friends and not intended for public view. Reading them, one feels one is looking into Kit's true character. The overwhelming impression is of great impatience. The letters are little better than a scrawl, slashing up and down strokes, the pen hardly leaving the paper between words, the words often illegible, tumbling out, sometimes grammatically incorrect – a man in a tearing hurry. Several are folded into four parts, which Kit fills in the curious page order one, three, four, two, as if he hadn't worked out how the letter would flow. On one he scrawls in a different pen on the obverse with a new (and unintelligible) idea.[6]

Kit served on *Britannia* for two years and 209 days; but England was again at war, this time in South Africa with the Boers. Once again he was called to military duties, assigned as Transport Officer, Thames District, attached to the drill ship HMS *President* and supervising the loading of soldiers, horses and supplies bound for the Cape, work that later gave him material for his third and final book. His more martial qualities were not required however, and he was sent on half pay leave until January 1900.

Then on the 31st he was posted to the China station and the biggest adventure of his career so far – one that would become his defining moment.

7

Cradock in China, 1900–1901

The culmination of his land-based combat, and the crowning moment of Kit's career, came during the Boxer Rebellion of 1900. Chinese rebels (the Boxers or Fists of Righteousness) were besieging Peking, and especially the legation compound where all the foreign diplomats lived and worked. A mixed nationality force of 2,000 men was assembled to rescue the situation, mainly naval personnel and marines under Vice Admiral Edward Seymour (or 'see-less' as he was known to his men), who managed to get them trapped in Tientsin. Kit was in Chinese waters as a commander and ship's captain in HMS *Alacrity* (a third-class cruiser, really just a glorified gunboat, built in 1885 and serving as a despatch vessel and admiral's yacht) and joined the naval brigade, distinguishing himself in a number of major incidents.

The background to the rebellion is complex. China in the latter part of the nineteenth century was a troubled country, a backward state living in the past, preyed upon by its neighbours and racked by internal strife both as a result of fractured leadership and of poverty and starvation. The Boxer rebellion was but one, although a culminating one, of a number of quasi-revolts reflecting the frustrations and dissent of the populace. There were probably three main causes of the uprising: first, the imperial ambitions of the great powers and especially Britain, Germany, Russia and Japan; second, the Christian missionary activity by US, British and German Protestant and Catholic churches; and third, the general belief that the ills of the populace and of China were caused by foreigners.

With the general partitioning of Africa, and the Munroe doctrine being rigorously enforced by the USA to keep the Americas free of European influence, there was little of the world left of value as an addition to empire and an outlet for trade, except for China. With its huge population and urgent need to modernise, China was a market and a territory of great value to all. Through various pretexts Russia, Japan, Germany and Britain had all acquired territory in China and all were jealous and suspicious of each other's ambitions in acquiring more land, influence and trade. The ambassadors and emissaries of these great powers lived together in their own cantonment – the legation quarter – adjacent to the seat of government in Peking. They lived a life of European splendour, shut off from the realities of the world outside their walls.

A second type of imperialism was being practised by the Christian churches, anxious to gain both heavenly and temporal power over millions of pagan souls. As a part of various treaties during the nineteenth century, missionaries had gained legal protection from Chinese law and could only be tried and judged under the laws of their own country. Their converts from the local populace found that some shadow of these rights attached to them and that, because of their protections, missionaries would intervene on their behalf in a manner which the Chinese could not. Criminals and other undesirables as well as true believers found this shield of value, and flocked to the church causing much resentment amongst the general populace who had remained true to the faith of their ancestors.

Foreign influence was everywhere apparent to the ordinary Chinese citizen. Foreigners were building the new railways, canals, roads. They were gaining trade advantages and wealth. And they were seen as undermining the Qing dynasty and the governance of the country. As such they were a powerful focus for dissatisfaction and the Boxers – with their slogan 'Support the Qing, exterminate the foreigners' – were able to prey on these feelings.

The Boxers – 'Righteous Fists in Harmony' in Chinese – were a mystical nationalist grouping with no real leaders, a little like the peasants' revolt in England of 1381. They wore red sashes as their only uniform, performed mystic devotions of both a physical and religious nature and believed themselves impervious to bullets. By summer of 1900 they were tens of thousands strong and began to march on Peking, killing missionaries and their converts as they went. The Empress initially sought to oppose them but when she realised that they might be powerful allies in her own power struggles she changed her view. Little by little the official Chinese army began to ignore and then side with the advancing hordes. They entered Peking and set up camps around the legation district. Under the aegis of the British ambassador, MacDonald, the Europeans sent to the coast – where the navies of several nations were gathered to protect their local interests – for help. The German consul was shot and killed by an imperial soldier, and suddenly the legation compounds were under siege. A shooting war started which lasted for 55 days.

Admiral Seymour was asked to lead the relief column. He decided to travel by train from Tientsin to Peking, using five trains in all, a plan which Beatty – a future first sea lord, then a captain and serving under Seymour – would later call 'the maddest, wildest, rottenest scheme that could emanate from the brain of any man'.[1] Seymour was also unaware that the imperial forces were at best neutral. As he set off towards Peking, the Empress Cixi and her court took the view that this was an invasion column designed to replace her on the throne. She ordered the imperial troops to support the Boxers in destroying the force, and declared war on the foreign powers. Digging up the rails behind and in front of him slowed Seymour's progress to nothing and he eventually chose to retreat back to Tientsin – which he did not reach, capturing instead the Xigu arsenal and taking refuge there.

To effect his rescue and to relive Peking the coastal forces first had to reduce the powerful forts at Taku which commanded the access to Tientsin via the Pei-Ho river. Cradock was put in command of the British assault force at the urging of his friend Roger Keyes (because 'he kept himself very fit and would see to it that our men were first into the fort').[2] The British contribution to the force was 321 men culled from those ships at harbour nearby and armed with rifles, cutlasses, pistols, tomahawks and boarding pikes, who were joined by 244 Japanese sailors, 133 Germans and 159 Russians.

The German and Japanese commanders proposed that Cradock direct this polyglot force and after an initial hold-up whilst further naval bombardment was directed at the forts, he led the advance, charging with his men and the Japanese contingent down the road to the forts and under heavy defensive fire. Kit was soon ahead of the column and, fearful of the Japanese getting the honour of being first over the threshold, he led his men past them and over a moat into the fort, closely followed by the Japanese commander (Captain Hattori) who was killed on the parapet by a shot to the head (according to some sources, but Cradock himself noted that it was a Japanese rating). Both the Japanese and British ensigns were run up over the North Fort but Cradock was determined that the British flag would be first up over all of them, and whilst the Russians and Japanese occupied themselves in looting he carried on the charge. The German commander, who then arrived on the scene, asked for the honour of leading the next assault which Cradock granted, but told some of his men to see that the British flag went up first and that he would 'shoot them if they failed and give them ten dollars if they succeeded'.[3] They succeeded. Keyes later wrote 'the honour and prestige of the British navy at the taking of the Taku fort was worthily upheld thanks to the imperturbable gallantry and initiative of ... Kit Cradock'.[4]

Cradock was next engaged in the relief of Tientsin, which was under siege by the Imperial Chinese Army who were firing into the foreign concession with artillery. The British consul's last message out stated 'reinforcements most urgently required'.[5] Additionally, Seymour's force was trapped nearby. Again Cradock was placed in charge of a force comprising 250 British sailors and 23 Italians and entrained at the port of Tongku for the journey to Tientsin. He had been preceded by 400 mixed American and Russian troops who had advanced before Kit's arrival but who were thrown back with heavy losses. Cradock advanced with his men, turned the Chinese left flank and was able to cross the river on sampans and enter Tientsin a long time ahead of the rest of the relieving forces. In Keyes' words, 'Cradock always charged at the earliest possible moment'.[6]

Finally Kit led the naval brigade at the taking of the Tientsin (Pei-Yang) arsenal, in which Seymour and his men were holed up. Having failed to get the Russian commander to stir his troops into action, Cradock sounded the charge and, mounted on a pony, doubled his men forwards in short rushes. His pony was shot from under him but Kit recovered his position in the van and the naval brigade drove the Chinese from the field at bayonet point, killing 400 Boxers in the process.[7]

Admiral Seymour noted that '[Cradock's] performance was undoubtedly very satisfactory and for the credit and benefit of the service'.[8] Oddly, Kit received a German decoration (the Crown of Prussia, 2nd Class with Swords) for his bravery, to go with his China Medal with Clasp and a 'Mention in Despatches'. This brave performance also earned him his promotion to Captain 'specially promoted for services in connection with the capture of the Taku forts';[9] Keyes too was promoted to Commander for his contribution.

Kit had some distinguished colleagues in the Boxer Rebellion adventure, including some of Britain's future best commanders. David Beatty (to command the battlecruisers at Jutland), Jellicoe (to command at Jutland), Roger Keyes (who was to devise the Zeebrugge raid), Warrender (eventually Commander in Chief Plymouth); and also Herbert Hoover, future American president (who constructed the defences at Tientsin), von Pohl (who commanded the German High Seas Fleet) and von Holtzendorf (who was the chief of staff who led the unrestricted submarine campaign of 1917).

Cradock had proved his mettle, if proof were needed. Bold and fearless on the hunting field, he had shown the same characteristics on the battle field. His courage inspired others: Lieutenant John Tanca, of HMS *Algerine* wrote to Kit on 17 June, after the capture of the Taku forts, '... I have the honour to thank you very much for your kindness, in the same time that I cannot find sufficient words to praise the conduct and direction of your troops which I tried, very poorly, to emulate. Hoping that in any other occasion may [sic]

I have the honour to be put under your orders ...'.[10] The future Admiral Roger Keyes, who fought with Cradock at the Taku forts, wrote of Kit's 'fiery, ardent spirit in action'.[11] Kit Cradock was a fighter.

Kit wrote a journal of his two weeks of action immediately after the event and, whilst adding a little more detail to the events that took place, it is more revealing of his character and personality. From the first page it can be seen that Kit bears a good grudge. He writes, 'the personal pleasure of the experience was somewhat marred by a series of petty jealousies – from which I am afraid the navy is no more free that are any of our other public services'. On the very next page he takes on Admiral Seymour '[after] releasing the Peking Column from their tight place 48 hours earlier than expected he never uttered one word of grateful recognition; he appeared to be wrapped up in his own unfortunate failure' (this can be read alongside Kit's letters to Keyes in which he complains of lack of recognition). Seymour is also castigated at the end of the journal: 'even on his relief he allowed no expression of gratitude to pass his lips, all the thanks I got from him were "where's your ship?" ...'[12]

Captain Bayly, the Commandant of Tientsin, becomes a particular bête-noir – a stickler for protocol, and in Kit's eyes indolent. They cross swords on numerous occasions, commencing on 23 June when Cradock leads his forces into the town and relieves the siege. Bayly has made no efforts to prepare for their arrival and when Kit returns the way he had come to check for wounded and carry the message of relief back to the railhead, Bayly makes no provision to continue the advance. 'I suppose he judges others by his lazy self,' Kit remarks, adding in another part of the record that Bayly was 'a fat, alarmist Post Captain' and 'a small mind in a fat body'.[13]

Their feud was not ended by Kit's recall to his ship on 1 July, for four months later Cradock writes, 'the cause of my one Tientsin unpleasantness has now come to light. It is all too despicable but would that I guessed it before. After this long interval of "bottled wrath" I have received a most violent letter from Captain Bayly containing an accusation of self-advertisement on my part at his expense i.e. that I sent a telegram that Tientsin has been relieved (an announcement to that effect was read out in the House) instead of leaving him to do so that apparently his name might appear.'[14]

Kit responds in high dudgeon that first he had no intention of so doing but rode back to the railway camp as he had promised to do; and second that any fool could see that the telegraph lines were all down and had been for days. Cradock 'remonstrated very strongly and threatened to lay the letter before the Admiral'[15] and his detractor takes fright and apologises. But Kit does not forgive him and takes to his grave his umbrage at a particular paragraph. 'I cannot help quoting one sentiment contained in this extraordinary letter, it was "that of course he did not wish to impute anything against my personal courage, it was known to all". Did anyone I beg to state ever hear such infernal cheek! I replied "that I believed that all men hoped they were not cowards and that I outwardly, whatever I might have felt inwardly, tried not to be an exception".'[16] A very Victorian response, the chivalric expectation that every man would do his duty.

Kit's horse obsession shines through his prose from the beginning. 'I had two letters ... about a pony I had bought (which alas was never to leave Peking but nobly fulfilled a tragic destiny in providing soup for the besieged)'. Later, when marching to Tientsin, he writes, 'my pony was a ripper and with a rifle belonging to a disabled man I was making bad practice from his back with the greatest ease'. Having liberated Tientsin and riding back to the railhead, 'I found I had a good pony under me with a long rein and free galloping action ... As my pony and I sped for our distant goal I could almost fancy I was flighting along on the left – it's better than the right – of the flying pack and letting go one wild "view halloa" as some snipers fired at me I rode hard for the bridge.'[17]

Personal bravery was a Cradock hallmark and it shows through in his narrative. He has no hesitation in trying to get into the fight and, when told by Captain (later Admiral Sir) George Warrender that the Taku forts were to be stormed that night, he rushes off to see

Admiral Bruce and demands to go – and finds that he is already drafted. When they eventually storm the forts he notes, 'it was with a curious feeling that I ran across the bridge which spanned a ditch before the gate, we were sure it was mined and lo! what a fright I was in'. He was the first officer through the gate (but the fourth man) and found that both he and his men were 'porcupined' by the muzzles of blazing rifles ('it was amazing not many of us were hit'). Walking back along the rampart a 'a shell, which did not explode, pitched three feet in front of me and hurled away some tons of earth, covering me with dust and spinning me round'. He laconically adds, 'This, I fear, was somewhat imprudent', later crossed out and added in pen, 'idiotic'.[18]

When the train in which he is travelling to relieve Tientsin crashes and his carriage starts to overturn, he 'stuck to the lurching ship till I thought she intended to capsize over the embankment and then I tried to get out at the weather side but she righted herself just before turning over and I found myself lying on my back with the infernal thing coming right down on top of me! However providence interfered and though it's heavy side was literally brought within two inches of my face, so close indeed that when I was dragged out my head had to be hauled out of my helmet which was jambed [sic] between the truck side and the ground.'[19]

Approaching the city alongside a party of 400 American soldiers, he finds that they begin to waver under fire so, being the only person mounted, he rides to the front and from behind some brick kilns tries to identify the problem. 'There was little danger for me for although the bullets were flying past they were wretchedly aimed … All being practically clear ahead I made the signal and the line advanced to join me. We fixed bayonets – and the Chinese flew.'[20]

In the assault on the arsenal Cradock is frustrated by the lack of verve and courage of the Russians and the German contingent ('desperately slow and crawling like fat snakes') so he decides 'now we will show them what the British can do'. Leaving his pony aside he walks to the top of an embankment and, exposing himself to the enemy, orders his men: 'show the foreigners the way across'.

Cradock is brave but not unthinking. 'I do not hesitate to acknowledge,' he wrote, 'that standing there on top of the gap ... might have been more pleasant. I was in deadly fear but I hope I didn't shew [sic] it and twice to conceal my emotions I used the mild deception of blowing my nose. It was literally raining bullets ... I felt that, if nothing else, I was doing my duty and upholding our great country's traditions by the example our men set to the foreigners.'[21]

He resents being ordered out of the fight and back to his ship. 'The Admiral sent for me and told me he wanted me on board the *Alacrity*. He was very civil but I thought it better not to ask anything of him. It was a severe blow to us all but I told the men that their first duty was to the ship and there was nothing to it but to make the best of it.'[22]

On a lighter note he has a strong relationship with his food and drink. Before the assault on the forts he and a fellow commander enjoy some 'fruity'. On being awoken by shell fire he discovers that he has a hangover ('O what a head I had'). At Chen-Liang-Chung he has 'good food and excellent cocoa for breakfast'. At the consulate in Tientsin Mrs Charles gives him 'the best breakfast I have ever had – good bread with Yorkshire ham washed down with copious draughts of delicious tea'.[23]

And finally he never misses the opportunity to demonstrate the superiority of the British over the 'foreigners'. At the Taku forts Hattori, the Japanese commander, comes up to Cradock and says, 'Sir, I salute you – where the British go so do also the Japanese. I act under your orders.' Captain von Pohl, the German commander, 'made himself a great nuisance. He was in a curious state of "let me go but hold me back" and went like this. "I vill go on." All right said I, go on. "No I vill not I vill wait for you."' When it looks like the Germans will be first to enter the South forts – for they had got their boat away ahead of Cradock – he 'shouted to Captain Pohl to pull for a certain point and they ran on the mud as I knew they most surely would'.[24]

Cradock's voice rings clear from his journal. Impatient, ambitious, proud, brave, but not without qualms; convinced that, as Cecil

Rhodes once said, to be born British is to win the lottery of life, quick to take offence, decisive. His character was a reflection of his time – the British Empire, on which the sun never sets.

But he is not content. Suffering from an eye injury after the fighting and staying at The Shanghai Club he writes to Roger Keyes, venting his frustration at the lack of recognition and, more importantly, promotion, for his deeds and achievements whilst others have received theirs. 'Granville and Beatty are come over my head but I'm not going to fudge it. The worst of it is their use of their friends at home.'.[25] Beatty had been promoted captain on 9 November 1900 aged only 29 (Kit was 38 at the time and a commander). He has heard Keyes would be getting the DSO, personally awarded by the British Army Commander, Gravelee, (this wasn't in fact true but he was promoted to the rank of commander). Kit moans that '[people] see Commanders being promoted before me … they begin to think I have failed … it is a hard position'. Kit wanted his promotion to captain badly and he clearly felt he deserved it. In another, slightly later, letter he congratulates Keyes on being reappointed to command (of HMS *Fame*) on the China station but thinks Roger has been treated badly ('I don't think much of his platitudes to you') by Admiral Seymour who he claims 'doesn't care a ***** about anyone but his own people'.[26]

However, he takes comfort from the success of the wider 'band of brothers', writing that 'one great comfort I have is that all these people I have [referred to] have either been mentioned [in despatches] or promoted and that is the next best thing' (to his own promotion one assumes).

He never forgot his good fortune and his and Keyes' accomplishments in those two weeks of 1900. In a letter written to Keyes in 1906 he recognises his good fortune in China and the opportunity it created for him: 'it is so nice what you say of my luck. I have ridden it very many times … and I might have done better. I know how lucky I was to be where I was … others swear I was second or third'[27] (referring to the death of the Japanese sailor who raced with him to be first into the Taku forts).

He reminisces about their joint moments of glory on the Peiho River: 'I often picture you that dark night on the Peiho going to war ... for you meant to see it through' (this refers to Keyes' escapade in capturing three Chinese destroyers). In a later (1912) letter he again references Keyes' achievements in China: 'I shall never forget your honest anger when that Imperial boat was taken away from its jetty by the Russians' (referring to the Russians refusing to honour an agreement not to make off with a captured destroyer – Keyes returned and forced them to resile). In the same missive he thanks Keyes for some compliment and says it is undeserved, 'but I shall put it amongst my best service remembrances in a little drawer I have and I hope you will not mind'.[28]

Kit returned to England on 31 July 1901; by then he had received his most desired reward for his bravery – promotion to captain, effective 18 April of that year. He returned a hero and a full captain – a sort of God in the 'Vicwardian' navy. His service record had also been endorsed to the effect that he was 'to be prom [promoted] to flag rank when turn arrives irrespective of having comptd [completed] 6 years of qualifying service [i.e. sea service] in order prescribed'.[29] He obviously had supporters in the hierarchy. Note the 'Buggins' turn' phraseology too. But for now, and in the way of things, there were no open positions for a newly promoted captain and so he was placed on half pay leave again, this time for eight months. He returned to Hartforth Hall.

8

Bachelors

Kit was 39 and single. In fact neither Kit nor his two martial brothers ever married. This was unusual for the time, particularly in the case of Sheldon, the eldest, who would be expected to inherit the estate and continue the familial Cradock line. Kit might have argued that he was married to the navy but in fact he was an exception amongst his peers. Of the naval personnel we will meet in this book, Kit's peers or friends, all were married except Kit. Fisher (wed aged 25), Beatty (30), Jellicoe (43), Meux (54), Keyes (34), Troubridge (29), Luce (32), Arbuthnot (33), Battenberg (30), Bridgeman (41) – most of Cradock's peers were married men and had married at ages younger than Kit when he died. It was clearly possible to take a wife and be married to the job; why not Kit and why not his brothers? Admiral Charles Hope Dundas, a friend from Kit's Channel Fleet days, later wrote, 'Why he was a bachelor I never knew. Probably never met the girl he cared for sufficiently.'[1]

On the other hand, marriage was not exactly encouraged in the service. It was largely impossible for a lieutenant without private means, and no allowance was made for married men financially or in terms of leave. An overseas commission might last for four years and be quickly followed by another one. No wonder the saying was 'an officer married is an officer marred'.

Kit's mother Georgina died when he was three years old, his brothers being seven and six respectively. Their father never remarried and there was no female input to their upbringing bar the occasional governess and their grandmother. Their life was no doubt influenced by their father's example; hunting, horse racing, shooting and masculine company. Sheldon and Montague joined the army young and served abroad. Kit joined the navy at twelve-and-a-half years old and, as we have seen, lived a life both Spartan and tough – and exclusively male. From *Britannia* he was translated to the gun room and service at home and far away, again in exclusively male company. He had limited opportunity in his early years to meet the appropriate sort of woman and might well have understood virtually nothing about them (which was not untypical of his class at the time). For Kit and his brothers women would be a mystery, as would emotional expression. William Morris was typical of the buttoned-up men of the age when he stated, apropos his relation-ship with women, 'I am something of an Englishman and the words won't flow; it's one of the curses entailed on our blood and climate.'[2]

In the Victorian era the attitude to women amongst the upper classes had changed markedly from the Georgian age that preceded it. Undoubtedly the Victorian love affair with King Arthur and the Court of Camelot had much to do with this change. The age of chivalry was reborn in the latter part of the nineteenth century. Women were to be protected and subordinate to men, a view sus-tained by the laws of the land – in which a woman was 'femme covert', wholly subordinate to her husband and unable to own property, money or contract in her own right – until the Married Woman's Property act of 1882 gave them a full and separate legal status from their husband.

Chivalry and self-sacrifice, unspoken love and yearning, the pursuit of ideals and good deeds, the 'Venusiation' of women – these were the tropes of the age. The seminal novels were books such as *The Heir of Redcliffe* by Charlotte M. Yonge. Tennyson's *Idylls of the King* or the works of Swinburne (especially *Laus Veneris* and *The Leper*) were poetic exemplars; Malory's *Le Morte D'Arthur*, de la Motte Fouqué's *Sintram* the historical models. In art a plethora of Galahads, Lancelots, Guineveres and Arthurs decorated studios and drawing rooms alike. Burne-Jones's *Arthur in Avalon* – one of the grandest and, in his view, the defining painting of his long career – was the Arthurian apotheosis. Henry Newbolt (think *Vitai Lampada*

– Play up! Play up! and play the game), Sir Walter Scott and G.A. Henty were more prosaic popularisers. Scott in particular was responsible for evoking an age of personal honour, selfless courage and a romantic view of the protective feudal relationship through novels such as *Ivanhoe* (published as early as 1820). William Morris was another powerful influence: his prose romance *The Well at Worlds End* (1896) – a tale of young Prince Ralph in search of the redemptive and healing well at the end of the world – was probably read by virtually every literate man in England immediately before the beginning of the war. Such medievalism became more attractive as the century developed, and people tried to avert their eyes from the growing industrialisation and despoliation of the country and towards a dimly remembered and even more dimly experienced Eden.

In these artistic and literary interpretations women were either temptresses or placed on lofty pinnacles of unattainability. The Victorians needed a woman to love and a woman to make love to and could not necessarily see that these requirements could be combined in one person. Women were either virgin or whore and the ideal was the 'Angel in the house'.

Chivalric behaviour could descend into the ludic. In 1859, Edward Heneage Dering, an officer in the Guards, fell for Rebecca Dulcibella Orpen. He sought out her Aunt and guardian, Lady Chatterton, a widow, to gain permission for marriage but whether deliberately or not the widow took the proposal as being directed at her and accepted. Dering, being an officer and a gentleman, was unable to cause her the distress and social embarrassment of disillusioning her, even though she was old enough to be his mother, and married her. Two years later, his real love – Rebecca – married one Marmion Edward Ferrers and they all went to live at his house in Warwickshire, Baddersley Clinton, a moated manor (and now owned by the National Trust). We may imagine the meaningful looks and deep sighs in that mediaeval, atmospheric house. Eventually Lady Chatterton died in 1876 but Ferrers lived until 1884 when Dering was finally free to re-approach Rebecca, 26 years after he had first wanted to. They married in 1885 and he died seven years later. There were no children from either union.

The idea of the quest was intimately tied in to the chivalric, as in the quest for the Holy Grail of Arthurian legend. It is perhaps no surprise that no fewer than thirteen different authors published translations of the *Odyssey* between 1860 and 1890. Searching for an ideal, a self-abnegation or self-fulfilment was a suitable occupation for a gentleman. And it was important to be a gentleman – truthful, pure, manly. Thackeray in his 'Four Georges' lectures defined the breed. 'What is it to be a gentleman? Is it to have lofty aims, to lead a pure life, to keep your honour virgin; to have the esteem of your fellow-citizens and the love of your fireside; to suffer evil with constancy; and through evil or good to maintain truth always?'[3]

These behaviours lay deep in the British psyche and continued into the twentieth century. Lord Annan (born 1916 and a late exemplar of the type), writing his memoir *Our Age*, described the 'ideal Englishman' that he and his peers were encouraged to emulate in the years immediately following the First World War. 'Every man's first loyalty should be to the country of his birth and the institution in which he served. Loyalty to the institution came before loyalty to people. Individuals should sacrifice their careers, their family and certainly their personal happiness or whims to the regiment, the college, the school, the services, the ministry, the profession or the firm.'[4]

The chivalric code also governed the Victorian approach to battle. In schoolrooms all over the country the texts were Hector and Achilles, Horatio and the bridge, Arthur and his knights, Childe Roland, Prince Rupert, Moore at Corunna, Nelson at Trafalgar, Gordon and the Dervishes. Newbolt's *The Vigil*, published on the day war broke out, probably earned him his knighthood. It was no surprise that in 1914 reports of the 'Angel of Mons' or the Agincourt bowmen seen helping British soldiers on the Western Front were accepted as truth, and claims that German soldiers had been discovered killed by arrows credulously believed.

Chivalry even cropped up in bar brawls. In 1892 the then Sub-

Lieutenant Roger Keyes was assaulted at a dance and defended himself with his fists. His assailant was found to be bleeding profusely from the cheek and Keyes was menaced by the crowd who accused him of using knuckledusters. He explained that the wound was caused by his new signet ring which the man had given him no time to take off as he had attacked without warning – and the crowd immediately took his side instead.

The chivalric ideal was not just promulgated in schools but also in Sunday schools, Boys' Clubs, Scout groups, even newspapers. The Victorians believed that to fight for a good cause was an honourable and desirable thing, and to die for one's country a great ideal. *Pro Patria Mori*. War was good. In the USA, too, this was true. Theodore Roosevelt, one of America's greatest presidents, summed it up in a speech made in 1897: 'No triumph of peace can be so great as the supreme triumphs of war,' he declared, 'all the great masterful races have been fighting races.'[5]

Kit the sailor was certainly a prisoner of this zeitgeist as his quixotic behaviour at Coronel would demonstrate. Might it also have caused him, Kit the man, when coupled with his lack of experience of women, to feel conflict and emotional insecurity when confronted by a lady of his own class? Or was it that he had no interest in women? The Victorian approach to homosexuality and homoeroticism was confused. The cult of 'manliness' was much valued and many Victorians accepted and admired the view of the ancient Greeks that male friendship was the highest form of relationship. The love between men and men, or boys, was praiseworthy and only problematical when it crossed over into sex.

Public schools were hotbeds of such feelings and many masters had what would today be seen as very improper relationships with their charges. Like the navy these were closed, self-regulating environments and exclusively male. Homosexuality, or at least homoeroticism, was tolerated or even encouraged. Often such tendencies converged with the chivalric – the older boy protecting the younger, the master 'mentoring' the pupil.

As artists like Simeon Solomon and Swinburne, the demi monde surrounding Oscar Wilde and the laxity of the public schools, became more overt it led to the search for a different expression of 'manliness' more in line with the teaching of 'muscular Christianity' where 'purity' in relationships was emphasised. Tom Brown, at Oxford, is about to embark on a sordid affair with a bar maid but is dissuaded by his pal Hardy on the grounds that real manliness is defined by purity.

Homosexuality had been rife in the eighteenth-century navy, with its press gangs and long voyages overseas. 'Peg boys' were sometimes put on the crew roll for the purpose of providing Greek style pleasure. Whilst that tradition disappeared in the nineteenth century the association between the navy and homosexuality did not. Churchill is popularly supposed to have said, 'Don't talk to me about naval tradition; it's nothing but rum, sodomy and the lash,' although he later denied it, but it sounds like him. Sodomy was a capital offence in Britain until 1861, as it was in the navy. The last execution for the offence in a naval context was in 1829 which suggests that tolerance was the rule. But to be 'outed' spelled social ruin as it did, for example, for Simeon Solomon and Oscar Wilde. C.R. Ashbee, the founder of the Guild of Handicraft, knew he was gay but to conceal it married, told his wife that his sexual orientation was a problem before he married, had four children and a thirteen-year-long unpleasant marriage.

Kit was fastidious in his dress and appearance, 'always immaculately dressed with a neatly trimmed beard'[6] and usually accompanied by a small dog. He set great store by using the correct titles, salutes and other graciousness. He had an obsessive knowledge of the trivia of naval procedure; he was diplomatic and socially well mannered. He was described as 'something of an exquisite'.[7] Exquisite is an interesting word, generally used as an adjective but here it is a noun. The *OED* gives the noun form definition as 'a person who is affectedly concerned with appearance'. From about 1819 the usage was 'one who is over nice in dress, a fop'. A fop is defined as 'one who is foolishly attentive to his appearance dress or manners'.

As a function of his background and experiences, the unmarried Kit might simply have found women difficult to relate to, or it might have been that he preferred the company of men. Or was there unrequited or frustrated passion? Was there someone special in Kit's life who had to be kept a secret? Did he have a mistress, as did so many of his class?

9

Mistresses

It was not unusual for members of the upper classes to take a mistress. Given the great store set by social standing and lineage in the Victorian and Edwardian eras, choosing the right marriage partner was not wholly the province of Cupid. Aristocracy and landed gentry alike were concerned to make the 'right' marriage rather than the romantic one. The pool of available talent for a young girl of standing was limited by wealth, social status and geography. An aristocratic bachelor would seek a wife of similar background or, if his family finances were on the downward slope (as many were due to land based wealth being eroded by industrialisation), he would look for a match from the rising mercantile classes who would bring a substantial dowry, thus ensuring a short-term stabilisation of his disposable income. Love was not enough. As Edward Bulwer-Lytton wrote, 'wealth is the greatest of all levellers ... the highest of the English nobles willingly repair their fortunes of hereditary extravagance by intermarrying with the families of the banker, the lawyer, and the merchant.'[1] Hence, when the necessary 'heir and spare' had been produced, the reluctant husband would seek pastures new and the abandoned wife, accepting her fate meekly, would nonetheless welcome the attentions of another lover. The landed gentry were somewhat trapped in the middle of this movement, being neither super rich and of great lineage nor possessing industrial quantities of money.

In the Edwardian age a married woman of society was an attractive proposition to a man, as she was demonstrably not in pursuit of a spouse and any progeny of the relationship could be passed off as the husband's. Women would take as lovers men from their own social set, and hostesses were practised at making provision for such liaisons. Casual visits were made to the woman's house between lunch and tea, and the husband would absent himself to his club or mistress likewise. For society weekends away, lovers were allocated bedrooms close to each other, and the husband given an outer dressing room so he could slip away easily. However virginity was a precondition of marriage and ruin fell upon the unmarried 'fallen woman'.

The tone was set from the top of society. Edward VII, both when Prince of Wales and after his marriage and coronation, was a libidinous man. It is estimated that he took over 50 mistresses, the most famous being the actress and singer Lily Langtry (The Jersey Lily), but his conquests included Lady Randolph Churchill (mother of Winston), the Countess of Warwick (Daisy Warwick, who he called his 'Daiseywife'), the actress Sarah Bernhardt and Alice Keppel (great-grandmother of the present Duchess of Cornwall). He was also a famous user of brothels and had a particular favourite one in Paris (named Le Chabanais) for which he was rumoured to have designed special bondage equipment..

Between 1877 and 1880 Lily was Edward VII's semi-official mistress and was introduced to Queen Victoria and to Edward's wife Alexandra. By 1891 Edward's affections were fixed on Daisy, Lady Brooke, Countess of Warwick which led to a public quarrel with Admiral Lord Charles Beresford (Charlie B) concerning Beresford's own relations with the Countess. These were threatening to lead to divorce proceedings, not least because Beresford had fathered one of her children, and Daisy told Beresford's wife she intended to run off with him. Kit, as his naval ADC, would of course have observed Edward's later entanglements from a first-hand perspective.

Lloyd George, Chancellor of the Exchequer at the outbreak of war, and a future prime minister had a long-term mistress in Frances Stevenson, who came into his life as a governess to his daughter. After he married in 1888 he carried on many affairs, gaining the nickname 'the Goat'. Field Marshall Sir John French, who was to command the British Expeditionary Force in 1914 with a mixture of incompetence and vindictiveness, maintained a string of mistresses and married twice, having divorced his first wife, and whilst serving in India was cited as co-respondent in divorce proceedings by a fellow officer. One of his opponents, Franz Conrad von Holzendorf – Chief of Staff of the Austro-Hungarian forces – was having an affair with a married woman and hoped that she would leave her wealthy husband for him if he came back from the war a hero.

As in society, so in art. Dante Gabriel Rossetti and Janey Morris, wife of one of his best friends William Morris, carried on a very public affair to which William patiently consented, transferring his own affections to Georgina Burne-Jones, wife of Sir Edward, the painter, who had had his own angst-ridden affair with Maria Zambaco. Charles Dickens carried on a long affair with Ellen Ternan, eventually deserting his wife for her after 22 years of marriage. Thackeray took as his lover Mrs Charles Brookfield, wife of a famous preacher and inspector of schools and well known for her literary salon. The poet and writer Wilfred Scawen Blunt, married to Lady Anne Isabella, 15th Baroness Wentworth, took many mistresses including Janey Morris after Rossetti's demise. Eventually he moved one mistress, Dorothy Carleton, into the marital home, causing Lady Anne to sue for divorce.

There was even a district of London famous as the abode of mistresses. The new suburb of St John's Wood, NW8, with its attractive mixture of low-density villa housing and blocks of mansion flats, was near enough to the centre of London to be convenient and yet far enough to be discreet. Gentlemen of means found it handy to install their mistresses there in rented or sometimes purchased accommodation, and the area soon developed a reputation for the presence of single ladies with gentlemen friends.

Obtaining a divorce was rare. Most couples chose to put up with the situation and go their separate ways discreetly. In 1908 there were only 638 divorce petitions and approximately 275,000 marriages (0.2%). Divorce brought social obloquy and disgrace, particularly to the woman. Thus to all concerned, the faithless husband or the angry wife, being or taking a mistress was generally felt to be a better solution.

If Kit had had feelings for someone else's wife, might taking her as his mistress have been the route he chose?

10

The Mediterranean, 1902–1905

Kit spent the winter of 1901–2 in Yorkshire. He hunted, rode, visited old acquaintances and caused a small bungalow to be built against the walled garden the Hall to house him and his limited possessions. In particular he resumed his friendship with Lawrence Dundas, 1st Marquess of Zetland, Master of the Zetland Hunt for 35 years, boon companion of Kit's father and fellow huntsman and friend to Kit.

The Dundas family had come to Yorkshire from Scotland in 1763 when Sir Lawrence Dundas (Bt) purchased Aske House and estate from Lord Holderness. Lawrence Dundas (1712–1781) was a self-made man who, on leaving his father's draper's shop and setting up as a military contractor, had amassed a considerable fortune supplying goods to the British army during the Jacobite and Seven Years Wars. As was the way of the times he took advantage of the corrupt and inefficient system of military procurement to underperform and overprice against his various commitments. He also developed the port of Grangemouth and was major backer of the Forth and Clyde Canal on which sailed the first practical towing steamboat, the *Charlotte Dundas*, named after his daughter. On locating to Aske he achieved one of his ambitions (to acquire the nomination of the pocket borough of Richmond) but not the other (a peerage) for the king took against him as a result of his pushy profiteering.

His son Thomas, in the traditional manner of nouveau riche trade gaining legitimacy through dynastic marriage, married Lady Charlotte Fitzwilliam, daughter of a family that traced its pedigree back to the Norman invasion. He thus acquired standing, social cachet and eventually a peerage, being created Baron Dundas of Ashe in 1794.

Thomas was succeeded by his son Lawrence, the 2nd Lord Dundas who by dint of providing much needed financial help to the Duke and Duchess of Kent (Queen Victoria's parents) was created 1st Earl of Zetland in 1838 (Zetland is an old name for the Shetland Isles where his grandfather had acquired substantial estates). His son Thomas became the second Earl but died childless and the title and inheritance passed to his nephew Lawrence who became 3rd Earl of Zetland and subsequently 1st Marquess of Zetland. He played an active role in politics, including a period as Lord Lieutenant of Ireland (for which he was promoted to the Marquesate) and MP for Richmond, and produced five children: four boys, and a girl named Maud.

Maud was a beauty. She was photographed by Lafayette and in 1911 was painted by Phillip Lazlo (whose sitters included Battenberg, Balfour, the Kaiser and Edward VII). The portrait shows that at age 36 she had lost little of her looks.

In 1896, at only 19, Maud married William Charles de Meuron Fitzwilliam, Lord Milton and soon to be 7th Earl Fitzwilliam, at St Paul's cathedral. She was his third cousin (meaning they shared a great-great grandparent, Lady Charlotte Fitzwilliam who had married Sir Thomas Dundas, noted above). Third cousin marriages were popular in aristocratic circles as it was the closest form of cosanguinity that would be likely to produce the lowest risk of genetic defects in the offspring and thus kept the ownership of land and resources within the extended family. William was handsome and dashing, a polo player, Eton and Cambridge educated and would win a DSO in the Boer War. On succession to the Earldom in 1902, following the death of his grandfather, William (known to his workforce as 'Billy Fitzbilly') became spectacularly wealthy, inheriting an estate of significant land holdings and mineral rights worth billions of pounds at today's values – his income from coal alone equated to over £6 billion.

The 7th Earl and Countess Fitzwilliam – Billy and Maud. (Sheffield City Council, Libraries Archives and Information: Sheffield Local Studies Library Picture Sheffield: s08883).

William had been born in remote Canada (Pointe de Meuron) where his father had been sent to hide his 'madness' (actually epilepsy), and all his life was dogged by rumours that he was a changeling, not the true heir but a substitute inserted to remove the stain of epilepsy from the family. Epilepsy was badly understood at the time and the 'cures' were often worse than the disease. For many years Billy had to fight his aunt, Lady Alice, who tried repeatedly to prove that he was not the rightful heir.

He was also a cad. Maud and Billy had married young and soon went their separate ways. Billy was a philanderer, as a teenager with the family's tenantry and as Earl with a succession of actresses, whom he would entertain on his yacht *Kathleen*. In 1913 he was cited as co-respondent in a divorce case, a charge which would have been highly embarrassing but was withdrawn at the last minute allegedly by reason of Billy buying off the plaintiff. His long-term mistress was the Marchioness of Headfort, a one-time showgirl called Rosie Boote with whom he spent the larger proportion of his time. His relationship with Maud was resultantly stormy and she would frequently lock him out of her rooms.

The feelings between Maud and her husband were also impacted by a succession of female births when all that was wanted was a male heir, although Billy was said to have fathered an illegitimate boy child. After the birth of his fourth daughter in 1908, the Earl apparently turned his back on the midwife in disgust.

But this was in the future. The 24-year-old Maud and the war hero Kit met and hunted together at the Raby and Zetland Hunts. She was taken with his charm and looks. He held her, according to the family's descendants' oral history in 'great esteem'.

But this was not enough to distract him from his goal. Kit hankered for a new sea appointment and his wishes were granted in March 1902 when he was given command of HMS *Andromeda* (the Handy Dromedary to its crew), Flag Ship of Rear Admiral Sir Baldwin Walker in the Mediterranean Fleet based at Malta, who was to shift his flag to the newly arrived *Bacchante* in December, taking Kit with him as his flag captain.

In the Vicwardian British navy the cynosure of all that was prized was found in the Mediterranean fleet. Based at Malta, sunny, cheap, far away from the travails of home, it was a posting much to be wished for. The Med was Britain's *mare nostrum*, a playground for its rich and for its navy. Here officers could live the life they lived at home, enjoying the privileges of their class, only at lower cost

The social life was superb. Admiral C.C. Penrose Fitzgerald, writing in his autobiography of his service in the Med in 1889, emphasised it: 'Very good opera companies used to come to Malta for the winter months ... then, it was extremely cheap – two-and-six for a stall and boxes in proportion. Several stars, including Albani, made their debut at the Malta Opera House. There were balls, parties, picnics, polo, gymkhanas, and golf. Many of the officers of the Mediterranean squadron got their wives out from England for three or four of the winter months, and as these frequently brought with them other ladies, there were plenty of dances, riding picnics, and other innocent relaxations from the stern routine of naval discipline. The great event of the season was the fancy-dress ball at the Governor's palace. The various and picturesque costumes of the East were always well represented ...'.[1] Better than home by far.

The fleet cruised up and down, its programme largely social and its practices based around complex and centralised 'evolutions' – manoeuvres. These choreographed routines were like an army parade-ground display and bore little or no resemblance to the likely needs of a shooting war. When ashore, officers could enjoy dinner parties, fancy dress balls, shooting, regattas, tennis parties, golf, cricket; and if you had the financial resource, polo and horse racing (Kit kept a horse in Malta for that purpose). A generation of future flag officers grew up in this environment, Kit included. Military 'bull' was the rule, a smart and clean ship the route to promotion, following orders and 'fitting in' socially the most important aspect of behaviour. Admiral Lord Charles Beresford commanded the Mediterranean fleet from 1905 to 1907 and this was still the routine. His reign was characterised by rigid training and discouragement of initiative.

The prizing of such character traits ensured that their roots sat deep in the navy's soul and, as in any closed system, it became a parody of itself; clannish, self-absorbed, complacent, convinced of its own superiority and untested by any foe. Seniority within this clan brought with it privileges and untrammelled power. Those who do well under such a system have an interest in perpetuating it. As Machiavelli recognised four centuries before, 'It must be remembered that there is nothing more difficult to plan, more doubtful of success, nor more dangerous to manage than a new system. For the initiator has the enmity of all who would profit by the preservation of the old institution and merely lukewarm defenders in those who gain by the new ones'.[2] Kit was becoming a prisoner of the system.

Kit's admiralty record, which details his service and ships, shows him taking command of *Bacchante* on 19 December 1902. The ship's log book confirms this: 'at 3.00pm Captain C Cradock took over command exchanging with Captain Brock who proceeded to *Andromeda*'.[3] Brock had sailed the *Bacchante* out, and conducted its 'shake down', for it was a newly launched vessel. But the same admiralty record also states that Kit 'broke his leg while in England Dec 02 and unable to return to his ship for about six weeks'.[4] These statements cannot both be true.

Perhaps Kit took over 'in absentia'. On the 20th of December Rear Admiral Baldwin Walker transferred his flag to the *Bacchante* but the day before a Commander Chambers had replaced the second in command of the passage crew, Lieutenant P.B. Garrett, on *Bacchante*. A more senior man – had he been standing in for Kit on *Andromeda* and now on his new command? When did Kit return – presumably mid-January? Or did he take passage out with his broken leg and recuperate on Malta? He was certainly on board and on the island by April, for that is when the royal visit to the fleet took place. Edward VII arrived on the 8th in the royal yacht *Victoria and Albert* and departed on the 23rd, by which time the king had invested Cradock with the CB – Companion of the Bath – during his visit. Throughout June, July and August the fleet was heavily engaged in manoeuvres, as was *Bacchante,* calling at, *inter alia,* Cartagena, Alicante, Lagos, Gibraltar, Corfu and Patras. But for the whole of May *Bacchante* was at Malta doing nothing much, according to her log. Did Kit take some leave then? Kit's movements are never mentioned in the ship's log. Baldwin Walker is recorded as transferring his flag back and forth, and officers and men are noted when they join or leave the ship. And yet Kit must have come and gone regularly – we know he liked the social life on Malta and kept racing and polo ponies there. He would often have been off ship and on shore; yet his movements are never recorded.

The question of his movements is germane, for Kit obviously felt the need to return to England. In late 1903 Kit requested – and was granted – 30 days' paid home leave in England for 'urgent private affairs'.[5] He left for home on 17 November. He did not, in fact, return to his ship until 13 February 1904, a rather longer leave than originally suggested. What were these urgent private affairs? For a man in his position to request abnormal leave was most unusual, and in any case he much enjoyed his social life on Malta. Sheldon was running the estate; his father was long since dead, his other siblings in rude health. What drove him to return?

On 14 March 1904 Maud Fitzwilliam gave birth to another daughter and named her Donatia Faith Mary. Donatia means 'God's gift'. It is not a Fitzwilliam family name and the family were not Catholic. The names chosen for her other children were much more mainstream and family related – Maud, Marjorie, Helena, William. Was there something special about Donatia? Could there have been something special about the father? Conception would have been around June and the pregnancy would have been evident by October. Was Kit and Maud's relationship rather more than hunting companions?

For Kit to have been Donatia's father he would have to have been in England around May or June 1903 – or Maud would have to have been in Malta. As noted above he could have been. That Kit and Maud were close will be returned to and perhaps proven later, in Chapter 26.

The year 1904 bought new fame for Kit. The Crown Prince of Siam, Prince Vudijai, heir to the throne of Rama V, Chulalongkorn, had been sent to Britain at the age of ten to be educated, attended the Royal Military Academy at Sandhurst and was attached to the Durham Light infantry. Later he read history at Christ Church, Oxford and graduated in 1901. In April 1904, while serving as a midshipman in the British navy, he was rescued from drowning off the coast of Sardinia, by Kit Cradock. A grateful father gave Kit a diamond-studded gold presentation cigarette case, oblong in shape with a curved section. The cover had crowned initials in a foliate surround and a cabochon sapphire push-piece, and it was inscribed on the reverse 'To Captain Christopher Cradock, C.B., H.M.S.

Bacchante from H.M. King Chulalongkorn of Siam, for jumping overboard at night and saving the life of Prince Vudijai in Palmas Bay, Sardinia, April 1904'. It measured 9.2 cm in length and came in a fitted green leather case with the retailer's address of Child & Child, 35 Alfred Place West, London SW and a tooled sunflower mark on outer cover.

Kit treasured the gift, but it was not with him at Coronel and survived in the possession of his sister's family until 1995 when, sold at auction, it realised £17,500. He also received official recognition in the form of a testimonial from the Royal Humane Society for his selfless action. His fame was growing.

In October 1904 Kit was still Flag Captain to Admiral Sir Baldwin Walker when that officer was in command of the cruisers sent to shadow the Russian fleet after the infamous 'Dogger Bank' incident, when Russian Admiral Rozhestvensky's fleet – en route to its destruction at Tsushima – fired on a fleet of Hull trawlers causing loss of life and general public outrage.

Then, in January 1905, Kit took command of HMS *Leviathan*, another cruiser of similar type to *Bacchante* and sister ship to HMS *Good Hope*. In her he returned to England, and between June and September was absent on sick leave before once again being placed on half pay, this time for 11 months.

11

The Vicwardian Navy

In order to understand Kit it is necessary to understand those vectors which would have formed his personality and character. His family and class background certainly, the social and societal mores of the time surely, but most importantly the navy in which he grew up, lived his life and found his calling.

For Kit the navy was his life, with only hunting coming close in his affections. The navy was a top-down, controlling, ordered world. All aspects of life were regulated and subject to routine. But for the officers it also provided a 'home away from home' – a life which paralleled the one they left behind and reflected the social class from which they were drawn.

The navy was a private club with strict criteria for membership, a sort of glorified yacht club for the aristocracy and landed gentry. Just as with a private members' club there were rules to keep out the riff-raff, and promotion to the officer caste from the lower deck was strictly forbidden. The navy's ruling class was drawn from the same families as ruled the country at large and they fought hard to protect their privileges. As one titled lady remarked to an aspiring officer from the lower deck, 'The navy belongs to us and if you were to win the commissions you ask for it would be at the expense of our sons and nephews whose birthright it is.'[1] Membership of this club was almost 'by invitation'. Would-be officers had to be 'recommended' by friends of the family who were naval officers (as Jackie Fisher was by Admiral Sir William Parker in 1854 or Roger Keyes by the then First Lord, Lord George Hamilton, a friend of the family). Engineers were not allowed to be officers until the 1840s and then had to mess separately from their peers. The engine driver did not want to talk to the oily rag. As a letter to *The Times* put it, engineers 'were a most useful class of men but they were not "gentlemen".' The 1852 Manning Committee had recommended that warrant officers (NCOs) who displayed great bravery in action could be promoted to lieutenant – but none was until two such promotions were made in honour of the Queen's Golden Jubilee in 1887, and then no more for the rest of the century.

In 1890 the navy issued an appeal to recruit 100 more lieutenants and Henry Capper, a warrant gunner, led a campaign to allow these to be selected from the lower deck. There was strong public support but the idea was opposed by many officers and defeated in parliament by their 'interest'. During the Boer War one warrant gunner was promoted for valour, but the way up from the lower deck was not officially cleared until general access to lieutenancies for warrant officers was declared in 1903.

So Kit Cradock, growing up through the ranks of the navy, served and messed with the same sort of person that he would meet on the hunting fields of Yorkshire or the dinner parties of his friends and neighbours. A small, self-perpetuating, self-regulating world with common values, background, beliefs and rules. And a controlling one, where everything had to be done a certain way and initiative or deviation from the norm was unacceptable. Take the examples of facial hair, dress and smoking.

Beards

Kit Cradock sported a beard (a 'full set') all his adult life. His 'neatly trimmed beard' drew comment in the *Dictionary of National Biography*. In the Victorian and Edwardian navy this was not unusual; most people would associate the navy and beards, and popular culture and advertising has endorsed that view – remember the famous matelot on the tobacco brand Players Navy Cut (hat band HMS *Excellent*, in fact the navy's gunnery school) and the sailor on the Players Senior

Service (itself a reference to the navy) packet? The navy was popular in the late nineteenth century. At Victoria's Diamond Jubilee fleet review (1897), *The Times* said, '... this unexampled scene ... nothing could be more impressive than the long lines of ships anchored in perfect order, spreading over miles of water in apparently endless array'.[2] Perhaps as never before the navy was the source of much public interest and the press built on this by presenting warships as the most advanced products of the new technology of the machine age. To the public it became *their* navy and admirals became stars, as sportsmen are today. The popular entertainment industry took up the cry, and songs and verse praised the navy and its ships. ('Stand by to reckon up your battleships, ten, twenty, thirty there they go ...' was a popular song of the time by Henry Newbolt and Charles Villiers Stanford). People responded to and copied the navy's tropes such as beards and the, to us toe-curling, sailor suits that little boys and girls were forced into.

The Victorian era was a famously hirsute period, in contrast to the fashion of the previous century. The Georgian era saw a clean shaven look in vogue, but the Victorians revolted against this, as they did against many aspects of the 'age of enlightenment'. The typical stern, bearded *pater familias* stares at us from many portraits and pictures. The three great prime ministers of the time – Gladstone (a wispy beard in later life), Disraeli (a goatee) and Salisbury (a full set) – led the way. The artistic elite endorsed beards – Morris (a full set), Burne-Jones (a long, two-pointed affair), Leighton (a full set), Poynter (a full set); Dickens and Tennyson too. Scientists were not immune, James Clark Maxwell was fully bearded and Darwin had grown a beard by 1866. The Victorians saw beards as symbols of manliness and male courage; in this they were following the Ancient Greeks (who inspired so much of Victorian culture and education) who saw clean shaven-ness as a sign of effeminacy.

Until the middle of the nineteenth century beards were in fact unusual in the services except for sappers. In the navy the fashion had been for queues or pigtails, made glossy with gun oil and worn to inordinate length (a long queue being the sign of a long service hand). Beards and moustaches were forbidden. Pigtails began to go out of fashion around 1825 and pressure grew in the service to be allowed to wear facial hair.

There were certainly practical reasons, as well as the dictates of fashion, to support beards, as water for washing and shaving would be in short supply on a long voyage. Being *à la mode* probably played a part too. In 1869 the Admiralty finally bowed to such pressure and in June issued an ordinance that 'officers and men on board Her Majesty's ships, including Royal Marines when embarked, will in future be permitted to discontinue the use of the razor on board ship ... moustaches are not to be worn without beards or beards without moustaches ... Captains will direct such that a uniformity as to length is maintained.'[3] This was amended in December to allow marines who had grown a beard to keep it when ashore (marines, like all soldiers from the late nineteenth century to 1916, were not allowed to shave their upper lip or to wear a beard – with certain exceptions). Reservists were allowed a moustache; otherwise it was a full set or nothing. The permission of an officer had to be sought and granted for a sailor to either grow or shave off a beard.

In his writings Kit advises, 'Keep the men's hair short, and those that shave should have clean faces on Thursdays and Sundays, if not on other days. To be shaved on Sundays is an order in the merchant service which is adhered to. Men are not to grow or shave without permission of the officer of their division, and all coxswains of duty boats, quartermasters and sentries should be shaved every morning'.[4] This was written in 1908.

Dress

Officers in the Royal Navy of the late 1890s, when Kit held a commander's rank, had no fewer than seven different dress codes to follow depending on the occasion. The garments and their usages were all listed in admiralty regulations. Just buying the clothing necessary would put a strain on many bank balances, and to be inappropriately dressed would lead to a reprimand at best and punishment or restriction of privileges at worst.

Number ones were the full dress uniforms, which included coat, epaulettes, laced trousers, cocked hat, sword, decorations and medals. It was used at state occasions or when the senior officer wanted to dignify an occasion appropriately. Number twos – 'Ball' – were similar but with a tail coat, no sword and a white waistcoat. It was worn at official or public balls and dinners/evening receptions. Numbers threes – 'Frock coat with epaulettes' – included a morning waistcoat, plain blue or white trousers, cocked hat, sword, ribbons (KCVOs, as Kit became, had to wear their badge of the order). It was for formal occasions such as courts martial, boarding a foreign warship and other such ceremonials. Number fours – 'Frock coat' – was similar but discarded the epaulettes. This was the dress standard expected if visiting, and returning visits, ship commander to ship commander for example. Fives specified an undress coat, morning waistcoat, plain white or blue trousers, cap, sword, undress belt, ribbons, and was for drills, patrols and dockyard duties. Number sixes – 'Mess dress jacket' – included a blue evening waistcoat, laced blue trousers and ribbons and fitted for dinner in harbour at the table of a senior officer or at a military mess dinner. Finally sevens – Mess undress – were the same but with plain trousers.

To dress incorrectly was to commit a solecism of a high order. When Edward VII, in the Royal Yacht, was visiting the King of Greece in Corfu, Admiral Beresford, as admiral of the Mediterranean fleet, arrived to escort him. Beresford welcomed the King of Greece onto his flagship without changing into his full dress uniform. Edward was furious at this act of discourtesy to a fellow monarch and made a formal complaint to the Admiralty.

This dress obsession extended to the ratings too. Men traditionally made their own working garments but as the nineteenth century progressed the number of 'inspection' outfits grew with it and the Admiralty saw fit to regulate the exact size allowed for a trouser leg or a collar. By 1891 an officer inspecting his division often carried a ruler with him marked with the various regulation uniform measurements. Small wonder that Kit became a man obsessed with the small detail of dress and appearance. It was the very stuff of existence and one could go horribly wrong just by wearing the wrong trousers.

Smoking

Like most of his peers, Kit was a smoker. Smoking was deeply embedded in Vicwardian high society and the navy. Cigarette brands made overt or covert references to the Service and smoking was universally popular with officers and men alike.

Tobacco came to England from the colonies in Virginia in the sixteenth century, apocryphally through the offices of Sir Walter Raleigh, more likely with ordinary sailors. James I abhorred smoking and personally penned *A Counterblaste to Tobacco*. More practically he raised the duty on it by 4000%. Despite this there were 7000 tobacco outlets in London alone by the early seventeenth century and by 1700 smoking was commonplace in the navy, although it had to be practised (for obvious safety reasons) over tubs of water in the forecastle only. Tobacco was imbued with many medical properties and navy surgeons would use it in a variety of treatments, including bringing drowned men back from the dead!

The famous Players Navy Cut brand of cigarette was introduced in 1900 and for many years carried an increasingly debased likeness of Able Seaman Thomas Huntley Wood from the 1882 battleship HMS *Edinburgh*. 'Navy cut' referred to the naval practice of buying whole tobacco leaf from the ship's stores which the sailors would wind into ropes. A plug would then be cut off for a pipe or a length for a cigarette. Until around the beginning of the twentieth century cigarette smoking was seen as somewhat effete and the smoke generator of choice was a clay pipe into which the plug was inserted and lit.

By the early 1900s mess dinners routinely finished with the handing round of coffee and cigarettes, and large supplies of tobacco were carried on board for the crew to purchase at discount prices. On long voyages its narcotic power was no doubt appreciated, hence tobacco's long association with things naval. In *Whispers from the Fleet* Kit records the standard case weights in which tobacco was carried on board – leaf in biscuit cases of 120 lb and casks of 80 lb, tinned tobacco in cases of 21 lb.

In eighteenth-century England smoking had been much frowned upon in polite society. On ascending to the throne Queen Victoria banned smoking in the court but Albert was an enthusiastic user and his son Edward, Prince of Wales even more so. When he took the throne in 1901 his first command was said to be, 'Gentlemen – you may smoke.' Under such royal patronage, smoking – particularly of cigars – became wildly popular amongst the upper classes. There were Smokers (smoking dinners) and Smoking Concerts.

Social life

The navy also provided a fine social life, at least for officers; and if one rose to the rank of ship's captain, or higher, it could rival the aristocracy for ease of living.

The officer class of the Vicwardian navy was made up primarily of the scions of the minor aristocracy and landed gentry. And whilst there were undoubted dangers to life at sea – ship wreck, disease and the occasional minor bit of gunboat diplomacy – there was a good life to be had as well. At sea and on land the officer class recreated the pastimes and pursuits that their kin would be enjoying at home in Britain. Hunting, polo, shooting and horseracing dominated the leisure hours of the navy's elite. Kit was, of course, inordinately fond of all of these, as was his best friend in the navy, Roger Keyes, who wrote several volumes of autobiography detailing his naval and social adventures. Keyes' memoirs can therefore reasonably be expected to reflect the lifestyle which Kit himself lived as a junior (and indeed senior) officer.

At the end of 1893 Keyes was posted to the South American

squadron as a sub-lieutenant and after some minor local difficulties with a revolution in Brazil, sailed to be based mainly off Uruguay and Argentina for the next two years. Here he bought retrieving dogs and would head off shooting whenever possible. Duck shooting on the islands off the coast bought bags of muscovy, teal, widgeon and mallard. Wading through the local marshes he bagged snipe (fourteen snipe and eleven duck in one hour). He played polo for the local teams, and estancia owners put strings of three and four ponies at his disposal. At the Hambledon club in Buenos Aires he played cricket, tennis and more polo. In May of 1895 Keyes took a fortnight's leave in Colonia and played polo, rode, and shot partridge, hares and a deer. At the Fray Bentos factory in Uruguay he shot deer and partridges. In other words, Keyes' life replicated the one he would have had at home in Kent.

In 1899 Keyes was in Hong Kong, commanding the destroyer HMS *Fame*. He enjoyed it immensely and had plenty of polo, cricket, golf and 'bathing picnics'. He bought a 'very good'[5] polo pony of his own and the commanders of two other ships asked him to look after and play theirs too while they were away. Keyes was a fine rider and would go to the Happy Valley racecourse in the early morning to catch a ride on racing horses. Captain Hedworth Lampton (soon to become Meux) was at Hong Kong commanding HMS *Powerful* and kept a string of polo and racing horses. Keyes rode several of Lampton/Meux's horses in steeplechases during the winter and in a cup race came in second against professional jockeys, winning a substantial sum for the owner and for his fellow officers who had backed him. Meux will feature in this narrative later.

A naval officer's life paralleled that at home in other respects too. Servants had been present in the eighteenth-century navy in large numbers and the tradition of naval servant continued in Kit's time. On board ship, admirals and ship's captains had personal servants, drawn from the crew. An officer's servant, in addition to his normal crew duties, would look after the officer's cabin, be his valet, wake him for his watches and serve him at wardroom meals, all for a little extra pay. In the officers' wardroom the standards were those officers would expect to find with their fellow gentry ashore. It was not a hive of intellectual activity. Marder comments that the only papers to be found in the average wardroom were the *Sporting Times* and one or two illustrated magazines. Breakfast was taken silently, then a light lunch and dinner in the evening. The president of the mess (the commander or first lieutenant) would head the table which would be set with silver service, spread with a white table cloth; servants would stand behind their officers for the *service à la russe*. The chaplain would say grace; conversation would be light and certainly not about technical matters. Wine was served to each officer by his servant and marked down on his mess account. On large ships a band might play. Guest nights when in port were similar but with the added advantage of new faces (almost always male).

By the turn of the century, it was commonplace for wardroom stewards to serve as waiters at meal times and serve officers as personal servants when not so employed. Senior officers had personal coxswains for their barge who followed them from command to command. In 1907 the admiralty issued an order enabling the commanders-in-chief of the three home ports to 'provide their own servants in place of the naval domestics allowed'[6] and granted a £500 per annum allowance in lieu. In 1912 the same officers lost the use of their private 'yachts' (small steam vessels in reality), again replaced with a £500 allowance.

Such was life in the Vicwardian navy.

12

Royalty and Promotion, 1905–1910

Kit was on half pay for 299 days from September 1905. He rode, hunted, socialised. Perhaps he saw Maud. He went to London and stayed at his clubs (he was a member of the 'Naval and Military Club' and 'Boodles' in St James'). The Cradock brothers owned (or more likely leased) an apartment at 90 Piccadilly in London for use when in town. Conveniently situated next to the Naval and Military club of which they were all members, the building had been erected in 1883 and comprised shops on the ground floor and 'residential chambers' above. Letters surviving from both Kit and Monty give it as their residential address and there still exists a wallet that belonged to Montagu inscribed '90 Piccadilly, London, 16 October 1926'.[1] No doubt it provided a convivial base from which to meet friends and a secure one in which to get away from prying eyes when necessary.

But generally Kit was frustrated. He was not at sea and that was what he liked best. He writes to Keyes from his sister's home at Hartforth Grange to congratulate him on his forthcoming nuptials. Keyes is a 'lucky man' and Kit 'looks forward to the privilege of meeting your lady'. He wants to host the meal when they do meet and encloses a 'small token of remembrance'. He reminisces about their joint moments of glory on the Peiho river; in a subsequent letter he writes that he 'shall be going to sea as soon as I can get a suitable ship'.[2]

Finally his ship came in. In July 1906 he was appointed to command HMS *Swiftsure*, a battleship of a type about to become obsolete overnight with the launch of HMS *Dreadnought*. She had originally been ordered by Chile and was launched in 1903. Following a collision with a sister ship she undertook a year-long re-fit, and it was Kit's task to recommission her as part of the Channel Fleet. That clearly did not occupy all of his time for in 1907 he published his last book, *Whispers from the Fleet*. From the book it is clear that Kit, at least by 1907, saw the threat posed to British maritime dominance by the growth of German economic power and its blue water navy: 'Our navy is not bellicose, it stands on the contrary a mighty instrument for peace; and may the day be therefore far distant which might cause this crushing factor of power, to fall like a thunderbolt on the back of a certain half fledged Eagle, which at times seems so anxious to fly, and bruise its talons on the armoured breast of poor battle worn Britannia.'[3] Regrettably things were not to play out quite like that for Kit.

He remained in command of *Swiftsure* for two years, but in August 1908 she was paid off into the reserve and once more Kit found himself unwanted and on half pay. But this time there was a pleasant New Year's surprise. In February 1909 Kit was appointed Naval Aide de Camp (ADC) to King Edward VII.

The role of the monarch's ADC was largely ceremonial – and Edward VII adored ceremony; he was obsessed with the correct forms of dress and address and with the petty distinguishments of rank and protocol. Kit, raised in the navy since childhood and imbued with its punctiliousness, would be a good fit. Edward loved shooting too and Kit was perfectly at home and competent in such a milieu. Unfortunately for his pocket it was an unpaid position and he remained on half pay.

Being appointed ADC to the king was often a good career move. Amongst the protagonists in this book the future admirals Sir Francis Bridgeman and Sir George Warrender both acted as ADC to Edward in 1901–03 and 1908 respectively. And it would appear to have been true for Kit too, for on 1 July 1909 he was promoted to the rank of Commodore Second Class and given command of Royal Naval Barracks Portsmouth, duties which he combined with those of ADC. A 'second class' commodore was one who did not have a full captain serving under him, and Kit's role was effectively to head the administration of the barracks and the supervision of the men quartered within them. It was not an overly taxing position and Kit had plenty of time for hunting and for visiting with his Barnes relatives in nearby Catherington. He also discovered the joys and pitfalls of the newly popular motor car. Clearly he was not afraid of the new or the dangerous for, in the same year as his promotion, he was fined £2 and costs at Havant petty sessions for failing to stop his motor car in a collision with a cyclist. A further summons for dangerous driving was suspended pending appeal. Motor vehicles were few and far between at the time. The Motor Car Act of 1903 had introduced the requirement for a driving licence, registration and numbering of cars and increased the speed limit from 14 to 20 miles per hour. The Ford Model T had commenced production in the USA in 1908 and the first Morgan was built a year later. Kit was in the vanguard of fashion.

On 6 May 1910 Edward VII died. The nation was plunged into mourning and a new king ascended to the throne. George V loved the navy, had been educated at *Britannia* and served as a midshipman and at Malta under his uncle. He had many naval contacts and friends, not least Kit who he knew through Kit's service on the *Howe* and the *Victoria and Albert*. George had not been fond of his father's circle but Kit bridged the gap and stayed on as the new king's ADC until the end of October.

And then hubris and nemesis in equal measure. On 24 August 1910 Kit was promoted to flag rank; a Rear Admiral at last, aged 48. In October he was replaced in his post and placed on half pay. Back to Hartforth and the wait for command and sea duty.

13

Cradock the Man

Kit was now a member of the navy's senior elite, but what sort of a man was he? How was he perceived by his peers and subordinates and revealed in his writings and behaviours? As a commander at the RN College *Britannia*, Kit reminded the future Admiral Andrew Cunningham (future victor of Taranto and Matapan) of Sir Francis Drake.[1] Another officer later described him in the *Dictionary of National Biography* as 'the very model of a Victorian Naval officer, who never married. Tall, alert, always immaculately dressed with a neatly trimmed beard, the well-spoken Cradock had a reputation as a fine sportsman and seaman'.[2] Not everyone was impressed, however. C.P. Scott, in his *Political Diaries* called him 'another society person, known not to be up to the mark',[3] whilst another writer described him as 'tall, handsome, an athlete and sportsman and something of an exquisite'.[4] He was famously gallant and had a reputation for impetuosity. The *National Review* described him as 'the beau-ideal of a British naval officer, as chivalrous, open hearted, gallant a gentleman as ever trod a quarter deck'.[5]

Cradock seems to have had charisma. People liked him. Admiral Roger Keyes and Admiral Charles Hope-Dundas both described him as their best friend in the service. Long after Cradock's death the (by then) Lord Jellicoe wrote to Kit's sister that 'your brother was in truth a man I admired with all my heart'.[6] Captain Alfred F.B. Carpenter VC, the hero of Zeebrugge, described Kit as 'a real white man' and said that he 'never ceased to be irresistibly attracted by his splendid personality'.[7] Allardyce, Governor of the Falklands, would later describe him as 'an extremely nice man, one of nature's gentlemen'.[8]

Kit's writings reveal much of him. As has been noted he was an author who had published three books: *Sporting Notes from the East* (1890), *Wrinkles in Seamanship or a help to Salt Horse* (1894) and *Whispers from the Fleet* (1907, which ran to a second edition in 1908). He writes in an avuncular style but with a detailed knowledge of seamanship and a sense of nostalgia for the days of sail. He pays particular attention to the traditions of respect in the navy and the etiquette of dealing with senior officers, one's peers and other ranks (a trait that would have stood him in good stead dealing with Edward VII and George V, who were both sticklers for correct dress, form etc.). He was a man to whom tradition, rules, the chain of command and orders were very important. How could he be anything else, having been in the Victorian and Edwardian navies since he was twelve years old? 'Obedience is the soul of the navy; he who has not learnt to obey is wanting in the first essential of command' is a chapter heading in *Whispers from the Fleet*. He must have been aware of his own tendency to rashness for he added, 'a naval officer should never let his boat go faster than his brain'.[9]

His excellent seamanship shines through with detailed instructions for the various tasks of an officer's life such as towing, mooring and leaving harbour; but newer technologies are of less interest to him. He admits a lack of knowledge of gunnery (and indeed in his last book he hands that chapter over to a co-writer), prefers battle to be fought from the open bridge rather than the recently introduced armoured conning tower and emphasises the importance of practice over theory. His experiences as a transport officer and an expert horseman are put to good use in a section describing how to load horses ('never turn round to look at a refractory horse and endeavour to pull him after you by the head as you walk backwards – if you want a horse to follow you, put the reins over your shoulder and walk away from him in the direction you want to go'). He claims he is bad at sums. He argues that speed is the most advantageous attribute when sea room is limited; and he is a romantic, writing of the 'swift ships of the cruiser squadron all drawing in to join their flagship ... like wild ducks at evening flighting home to some well-known spot, so are they, with one desire, hurrying back at the behest of their mother ship to gather round her for the night'.[10] Most of all one senses his love of the navy, hard to describe but shining through every word he writes. The navy was his essence.

A very fit man, Kit loved sporting pursuits. He rode to hounds all his life, an enthusiasm clearly inherited from his father and loved it beyond all other sports. Cadets in *Britannia* could hunt in their leisure time if they had the money and we can be sure that Kit did in the 'merry weekly hunts of the Britannia Beagles'.[11] As an Instructor Commander in *Britannia* in later years he was 'Master of the Britannia Beagles' and proud of it. Roger Keyes wrote that Cradock was very fit, often hunting on foot with a cadet bringing his pony along behind. In 1902 he was absent from duty for six weeks owing to a broken leg sustained on the hunting field. The then midshipman Harold Hickling remembered Kit at the Quorn hunt before the war. Kit had shouted him out of the way but at the end of the chase shared his flask with him, telling him it would do him good – and that it was Cockburns '76; his taste for port no doubt developed by many a mess dinner.

In his books Kit urges parents of potential *Britannia* cadets to have them taught to ride '... many opportunities for fun are lost in the navy to the boy who has been denied the Englishman's heritage – commune with a noble animal; and to the man later, the one spot on earth from which he can shout – begone dull care.'[12] After Kit's death, his friend Admiral Robert Arbuthnot, a martinet who was to die at Jutland rashly leading his squadron to destruction, commented, 'Poor Kit, poor Kit Cradock, he always hoped that he would be killed in battle or break his neck in the hunting field.'[13]

Kit also raced as a gentleman jockey and rode horses to victory in several flat and steeplechase races, including the Grand Military Gold Cup at Sandown on his own horse, 'Prizeman'. He was a keen shot too. In *Sporting Notes from the East* (1889) he writes of the pleasures of shooting snipe in Shanghai. Clay shooting appealed to him and he organised shoots for the ships and squadrons he commanded. Typically for the age he kept copious records of his kills, listing mammoth quantities of slain avian prey – and not just avian; his 'log book' for 1881 records that he shot nineteen 'couple' rabbits on one day and three opossums on another. On another occasion his bag included two wallabies.[14]

He enjoyed polo too and writes about it in his books. In Hong Kong he played with David Beatty before they went off to the Boxer War; he played in Malta, Egypt and back home. Malta was the home of the Victorian Mediterranean fleet – the epitome of the British navy at the time. An old polo team sheet from 1890s shows Cradock playing alongside Wemyss and Beatty (two future first lords) plus Lewis Bayley, Meux, Alexander-Sinclair, Mark Kerr, Evan Thomas – all of whom were to hold high flag rank. On Malta Kit kept a racehorse and reckoned that it cost no more than £50 a year to do so, including all entries and fees.

Cricket clearly exerted its magic over him too, as it should any true Yorkshire man. His journals show that he enjoyed playing and he uses its metaphors in his writings, for example 'some say it is immaterial which side you coal from – in this I do not agree. You might as well expect a man who has bowled over the wicket all his life, to bowl equally well round the wicket'.[15]

All his life he had dogs as pets. A photograph of him at the time of his appointment to flag rank shows him posed with a terrier and a retriever for company. When he went to the Falklands on his tragic last voyage he took his pet fox terrier with him.

Some authorities say Kit was a small man but this is not true.[16] The three brothers were fine-looking men, tall and slim. Three full length oil 'swagger portraits' of the brothers hung at Hartforth Hall, each depicting them mounted and in hunting pink. Kit was painted by Heywood Hardy, Paris trained, London based, a specialist in riding and costume paintings, who was often invited to stay at country estates to paint owners and animals. Montagu was rendered by James Lynwood Palmer, a sporting artist who never exhibited and only worked to commissions. He was a favourite of both Edward VII and George V and was considered one of the leading horse painters of his time. Sheldon's portrait is more complex. He chose the St Ives based academician and teacher Algernon Mayow Talmage, something of a society painter; but Talmage clearly struggled with depicting horses for Lynwood Palmer had to be called in to finish the job. None of these would have been cheap and today it is Heywood's works that bring the best prices – Kit chose well.

So who was Kit Cradock? A traditionalist, courageous, a man with a firm sense of right and wrong, well connected, diplomatic, tactful; perhaps not at the cutting edge of naval thought? Not overly intelligent. A man used to taking and receiving orders without question. A romantic for whom the sea and the navy were his pride and passion as well as his job. A man of his times, reflecting his Victorian background, convinced of the might of the British Empire and the navy's role in policing it. This was Kit the Rear Admiral.

14

The Great Schism: Fisher, Beresford and Royals, 1904–1911

As Kit was making his way back from the Med and embarking on his half pay leave a revolution had been touched off in his beloved navy which was to have lasting effects on the culture and relationships within the service The Edwardian navy was riven with feuds. These fault lines split the service, blighted careers and made newspaper headlines. The main axis of debate was the reforming zeal of Admiral Fisher (and the members of the 'Fishpond') and the influence of the royal court on appointments.

Jackie Fisher (Admiral of the Fleet Sir John Arbuthnot Fisher, First Baron Fisher of Kilverston, eventually) was the man who created the modern navy. With the launch of HMS *Dreadnought* in 1906, the first all big gun battleship in the world, he produced the definitive capital ship rendering all others obsolete – including the ones in Britain's navy. His modernising zeal changed training programmes for officers and men, introduced oil-fired engines, made engineer officer a respectable post and reconfigured the navy's forces. As First Sea Lord (1904–1911), he recalled ships from far flung postings (and the admirals who commanded them), concentrated the navy where he expected it to have to fight (the channel and the Med) and scrapped 150 ships (and, of course, the positions of commanding them) deeming them 'too weak to fight and to slow to run away'.[1]

Fisher was the son of a Ceylonese tea planter, from a poor background, a man who rose to high rank through ability not connections. He was volcanic in temperament, Old Testament in expression, intolerant of fools or anyone who disagreed with him and a compulsive and skilful dancer. If he liked you, he was easy to love. Winston Churchill loved him, invited him regularly on board the admiralty yacht *Enchantress* when First Lord (during Fisher's retirement) and corresponded with him regularly. But he was also easy to hate, especially if you thought that he was ruining the traditions of the navy and reducing the power one held or one's opportunities for progression. One man hated him with a passion – Admiral Lord Charles Beresford.

Charles William de la Poer Beresford, Charlie B to his admirers, was a man of limited intellect, great snobbery, a family pedigree going back to the Norman Conquest, a large estate in Ireland and an MP to boot. Charlie B believed that he should have the top job and that Fisher was preventing it. He saw Fisher as an inferior and social climber, while Fisher was jealous of Beresford's inherited wealth. Beresford did everything he could to rubbish Fisher and his reforms, was a frequent 'leaker' to the press and used his position in parliament to undermine Jackie which eventually led to a parliamentary enquiry. The war between these two outsized characters split the service, and officers had to take sides. If you were one of Fisher's chosen few (the Fishpond) the Beresfordites would attack you, and vice versa. Fisher called the Beresfordites 'the Syndicate of Discontent'.[2] The schism caused fault lines through the navy and continued even after Beresford left and Fisher retired.

It is difficult at this distance to grasp the ferocity with which the feud was pursued but it nonetheless ruined careers and reputations. Beresford was eventually able to force a parliamentary review, chaired by Prime Minister Asquith, and their mealy mouthed endorsement of Fisher caused him to resign his post in 1911.

Churchill regarded Beresford as an idiot. He said that 'when [Beresford] rose to his feet to make a speech he didn't know what he was going to say, when speaking he didn't know what he was saying and when he sat down he didn't know what he had said'.[3] Fisher also fulminated against the influence of the king and his circle on appointments that he believed were in his gift alone, and felt that promotion should be solely on merit, not social connections. His opposition to, and hatred of, Milne, Christian and Campbell was noted in Chapter six.

The story of Hedworth Meux will serve here as another exemplar, not least because he is to play a pivotal role in this story at a later date. Son of the Earl of Durham (and originally named Lambton) he was appointed PPS to successive First Lords from 1894 and antagonised senior naval officers who thought that he had far too much influence on decisions and showed a 'lack of consideration'.[4] A friend of Edward VII when he was Prince of Wales, from 1901 Meux was in charge of the king's yachts and promoted Rear Admiral. In 1903 he joined Charlie B as commander of his cruiser division in the Med and became an ally of Beresford in his feuds with Fisher (and succeeded Charlie B as MP for Portsmouth in 1916). George V supported moves to have him named First Sea Lord in succession to Fisher in 1911 and violently against Fisher's wishes. He was not chosen; but Fisher was then thwarted and the King pleased, by Meux's appointment to be Commander-in-Chief Portsmouth.

Officers had to take sides; promotional and social prospects were effected dependent on where you stood. A Fisherite serving under a Beresfordite would have limited chance of successful advancement and vice versa. So where did Kit stand in this debate? He was well connected to royalty. He had served on the China and Mediterranean stations, both reduced in scope and power by Fisher's reforms. He was a traditionalist of the old school, addicted to the pastimes and privileges of his class. We may suspect that he inclined towards Beresford.

If there were any doubt, Cradock confirmed it when, in 1907 as captain of the old battleship HMS *Swiftsure*, he wrote in *Whispers from the Fleet*, at the height of the Fisher reforms, '... we require – and quickly too – some strong Imperial body of men who will straightway choke the irrepressible utterings of a certain class of individuals who, to their shame, are endeavouring to break down the complete loyalty and good comradeship that now exists in the service between the officers and men; and who are also willing to commit the heinous crime of trifling with the sacred laws of naval discipline.'[5] Cradock the traditionalist, the sailor, the worshipper at the shrine to the Service did not like the new world that Fisher and his Fishpond were ushering in. Cradock was a Beresfordite and a 'Royal'.

15

Brothers in Arms and the Surtees Divorce

When on half-pay leave Kit always returned to Hartforth and his siblings, either staying at the Hall or with his sister Gwendoline and her husband. In 1891 she had married Herbert Straker from neighbouring Hartforth Grange, once a monastic farm, an iron-master whose family fortune was based on coal mines in Brandon and Brancepeth, County Durham. They produced two children, one of whom – Guy Herbert – was to carry on the military habit, serving in the Great War and becoming a major in the 15th Hussars. He won the MC for bravery and subsequently became an assistant district commissioner and magistrate in Kenya and Uganda.

Kit's brothers both served their country in its imperial wars. His eldest sibling Sheldon had served as a captain in the 5th Dragoon Guards in the Egyptian campaign of 1882 (where he had two horses shot from under him) and again as a captain in the Imperial Yeomanry (16th battalion) in South Africa 1899–1902 when he was mentioned in despatches and awarded the DSO. The Imperial Yeomanry was a volunteer regiment, drawn specifically from the hunting, shooting and fishing set of landed gentry to serve as cavalry in the Boer Wars.

The next oldest Cradock brother, Montagu, also took to soldiering. He fought in the Afghan campaign of 1879–80 with the Carabiniers (6th Dragoon guards) and in 1897 had emigrated to New Zealand (where he managed the 'Progress' group of gold mines on South Island's west coast), becoming a major in the New Zealand Second Contingent. He served in the Carnarvon Field force – commanding New Zealand and Canadian troops – in the Boer

War and eventually commanding 'Cradock's Corps' in 1901. He held the CB (Companion of the Bath, awarded 1900) and the CMG (Order of St Michael and St George, 1915). By 1917 he was a board director of the British Westinghouse Electric and Manufacturing Company and Metropolitan Vickers. Apparently he was an accomplished after dinner speaker. Like Kit he was a writer and authored *Sport in New Zealand*, based on his experiences there before the Boer campaign and telling of the abundant shooting, horse racing, yachting and polo to be found in that country. In 1913 he published *Diary of 2nd New Zealand Mounted Rifles*, an account of his experiences in the South African conflict. Monty was clearly the practical, business focused one. Family correspondence shows that he handled such issues as probates, investment strategy and, later, the defence of Kit's reputation.

Sheldon was obviously proud of his, and his siblings', martial achievements. In 1902 he installed a clock and plaque in the water tower at the Hall recording his family's involvement in five campaigns – Boer, Egyptian, Afghan, Sudanese and China. Sadly these deeds matter less today – the clock is only correct twice a day and the plaque is obscured by the storage of gardening machinery and oil drums. *Sic transit gloria mundi.*

The brothers would both re-join the army in 1914 and serve with distinction. Sheldon re-enlisted as a major in the 2nd King Edward Horse (a regiment raised at his own expense by 'Hell-fire Jack' , Sir John Norton-Griffiths, who travelled around the Western Front in a battered old Rolls Royce laden with crates of wine). Sheldon served until 1916 when, at the age of 58, he was sent home. Montague served as the outfit's commanding officer, holding the rank of lieutenant colonel until the regiment was sent to Italy. In both the Yeomanry and in the King Edward horse they were, to an extent, serving with their own kind, a sort of public school outing for ageing gentry.

The Cradocks were brave and courageous, dedicated military men, their roots deep in the traditions and soil of England. They were also bachelors and seemingly enjoyed their freedom. Montagu kept a mistress in London, one Gwendolyn Lees of Barrow Road, Streatham. And in 1908, whilst Kit was commanding *Swiftsure* and then at Hartforth on half pay, Sheldon became embroiled in a scandal that had the potential to ruin the family's good name and Kit's with it.

On 1 May Sheldon was cited as co-respondent in the divorce of Henry Siward Baliol Surtees and his wife Helen. The Surtees family was of a distinguished pedigree and Henry had, like Sheldon, served in the Boer conflict and risen to the rank of captain in the 2nd Life Guards. Their family seat was Redworth Hall, some sixteen miles away from Hartforth, where they kept their own pack of hounds. Henry, who inherited the estate in 1895, was a JP, a deputy lieutenant of Durham and a member of the Carlton Club, a bastion of the Conservative party. He had married Helen Winifred Muriel Thompson in 1898 and had sired three children by the time of the divorce. Sheldon and Helen had found romance and Henry, family motto *Malo Mori Quam Foedari* – Death before Dishonour – clearly decided that the situation was untenable and, possibly, dishonourable. At the time of the divorce petition Henry was 35 and Sheldon was 50, much the older man.

In the world in which Kit lived there were codes of behaviour for everything even, as described in Chapter 9, for extra-marital affairs. The tribe had rules and the balance, in romantic entanglements, between discretion and pride was a fine one to judge. Calling it wrongly could lead to disaster. Adultery was a game that had to be played by the rules and the first of these was 'never divorce'. Kit knew this and if he had romantic entanglements would have known both the protocol and the penalties for mistakes. His brother Sheldon nearly paid that price and could have ruined the family's name.

In 1906 Sheldon Cradock had been living in a cottage on his estate and renting the Hall to the Surtees family. He might have been short of money or he might have been tired of rattling around in the big house by himself with only the servants for company. Montagu was in New Zealand. Kit in was in the Med, and then home on half pay and staying with his sister. By 1911 the census shows that Sheldon was back in residence in the main house. The Surtees family had their seat at nearby Redworth Hall, a larger property than Hartforth, and also had properties in Brighton and Maidenhead. They might themselves have been renting out Redworth and needing somewhere local for their residence. Such rentals were not uncommon at the time and the families would certainly have known each other from the hunting field.

In 1870 Britain had been virtually self-sufficient in food production but agricultural returns had declined since then and times could have been harder for both families. The impact of refrigerated transport and the steamship, coupled with the removal of corn price protection in the first part of the nineteenth century meant that – for the landed classes – the latter part of the century saw a long-term decline in the amount of land under cultivation. Cheaper American and Canadian wheat and beef pushed returns down whilst the overhead of running a large estate was at best fixed. Many estates had been mortgaged in the boom years of the 1860s, but by the early 1900s things were tight and interest payments difficult to keep up; and after 1906 capital and income taxes bit increasingly hard. Possibly both Sheldon and Surtees were having to tighten their belts.

Whilst the Surtees were his tenants, or perhaps earlier on the hunting field, Sheldon had clearly developed a liaison with Helen. By 1908 Henry had had enough. He sued for the marriage to be dissolved on the grounds of his wife's adultery with Sheldon Cradock. Prior to the Matrimonial Causes Act of 1857 divorce had been possible only by gaining private legislation in the Houses of Parliament, a time consuming and costly (some £5,000) exercise. Subsequent to the Act a divorce court was established in London but the only acceptable ground was adultery for a man or 'aggravated enormity' for a woman (although marriages could be annulled due to non-consummation). Divorce remained uncommon into the twentieth century and brought with it considerable social disgrace; nor was the process easy. Many families 'liked it and lumped it' and maintained a facade of marital bliss whilst pursuing their affairs discreetly as before. For whatever reason, this was not the case with Henry and Helen Surtees. In the closed hunting community of northern England and amongst his peers in the gentry the affair was clearly a great embarrassment to Henry, the older man making a cuckold out of the younger.

The case was entered before the High Court of Justice, Probate, Divorce and Admiralty Division (what a curious mixture of responsibilities) on 1 May 1908.[1] Henry alleged that Helen had 'frequently committed adultery' with Sheldon and specifically on 27 November 1906. Additionally he applied for custody of the children to be granted to him. The Registrar asked for more detail and on 28 May Henry responded with enthusiasm. He stated that Sheldon frequently visited Helen at the Hall and that they walked in the shrubbery and woods near the house together. On one occasion they kissed in the shrubbery. On several occasions when Henry was away from home, Sheldon would lunch with Helen at the Hall and remain long after the usual time for dinner. Henry couldn't recall specific dates but it happened, he contended, between April 1906 and February 1907. On 28 November 1906 they had driven in a pony cart to dine at Mrs Straker's (Kit and Sheldon's sister Gwendoline) and returned together alone after dinner; and they corresponded with each other daily in November and December of that year. Finally he affirmed that in the month before Easter 1907 he had to go to Scotland on business and whilst he was away for three weeks Helen kissed Sheldon and dined with him at his cottage (away from the prying eyes of servants no doubt) on several occasions and that during this period they had intercourse in a room known as the 'Monkey Room' at around 9 pm on a day he could not remember.

This was dynamite. If proven, Helen would be permanently ruined socially and her children taken away from her; Sheldon would be branded a home-breaker and ostracised by the 'better sort'. Helen and Sheldon were in trouble and Sheldon's late-life fling would have serious repercussions on them both. Denial was the only course of action and on 23 July Sheldon and Helen did so, using the same firm of solicitors, Lewis and Lewis of London. This firm was headed by

Sir George Henry Lewis, one of the most prominent lawyers of his time. He had handled many high-profile cases, including acting for Charles Parnell and the Irish Party and had been knighted by Gladstone. He was a friend and confidante of Oscar Wilde and refused to act for the Marquess of Queensbury out of friendship in the fateful trial which destroyed Wilde's position and reputation. He acted for Edward, Prince of Wales, in shielding him from his many indiscretions. His obituary described him as 'not so much a lawyer, more a shrewd private enquiry agent'[2] and he was an advocate of the cheapening and decentralisation of divorce cases and an expert at libel cases. Expensive no doubt, but a formidable foe for Henry.

Helen and Sheldon went on the offensive. She counter-claimed that Henry had committed adultery in Paris on 24 February 1908 with an unknown woman and with one Renee Dorian. Now the gloves were off! Henry was quick to respond and denied the charge, reiterating that his original statements were the truth, but Helen was not to be countered and requested the court to appoint Special Examiners in Paris to find and take witness statements from Madam Renee Dorian. The court so approved on 27 October. She also requested that Col. Herbert Conyer Surtees, in Constantinople on government business, be deposed by the British Consul. Finally in November, all parties asked for a trial by 'special jury' (a jury composed entirely of high-status people).

At this point Henry seemed to be still ahead of the game. Helen's application for costs was struck out in December and Henry was awarded custody of the children, although they were to remain with Helen until a further court order and he was granted access rights.

Then sometime early in 1909 Henry seemed to get cold feet. The witness statements were in and, although they are no longer available to us, they must have caused Henry and his legal advisors to realise that they were batting on a different and difficult wicket from the one originally intended. In March, Henry applied for the order for a special jury to be discharged and indicated that he would not be proceeding with the action. But it was too late. Helen was made of strong Scottish stuff and – with Sheldon no doubt at her back and with an aggressive legal team – she was in no mood to accept a return to the *status quo ante*. In October she insisted on trial by 'special jury'.

Henry must have panicked that he would lose the children for he seems to have taken them away from her care and into his own residence. On 18 October a court order was made for Henry to return the children to Helen within 48 hours, or face the consequences. He was to have access to them once a fortnight and in their half holidays for two hours. Costs were awarded against him and his summons for custody dismissed with costs of £28-10s-8d. It was the beginning of the end for Henry. In a desperate last throw he submitted another affidavit and was given rights to have the children with him for three weeks from 28 December; but on 4 March 1910 the special jury heard the case and the verdict was unanimous. Henry was found to have committed adultery, a judicial separation was decreed and the children were given to Helen's custody, remaining within the jurisdiction of the court. Helen's witnesses were clearly more persuasive than Henry's unsupported protestations.

Costs were awarded against him in the sum of £830-4s-8d, a substantial amount at the time. Helen applied for, and was granted, maintenance: £50 a year for each child until they each attained the age of 21, or £150 a year for the next 18 years or so, a sum which would comfortably support a middle-class lifestyle. More costs were awarded against Henry, £28-3s-2d. He didn't have the money. His desire for revenge, for the recovery of his wounded pride, cost him his patrimony and his children.

As a consequence, Henry had to mortgage his ancestral home and lands at Redworth Hall. In November 1912 he entered into an indenture with Robert Lampton Surtees, a member of one of the many branches of the Surtees family all tracing their ancestry back to a seventeeth-century Robert at Redworth, and retired Admiral Reginald Hugh Spencer Bacon in which he mortgaged the property for £1,200.

Under the terms of the mortgage Henry was paid £300 per

annum, increased to £400 when he agreed to rent out the Hall itself, from the returns generated by the estate. Out of this he had to meet his maintenance commitments. Wartime inflation reduced the value of everyone's income and savings. In July 1916 Helen applied for an increase in the payments to her and the children. Henry was once again ordered to supply a summary of his income and outgoings, a request complicated by the fact that he was serving with the army on war duties. In response to the court order one H.H. Trotter, a solicitor of Bishop Auckland, set out the terms of the mortgage to the court. Trotter had been appointed to receive all the incomings and manage the outgoings of the Redworth estate. Out of those revenues he was to pay Henry £300 (later £400) per annum and all surplus revenues and profits were to go to Bacon and Lampton Surtees. Unfortunately there were no surplus profits and hence no part of the mortgage had been repaid. In fact there was a deficit of £447-14s-11d. Furthermore Henry had an outstanding creditor judgement against him for £625 and costs and the creditor had obtained a charge on the estate surplus and on the income allowance to Henry. Henry was broke and there was no more money for Helen either. He hadn't followed the 'rules'. How he must have wished he had turned a blind eye in 1906–7 to the relationship between Helen and Sheldon, as so many of his class had done before.

Henry Surtees did marry again but not until he was fifty-nine and his new bride, Emma Veronica Stone (nee Cunliffe), sixty. She married him one year after her husband, a fellow member of the Carlton, had died aged sixty-eight. Had they too been carrying on a clandestine affair, in this case preserving the niceties and waiting for her husband to do the decent thing and die?

Sheldon didn't marry Helen and no children can be traced, even born out of wedlock, of whatever liaison took place. However, in the Cradock family papers there is a picture of an attractive young woman, aged perhaps sixteen, marked on the back in pencil 'Joanie Surtees'. It is Dorothy Joan Surtees, born 27 April 1899, Helen's daughter. The Sheldon/Helen relationship was not a flash in the pan – it seems they continued to have a relationship of some description.

16

Recalled to the Fleet and the Delhi Affair, 1911–1912

The year 1911 did not start well for Kit Cradock for on 24 February, still on half pay, he admitted himself to Haslar Hospital (the navy's own medical centre at Portsmouth) with a kidney complaint. The nature of it is unknown, but it was clearly debilitating as Kit suffered from it on and off throughout the first half of the year. Discharging himself on 6 March (at his own expense) to attend the Royal Naval War College staff course (a relatively recently introduced educational initiative, owing its genesis to the Fisher reforms) he nonetheless missed a great deal of the programme. He passed sixth out of seven and his report was endorsed with the comment 'very attentive but sick a third of the time'.[1]

The course ended in June and Kit, although still without a posting, was asked to escort visiting VIPs at the Spithead Review of 24 June, an endorsement of his social and diplomatic skills if nothing else. This was the 'Coronation' review, the first of George V's reign, and featured a visit by the USS *Delaware*, an American battleship.

Kit entertained the guests from the decks of a chartered merchantman, the SS *Rewa*, no doubt seething inwardly that he was not in one of the great grey ships slowly progressing along the Solent, dressed all over with flags, in front of the King and Queen Mary. And for his efforts the Lords of the Admiralty allowed him a commodore's pay and allowances – for the day! But all things come to he who waits. Kit was finally rewarded for his patience with the plum appointment as second in command of the Atlantic fleet on

29 August and at long last raised his flag in the pre-*Dreadnought* battleship HMS *London* at Sheerness.

September 1911 found Kit involved in land exercises with the naval brigade, when 7000 sailors played defending and attacking armies near Berehaven in Ireland. Kit, as Admiral of the Red, commanded the defending forces and won the day. The *Irish Times* of 9 September noted that the day's manoeuvres were considered very important and that 'the Fleet holds its annual regatta next Monday, Tuesday and Wednesday and capital sport is promised'.

Kit returned to his post in the fleet, and it was here that he was to take part in the third and most high-profile rescue of his career – one which eventually played a part in the circumstances of his death: the *Delhi* affair.

On 13 December 1911 at 0200 hours the P&O passenger liner SS *Delhi* grounded off Cape Spartel, northern Morocco; she stranded, eventually breaking up and sinking. The ship ran aground in thick fog and heavy seas. In the course of the grounding all her lifeboats were smashed. Among the passengers were the Princess Royal, Princess Louise of Wales and her husband, Alexander William George Duff, 1st Duke of Fife. She was the eldest daughter of Edward VII, the late king, and sister to the new one. They were well connected and important and their lives were now in peril, as were those of their children, both also princesses.

In response to distress calls a rescue attempt was launched by the French and the British Atlantic fleet, based in Gibraltar and com- manded by Vice Admiral John Jellicoe. Three warships responded to the SOS: the French cruiser *Friant*, and the British ships HMS *London* and HMS *Duke of Edinburgh*. Kit, as Rear Admiral, was told by Jellicoe to shift his flag from the *London* to the *Duke of Edinburgh* (a cruiser) and command the operation. Kit sailed at 0630 and was in position at 0900 in foul weather. It was a difficult task with a very heavy swell coming in from the Atlantic and it took five days to complete, with one British cutter capsizing, the Gibraltar lifeboat stove in and three French sailors lost. Sixty naval officers and men, including Kit, landed to effect the operations. Survivors could only be taken off by cutter or by rocket apparatus, six to eight an hour, and had to live under canvas (provided by the French army) on the sandbar until transfer to a ship or dry land. Naturally, women and children went first, as did, perhaps less naturally, the royal party.

Kit had no hesitation in landing himself and directing operations from the peril of the mudbank where several cutters' crews and their boats were stranded and some boats damaged. Lacking any facilities he detached HMS *Implacable*, a battleship, to Tangier for transport; she later returned with 50 mules.

The Princess Royal, her children Alexandra and Maud, and the Duke of Fife were transferred onto a boat at 1100 on 13 December, Cradock personally accompanying them. Because of the heavy seas it was extremely difficult to effect the transfer; the ladies were dropped from the liner and caught by seaman in the navy's cutter. Some distance from the shore the boat was overwhelmed by the seas, filled and sank. Princess Alexandra disappeared under water and after a short panic was recovered. Eventually all the group made it to the shore. It was pouring with rain and the party, cold, drenched and wearing only their nightdresses and coats, were suffering. They then walked four miles in the rain to the Cape Spartel lighthouse where such clothing as could be found was made available. The British minister, Lister, arrived shortly with further wraps and hot drinks, discovering the Duke clad in his nightshirt and a pair of lighthouse-keeper's trousers. They then set out for Tangiers, some ten miles away, mounted on the mules, cold, wet and miserable. By the next day there were still 200 crewmen on board the *Delhi* although most passengers had been transferred to the shore.

Winston Churchill had only been appointed First Lord of the Admiralty (and thus the political head of the navy) in October of that year, and no doubt felt the hot breath of royal concern as George encouraged the rescue of his sister and brother-in-law. The time taken to get the survivors to safety was an aggravation for him, as no doubt was their condition and less than elegant mode of transport, and in Churchillian style he prodded Jellicoe and Cradock to greater efforts. Tempers might have frayed a little. Lord Beresford (no friend of Churchill's) asked repeated questions in the house about the wreck and the progress of the rescue thus aggravating to Churchill's already short temper.

Duff survived, as did the Princess Royal, but he fell ill with pleurisy, probably contracted as a result of the shipwreck and his subsequent ordeal, and died in Egypt weeks later. George V would not have been human if he did not show an aggravated interest in the rescue and its likely impact on his relative's health. Perhaps Churchill felt this anger reflected on him personally. Certainly, Kit believed that the *Delhi* affair explained why Churchill took against him, as will be seen later. But why? Two reasons are advanced above but there is a compelling third. Churchill at this time was a young (37) and pushy politician, always keen for the limelight and for personal aggrandisement and advancement. This was a very high-profile rescue and had happened under his watch; he thought that there should be recognition and praise for it – for him. But George V disliked Churchill (and Fisher) and did not trust him; he saw him as rather 'on the make' and lacking in principle; and Cradock had been George V's naval ADC.

There was recognition for Kit; he was received by the king for a personal interview on his return – a signal honour in those precedent obsessed times – and in February 1912 was made a Knight Commander of the Royal Victorian Order (KCVO), an order in the personal grant of the king for 'distinguished personal services to the monarch' which granted the titles of knighthood and distinctive pre and post nominal letters. Kit became 'Sir Christopher'. Kit had been individually and personally received by the king; Churchill had not – and was still 'Rt. Hon. Mr Churchill'. Could it be that this perceived slight to Churchill's sense of entitlement caused the animosity that Cradock detected between Churchill and himself? It would be very much in character for a man whose sense of his own importance was frequently commented on.

The king was not alone in demonstrating his gratitude. Kit received the Appreciation of the Lords Commissioners of the Admiralty for the 'courage and energy' displayed during the rescue.

Along with other participants in the rescue, he was awarded the Board of Trade Silver Medal for saving Life at Sea in October 1912. The wreck was the subject of a painting by Sir John Lavery RA. And the directors of the P&O Company further recognised Kit by presenting him with the *Delhi*'s ship's bell which remains in the possession of his sister's descendants to this day.

Kit's kidney problems seem to have cleared up by the beginning of 1912 for he wrote to Keyes that, 'I was sick, well again thanks. I fasted for 13 days on water.' But he continued to worry about the changes to his beloved navy. In another letter to Keyes he showed his disaffection: 'I am sure you like many of us are dying to do away with all these endless memos, notices, jealousies and feel the air cleansed by the North Sea'.[2]

In May Kit transferred his flag to the old battleship *Hibernia* and took command of the British navy's first experiments with manned flight from a ship. How conflicted Kit must have felt we can only guess – here was an entirely new technology which would eventually transform naval warfare; it involved new *materiel* and new men, and had nothing to do with the Nelsonian traditions of the navy. But as a good officer and seaman, obedient to his orders, he would surely have done his best to make the experiment work. And so it did.

The Atlantic fleet had begun aviation experiments at Sheerness in January 1912 aboard the battleship *Africa*, during which the first British launch of an aeroplane – a Short S27 biplane – from a ship took place. *Africa* transferred her flying-off equipment, including a runway constructed over her foredeck above her forward 12-inch turret and stretching from her bridge to her bows, to *Hibernia* in May, and *Hibernia* and Kit then hosted further experiments. Among these was the first launch of an aeroplane from a warship underway. A Commander Samson, again flying a Short biplane, became the first man to take off from a moving ship by launching from *Hibernia* while she steamed at 10.5 knots at the May 1912 Royal Fleet review in Weymouth Bay, in front of George V.

Kit Cradock wrote his last will and testament on 21 August 1912 on board HMS *Hibernia*.[3] It was witnessed by Cyril H. Brooking and George B. Owens, the latter being his secretary and fated to die with him at Coronel. Kit signed it 'Chris GF Cradock' and 'Chris' is a new usage not previously seen. 'Maurice' is omitted entirely. He gives his address as being the Naval and Military Club, Piccadilly.

The will is an interesting document in several ways. It is short, informal, almost chatty and very unlike the documents that lawyers would draw up today. The document is divided into two parts, A and B. A is concerned with Kit's property. He wishes his belongings, guns, animals, proceeds from sale of stocks etc. to go jointly to his sister Gwendolyn and to Montagu (note, there was no bequest to Sheldon; had there been a distancing between them?). His Japanese china 'in the strong room' is to go to his sister. His medals, swords, epaulettes etc. are to be placed together and 'perhaps my brother Sheldon would like them at Hartforth'.[4]

Part B is directly addressed to Montagu, 'Dear Mon', confirming the apparent view of Monty as the brother best suited to business and administration (and the use of the diminutive also giving a sense of closeness between them). Kit encloses six letters (which will be discussed here in later chapters) which are to be sent to the intended recipients together with some 'little things of mine' as remembrances (see also Appendix 2). In this section Kit once again demonstrates his concern with the correct form and with his awards and medals. He wishes to be cremated and the ashes interred in the family vault at West Gilling church and a tablet with 'my honours inscribed thereon Foreign as well as British. Also ADC to King Edward VII i.e. Knight Commander Victorian Order, Commander of the Bath, Royal Order of the Crown of Prussia, Knight of the Royal Spanish Order of Naval Merit, Member of the Imperial Ottoman Order of the Medijie'. In spelling out the list he indicates both his pride in them and perhaps his belief that Monty might not remember them all! (For a full list see Appendix 3.) As a predella he requests the phrase 'The darkness falls at Thy behest' taken from the hymn 'The day thou gave O Lord is ended'. Intriguingly, Cradock does not want all his names on the tablet, just 'Rear Admiral Sir Chris GF Cradock'. He then apologises to Monty for his lack of detail and that he is sure he has forgotten lots of things but is confident that Monty will do 'the best for everything'. He has arranged for £1,000 to be sent to pay for funeral expenses should he die. Finally, and proving that tax avoidance is not a new thing, he tells Montagu that he has shown his Canadian investments on a separate sheet (he owned property in Winnipeg, which he acquired in 1912) so that 'you may destroy it and no-one (revenue officers etc.) know of any money of mine in Canada'.[5]

The will gives further insights to the character traits that have already been identified. It seems rushed and ill-thought through. It is lacking in detail. Kit is greatly concerned with how he will be remembered and with his status; and he is concerned that his closest friends have permanent reminders of his life.

Kit hauled down his flag on 29 August and once again went on half pay. He must have wondered if he would ever get his own complete command – and puzzled over his role in the genesis of naval aviation too.

17

4th Cruiser Squadron and Mexico, 1913–1914

Kit had to wait until February 1913 before he gained the much desired independent command. He was appointed Rear Admiral and Senior Naval Officer, West Atlantic and given command of the 4th Cruiser Squadron. Before sailing to his base, he took a jaunt in one of Keyes' submarines (Keyes was Inspecting Captain of Submarines), commanded by Lieutenant Fraser. Kit wrote to Keyes, 'It was most instructive and I enjoyed it.' He goes on to suggest that after the trial attack, 'it would be far more satisfactory to these "playthings" to know whether they were observed or made hits or misses … I am sure you will know what to do.'[1] Note his (common amongst his peers) rather dismissive view of subs. The flotilla captains dined with him that evening and he reports their 'great affection' for Keyes.

Previously designated the 'Training Squadron', his new command did not represent the ultimate in naval construction. Hoisting his flag in the *Donegal* and then the *Suffolk*, Kit presided over a collection of county class cruisers laid down in 1901 and sadly lacking in armament or armour but requiring a considerable crew. Kit sailed for the North American coast and to his base (and free mansion) on Bermuda, where his handsome demeanour and urbane personality made him a hit on the East Coast society circuit. He was not to enjoy his leisure for long.

With a strong presence in the Caribbean and the necessity for coaling bases for the navy in the Pacific and Atlantic, the British had always had half an eye on South America, not so much for Empire as for trade. Germany too had developed South American ambitions and was beginning to build both trading and political relationships, especially in Mexico. Britain therefore kept a wary eye on Mexican affairs too, a posture that much excited the American government of Woodrow Wilson. Oil fields were another attraction for all parties. The governance of Mexico was unstable (and had been for many years) and all the aforementioned countries vied to ensure that they had influence amongst the various contending players. The prime minister of the day, H.H. Asquith, had little ambitions in the area but not all of his ministers supported that view, and the Americans – hyper-sensitive to Britain's imperial past and potential future – were deeply suspicious of the role that Britain might be playing.

In 1913 the Mexican army supremo, General Huerta, had connived with the then American ambassador, Henry Lane Wilson, to lead a coup against the incumbent government and take over executive power, promising to introduce policies more favourable to American interests – a pact agreed and actually signed in the US embassy in the Mexican capital. However, Huerta soon introduced a harsh military dictatorship and lost the confidence of US President Woodrow Wilson. Ambassador Lane Wilson was recalled and the US president demanded of Huerta that he step aside to allow democratic elections, a request that Huerta found easy to ignore. Civil war broke out, a state of affairs never far away in the Mexico of the time, and Huerta found himself threatened by the forces of Zapata in the south and the opposition Constitutionalists in the north.

America had significant oil interests in Mexico, especially around Tampico and Vera Cruz and so too, to a lesser extent, did Britain. The British consul, Carden, believed both property and personnel were threatened and in late 1913 requested British naval support, alongside that being provided by the USA to support their own citizens and interests. The Admiralty ordered Kit to Jamaica to be nearer the potential action and then, as the unrest grew, sent him to the Mexican coast.

Cradock now found himself with a rather tricky problem. The

Americans were deeply suspicious of British intentions in Mexico which they regarded as their back yard and sphere of influence, arrogated under the Munroe doctrine to them only. All of his diplomatic skills would be needed. In Mexico he conferred with Carden, who disagreed with the Foreign Office policy of no support for Huerta and felt this was leaving the Americans a free hand. Through Cradock and the military attaché he tried to paint a lurid view of what might happen if the rebels were able to reach the oil rich areas before the Constitutionalists arrived to restore some sort of order, and hoped to use these official feedback mechanisms to get the FO policy changed. In fact Cradock had, in his dispatches to the admiralty, assessed the situation well, saying that it was most confused and that in the event of a worsening situation he would send only 'a Maxim gun and ammunition'[2] to the British legation for self-defence only.

Restored to his ship, Kit left for Tampico where on arrival he was presented with another tricky situation. The American admiral present, Fletcher, was his junior but reported to Washington that Cradock had waived his right to seniority, which Cradock protested strongly he had not. Nonetheless, when Tampico was finally besieged four days later the two admirals cooperated successfully in rescuing some 2000 threatened American and British (and some German) nationals. The admiralty then solved the problem by splitting Kit's forces and sending him to Vera Cruz with half of the squadron, where he was witness to the American invasion. Kit came out of the affair well, having managed a difficult brief effectively and 'kept Britain's nose clean'. And the Americans later recognised that in communications to the FO and the Admiralty.

Kit kept his letters and journals of his time in Mexico.[3] Like those from China 13 years before, they serve to give a better picture of the man; his obedience to orders, his charisma, his humour, his chivalric turn and his magnanimity.

The first is his response to the pleadings of British Consul Carden. Based at the legation in Mexico City, Carden is disgusted at the Foreign Office's policy of non-intervention. He hopes that, through

Cradock, or through getting Cradock to take some precipitate action, he may involve Britain more deeply in the future of the country. Kit's orders are to the contrary. He is instructed to protect British lives and property but not to take any position that could be construed as British interference in the affairs of state.

On 7 February 1914 Carden writes from the British legation. He tells Cradock that a defence force has been formed of British and other foreign legation members to defend the legation district in the event of violence and that they would benefit from having 'one or two Maxim guns'[4] (a heavy machine gun). Kit sends a lieutenant, a rating, two guns and 24,000 rounds of ammunition but his orders clearly state that they are there to train people to use the guns, not take an active role in leading the defence forces. He requires a receipt for the armaments. He then informs the American and other foreign captains present of what he has done. The former asks if they are there to protect all people including Americans – Kit replies 'most certainly'.[5]

Kit is suspicious of Admiral Fletcher, the American commander, who tries to persuade Cradock to send more men to the legation, so that he can do the same. Kit demurs saying that Fletcher should ask the Mexican government to protect the embassy and if that produces no response they should telegraph home for orders.

On both occasions Kit acts as his orders would have him, despite his own personal desires. His true views can occasionally be discerned. He writes, 'everyone wishes well to America if only they could bring peace – for all are being slowly ruined'. His views of the Mexican participants are also instructive; of Villa, the rebel commander who dominates the north of the country he writes, 'arch scoundrel, torturer and ravisher ... the Americans could never wish, it is hoped, to put him forward ... the man is a low peon born [sic] and cannot write. There are stories enough of horrors perpetrated in Mexico to fill many volumes; the wise man believes but few, but I possess knowledge (on unimpeachable direct authority) of the abominations committed on well-born Mexican ladies in the early days of Torreon and Durango which are unspeakable – and Villa was in command.'[6] Villa was no gentleman, then; and that was guaranteed to offend Kit's code of chivalry.

Carden took Cradock to visit the president, which Kit did in full dress uniform. This was taken by the Americans to infer an official visit was in train, but of course Kit could no more fail to observe the protocols of necessary dress than he could dishonour his own flag. The interview lasted 90 minutes, which also excited American beliefs that arrangements were being made for British support to be lent to Huerta. Then an American newspaper published a totally fictitious version of the conversations between Cradock and the president which had to be strongly rebutted with a verbatim text of the conversation. But the suspicion of collusion remained in the mind of the US Secretary of State, O'Shaughnessy.

Kit was ordered to Galveston, Texas, where many of the evacuees from Tampico had been taken, and sailed in HMS *Essex* in company with Carden. He arrived at the end of March with much trepidation, for the American newspapers had been virulently anti-British and suspicious of British intentions in the region. But his personality turned the visit into a PR success. He was invited to visit the governor in the state capital, Austin; he was entertained at the governor's house. Asked to review the American army, Kit took the salute from 8000 troops in Texas City; he inspected the latest artillery. He held a dance on board *Essex* for American guests and in return the ship's company were entertained on-shore to an 'oyster feast' and Cradock and his officers given dinner by a committee of Galveston's prominent citizens. 'Many loyal toasts between country and country were proposed and perhaps good may have been done,' he reported. At the end of the dinner he gave a speech in which he asserted that 'there is no ill-will – there never could be any ill-will borne in Great Britain against the United States and in all things Britain wished them well'.[7]

It was a triumph, a royal progress, with Kit's charm winning American hearts and minds. He reported that 'on leaving Galveston my principal impressions are these. Unfortunately a wrong impression had been fostered in Texas regarding Great Britain's attitude towards the United States in the Mexican affair. I think now, after all this friendship and "understanding", a very different atmosphere might prevail.' So impressed were the citizens of Galveston that they offered to pay the expenses incurred by Cradock on his journey through Texas, but he refused and 'settled the matter from my private purse'.[8]

You can take the sportsman out of England but he's still a sportsman. In a letter to the king Kit wrote that in the US 'their game laws are all wrong. Close season starts on 1st February, which is their best time for Canvas Back Duck and is just before the Snipe come in.'[9]

There is a wistful note to a comment in a letter written in March to Arthur Nicholson: the President of America has sent his yacht *Mayflower* down to Mexico for use by Admiral Fletcher and his wife and family. Kit comments, 'alas I have neither yacht nor wife'.[10] And in a letter to Admiral Dudley de Chair (with whom he served on the *Cleopatra*) requesting when supplies may be expected he writes, 'the many foreigners here afloat – let alone British subjects – have eaten nearly all my stores and drunk most of the champagne, hence my call of distress'.[11] Entertaining in style was expected of a British admiral, obviously, and Kit kept a good table. He introduced Fletcher to the Spanish navy commander in the area at a dinner on board the *Essex*.

After a so-called insult to their flag, occasioned by the arrest of some US marines, Admiral Fletcher determined to invade Vera Cruz. He warned Kit of this and said he saw no objection to *Essex* remaining in harbour at her own risk. Telling Kit he would give ample warning, he left – and immediately triggered an invasion by 4,500 men. Kit noted that Fletcher was spoiling for a fight and – realising that his senior officer was arriving soon to take command – decided to have his day. Kit sent an officer and ten men to assist in the defence of the legation but otherwise stayed out of what was a one-sided fight. The only Mexican resistance came from the Naval College at Vera Cruz where the naval cadets put up a stout defence. Kit Cradock, the chivalric admirer of a fight in a lost cause, noted to the king, 'heavy firing on the Naval Academy which was most gallantly defended by the cadets. They beat back a whole US Naval regiment before 21 of them were hurled into the next world by the *Chester* taking the roof and the *Prairie* taking the windows with their guns at point blank range.' He also sees the humorous side to the position. 'The situation, the knots to unravel, the extraordinary relation of everyone to everyone else in these waters ... Were it not for the seriousness of it all and all the great matters entailed and the blank uncertain future ahead, might be compared to a comic opera.'[12]

His ships take 1,500 people out of Tampico without incident but there are nationals trapped in Mexico City too. No problem for Kit. He discovers an abandoned locomotive and sets his engineers on it to make it function. They succeed and Commander Hugh Tweedie is made captain of the train, gets through to the beleaguered nationals and brings them back to Vera Cruz. The Americans try the same thing but have difficulty getting the train to work – obviously British engineering is superior.

Finally came the ultimate irony: German interests are represented on the Mexican coast by the light cruiser SMS *Dresden*. On 14 July, only three weeks before the outbreak of war, Kit wrote to the German ambassador by hand. He noted that the *Dresden* was absent from the coast for a short time and offered, in her absence, 'to place under your Excellency's command the services of the British cruisers for duty in the Imperial German State's interests during the absence of SMS *Dresden* on her mission' (which was in fact to convey the now exiled ex-President Huerta to Jamaica). Von Hintze, the German ambassador, replied on the 17th expressing his deep gratitude for the offer of protection. He wrote, 'I take your Excellency's offer for another proof of the constant goodwill you have shown his Imperial Majesty's ships and subjects during all these troublesome times and, over and above, for indicative [sic] of the excellent relations and of the good comradeship happily existing between our two navies.'[13]

Three weeks later the world blew apart. The sailors who had

worked together in a humanitarian effort to save lives became bitter enemies. *Dresden* joined von Spee's squadron and fought against Kit's ships at Coronel, only to die herself under the guns of HMS *Glasgow* and *Kent* off the coast of Chile in 1915.

Kit was not a materialistic man. He had nothing much in the way of possessions; he owned some property in Canada but no large house in England where he could establish a home or leave the legacy of his existence. His life was a peripatetic one, living on board ship or in rented accommodation abroad – or at his and other clubs on the stations he visited. He leaves little trace behind. There is no vast archive of letters and documents and no treasure trove of possessions to trawl. Most of what he valued was with him in the little 'drawer' where he told Roger Keyes he kept his most treasured mementos. Being the youngest son he could only expect to inherit Hartforth Hall as a very old man, if at all, and it probably didn't matter to him much. His home was a cabin on a ship and from his earliest years in the navy he would have had servants, initially seamen, but as commander, captain and admiral he would have his own personal servants and secretary. He had no need of terrestrial assistance. At sea he was in no want of house and livery – everything and everyone he needed was there at his beck and call – and when on shore clubs and friends and family provided the lodging and support that he needed. Being unmarried meant there was no need for him to provide a family home. He lived as a gypsy carrying his small and treasured possessions around with him. He was free to come and go as he pleased. The navy was his life and his life support, and as long as he could afford to shoot and hunt it suited him.

It's possible that this was another reason for his bachelor status. Perhaps he just enjoyed being footloose and fancy free too much. It had been his life for so long he could think of no other. Certainly, from what we know, he was impulsive and precipitate in his character, as reported on by many observers. An unburdened lifestyle would fit.

Nor did he necessarily have the opportunity to put down solid roots in Britain. In his forty-year naval career he had few home postings. He probably spent no more than a third of his whole naval career in appointments which required him to be based in England. Service overseas was usually for a period of three to four years and after accumulated leave an officer could be deployed to a distant station again for another long stint. On return from extended overseas duty the country would have changed noticeably each time; this was the age of technology and rapid change. Perhaps nothing would ever feel familiar or quotidian, except the hunting field.

So Kit was not a materialistic man. The evidence of this can be seen in his will and those of his two brothers. At probate Kit left effects valued at £1,055-4s-11d – perhaps £100,000 at today's values. Not a trifle but a relatively insignificant sum for a man of his class and background (although we know that he instructed Monty to try to hide his Canadian property from the taxman). By contrast in 1922 Sheldon left £43,257 (at today's values £1.6 million) and Montague £63,335 (£3.2 million) – although this would include some element of the Hall and estate. Kit's brother-in-law, Herbert Straker, left £226,909-3s-11d in 1929 which today would be worth the staggering sum of £13.2 million.

Which is not to say that Kit didn't need money. Admirals were paid allowances when serving on station in recognition of the fact that a British naval officer had to maintain a certain style and table, to demonstrate the clear superiority of the British navy in everything, including entertaining. Kit's experiences in Mexico illustrate this well. Hunting, polo ponies and shooting all cost money too. We can envisage him to be a generous man, warm hearted and unstinting in supporting his friends and family. But not a businessman – he owned a few stocks and shares and the Canadian property, but turned to Monty, it would appear, for business and financial advice.

There is sufficient detail now, perhaps, to be able to see Cradock for what he was. His personality is writ large in his sayings, actions and writings. He reflects the time in which he grew up. Brave, fit, athletic; proud, soaked in the lore and traditions of the navy; a Victorian by chronology and values; not an intellectual, impulsive, quick to take offence; good company, accomplished socially, perhaps a little vain; chivalrous, loyal, generous. This is Kit Cradock. This is the man who went to war in 1914.

18

War: Coronel in Context, June to October 1914

On 28 June 1914 at around 1030 a 19-year-old Bosnian Serb named Gavrilo Princip fired the shot which started the First World War. His assassination of Archduke Franz Ferdinand of Austria, Heir Presumptive to the throne of Austro-Hungary, and his pregnant wife Sophie, set the fuse to the gunpowder keg that was Europe. Austro-Hungary was spoiling for a fight with Serbia to reassert its dominance in its own back yard. This was the *causus belli* she wanted. Despite Serbia giving in to most of the reparations demanded of her, Austro-Hungary began to mobilise. That led the Russians to mobilise to protect Serbia, Germany to protect Austro-Hungary, France to protect herself, and finally England to protect Belgium. That is the accepted history. In fact the German General Staff and some members of the Kaiser's government badly wanted a war with Russia, before the sleeping giant to their backs modernised and became too big a threat to their eastern borders. The Germans gave a 'blank cheque' to Austro-Hungary to deal with Serbia as they wanted and government officials constantly egged on their Austrian counterparts. Germany drove the world to war.

War on Germany was declared by Britain on 4 August 1914. But not everybody noticed. It was a beautiful summer, hot and cloudless and a bank holiday weekend. Many people were away from home; many politicians had been out of touch expecting a long break. The composer Edward Elgar and his wife were on holiday in Gairloch, Scotland. They only realised something was amiss when they could not get transport home and everywhere they saw marching bands of soldiers. It took them a week to get back to London.

Up until a few days previously Britain had been more concerned that there would be a civil war over the issue of home rule for Ireland. The Curragh Mutiny of March, when the majority of British officers ordered to Belfast to quell resistance to home rule threatened to disobey orders and resign their commissions, had called into question the ability of the government to resist civil disobedience and paralysed parliamentary decision making. On 24 July Churchill reports that the cabinet were discussing the Irish Home Rule bill when Sir Edward Grey interrupted them to read out Austria's ultimatum to Serbia. On the declaration of war, Redmond the Nationalist Irish leader offered his full support to the government and said that they could 'withdraw every one of their troops from Ireland'[1] without fear of trouble.

There were some who – following the works of Professor Norman Angell – thought that war was economically impossible. His thesis, given in his book *The Grand Illusion* and widely believed in intellectual circles, was that war would be unprofitable for all, the victor would suffer with the vanquished and therefore no nation would be so foolish as to start one. But many welcomed war. There was a feeling that a short sharp European war could clear the air and provide an outlet for nationalistic feelings everywhere. In London, Paris and Berlin crowds took to the streets singing patriotic songs and cheering. The German writer Thomas Mann opined that the war would be a 'purification, a liberation an enormous hope'.[2]

The years 1910–1914 had seen growing industrial unrest in Britain with strikes in every significant industry and in every part of the country, a pattern mirrored across Europe, the USA and Russia. Additionally the UK had seen turmoil caused by the suffragette movement and the battle over House of Lords reform. Again, some, especially in parliament, saw the outbreak of war as a way of cauterising, and deflecting attention from, these upheavals of popular feelings. Few people thought it would be a long war. 'Over by Christmas' was the commonly held view. The Kaiser, reviewing his departing troops, assured them they would be back in three months ('you will be home before the leaves fall').

David Beatty and Ernle Chatfield, both future First Sea Lords, were longing for war. Beatty bet Chatfield £5 that it would not come. Beatty longed for it. 'We had not fought for over a century; it was time we repeated the deeds of our forefathers.'³

Harold Macmillan, the future prime minister, wrote that he and his friends were desperate to join up to get some fun before it was all over. Macmillan, incidentally, got his wish. He served as a captain in the Grenadier Guards, was wounded three times and once spent an entire day in a slit trench reading Aeschylus in the original with a bullet in his pelvis. His hip wound took four years to heal and he was left with a slight shuffle in his walk plus a limp grip in his hand. Of the 28 freshmen who started with him at Balliol only he and one other survived the war.

For some it was intolerable not to be able to join up. An ex-captain in the Rifle Brigade, Arthur Annesley, aged 49, committed suicide by throwing himself under a truck because, according to the London Coroner, he was worried that he would not be accepted back into the army to fight.

The British sent the British Expeditionary Force (BEF) to France – four divisions under Sir John French to join the sixty-two French and eighty-seven German already engaged. At 160,000 men it represented virtually the entire British army. The German plan (the Schlieffen plan) was a massive right wheel through Belgium and northern France, brushing the coast and turning in to take Paris. The French were already being badly beaten. Falling into a German trap they had launched their forces into the Ardennes and Alsace, the promise of liberating their former possessions taking precedence over logic. In the Battle of the Frontiers, France lost 300,000 men in a fortnight; 27,000 were lost on one day, 22 August; 40,000 in three days. By Christmas, France would have suffered a million casualties (by the war's end, one in every twenty-eight of the total French population would die in the fighting; the comparable figure for Britain was one in fifty-seven).

The BEF was thrust into the line at Mons, in Belgium. Out-numbered by three to one, 100,000 men took on the entire German

First Army. They fought a running battle without rest as they retreated 170 miles, but they held on and the damage done to the German plans caused von Moltke, the German supremo, to lose his courage and turn in towards Paris too soon. This exposed the German flank to a French counter attack which bought two million men into conflict. The German advance was stopped and the 'race for the sea' began – each side trying to outflank the other. A last German thrust for the sea was halted by the British at Ypres. The first Battle of Ypres began on 20 October and lasted to the middle of November. The BEF held but the cost was awful and they were wiped out as a fighting unit. British casualties included 80,000 dead. Battalions of 1000 men were reduced to thirty. The 7th Division, 12,000 men strong, lost 9,000 in eighteen days. At the beginning of the war the minimum height for entry into the British army was five feet eight. Such was the need for replacements that it was reduced to five feet five on 11 October (and five feet three on 5 November). The war had reached a dreadful stalemate. Across Europe, from Switzerland to the sea, a maze of trenches sprang up and a war of movement stopped. No one was coming home by Christmas. The war on land had gone badly for the allies and casualties were frighteningly high; and Kit would have known this.

Nor was there any solace to be gained at sea. Before the outbreak of war the Royal Navy was hugely respected by the public. It was the Senior Service and 'the sure shield of empire'. For centuries the navy had defended Britain from its enemies; the names of Drake, Jervis, Howe, Nelson rang through the minds of schoolboys everywhere. Immense sums of money had recently been spent on providing eight new capital ships (initially opposed by Churchill before he became First Lord) and the naval construction race with Germany was headline news and subject to frequent parliamentary debate. The navy would save the country from Germany, as it had often done in times past from the French and the Spanish.

The truth was more prosaic. Although the Fisher reforms had removed or reduced some of the worst of the old-fashioned practices, the navy was still largely a Victorian body. Intelligence was not

a criterion used to select officers for high appointment and braini-
ness was disapproved of. What mattered was a smart ship, a con-
genial personality, a brave heart and a willingness to do as ordered.
Firing practice was disapproved of as it caused a mess and dirtied
the ship. Rigid adherence to sailing orders and a lack of any desire to
take one's own initiative mattered more. Admirals decided the plan
and officers implemented it to the letter. The navy, like the army, had
twentieth-century weapons but a nineteenth- (or in the case of the
navy possibly eighteenth-) century brain. Worse, improvements in
signalling technology meant that men could sit in the Admiralty in
London and issue instructions to the man on the spot, removing his
local decision-taking ability; and the men in Whitehall were not
necessarily there because of their competence.

The first naval shots of the war were fired on 5 August when the
cruiser *Amphion* and the destroyers *Lance* and *Landrail* sank a German minelayer. The following day the *Amphion* went back to the
exact location of the exchange and sank herself on a mine. The first
success turned by carelessness into the first loss.

Then the navy's reputation for courage took a blow. In the
Mediterranean the British fleet was commanded by Admiral
Archibald (Arky-Barky) Berkley-Milne, a 'royal officer', pleasant,
harmless and incompetent, friend of the late King Edward VII
and his wife Alexandra. Commanding a force of four armoured
cruisers under him was Rear Admiral Ernest Troubridge, a descendant of one of Nelson's 'band of brothers', much liked but not
famous for his cleverness. They had a number of missions to fulfil,
not the least of which was to prevent the modern German battlecruiser *Goeben* (accompanied by the light cruiser *Breslau*) from
escaping. After a series of tactical moves and mischances, the *Goeben*
began a run for Constantinople with the mission of becoming part
of the Turkish navy and catalysing Turkey's entry into the war on the
German side.

On 7 August Troubridge found himself in a position to stop
them. His four armoured cruisers together packed a broadside of
8,480 pounds compared to 8,272 of the *Goeben*. Despite his

numerical superiority in ships and the ability to divide *Goeben*'s fire, Troubridge allowed himself to be persuaded not to fix and engage the *Goeben* and she made good her escape into Turkey.

The public regarded this as a great naval disaster, and Troubridge and Milne were widely vilified. Battenberg wrote, 'none of the excuses Troubridge gives can be accepted for one moment. The escape ... must ever remain a shameful episode in the war.'[4] A court of enquiry on 22 September stated that Troubridge's actions were 'deplorable and contrary to the traditions of the British Navy'.[5] Troubridge was court-martialled on 5–9 November 1914 and charged with '... forbearing to pursue the chase of the *Goeben* ... being an enemy then flying'[6] (a similar charge to that for which Admiral Byng was executed in the eighteenth century, for losing Minorca in 1756; Fisher said he would like to see Milne shot like Byng). Although acquitted (on the basis of confusing orders from the Admiralty), Troubridge was posted to a desk job and never received another sea-going command again.

It is important to note that he was charged before Cradock's death and acquitted after it. Kit would not have known of the result of the court martial. Troubridge himself retained a dislike of Churchill for ever. He was enraged that his 'real accuser' had not been his fellow naval colleagues but 'an amateur'.[7]

Milne was left unemployed and on half pay, never to receive another appointment; both officers were reviled for the rest of their lives. It should be noted that the court, and later observers, put much blame on the Admiralty for the confusing signals they sent to Milne, some of which, through their flowery and imprecise language, bore the stamp of having been drafted by Churchill.

Preparedness was poor. Of the navy's three east coast bases Rosyth was too small, Cromarty incomplete and Scapa Flow undefended. At the outbreak of hostilities Jellicoe, the British commander (himself precipitated into the job in controversial circumstances), had nowhere safe to base his fleet. He was obsessed by the danger posed to the Grand Fleet by submarines and on 6 September had an early confirmation of his concerns when the flotilla leader *Pathfinder* was sunk by *U-21* with heavy loss of life. Worse was to follow.

In the Indian Ocean the German cruiser SMS *Emden*, detached from von Spee's squadron for trade interdiction purposes sank 70,825 gross tons of Allied shipping, including warships, between August and October and paralysed trade in and around the major Indian trade and supply routes. No one seemed able to catch her.

On 22 September three old armoured cruisers were patrolling off the Dutch coast. They had been, as Battenberg put it, 'peddling up and down' there since the outbreak of war to keep an eye on possible German light craft activity. They were elderly, vulnerable and predictable. Officially called 'Force C', they were known in the navy as 'the live bait squadron'[8]. At 0630 the *Aboukir* was hit by a torpedo and sank. The *Hogue* was trying to rescue survivors when she too was hit and sank in 10 minutes. The *Cressy*, which by now should have been running for her life, unbelievably hove to and at 0717 capsized having been hit by two torpedoes. Sixty-two officers and 1397 men (mostly middle-aged reservists and cadets straight out of the Dartmouth naval college) went down with the ships – ships which in any case were of little or no value; but the men were. Keyes, amongst others, had pleaded for the ships to be withdrawn but Sturdee had dismissed his request contemptuously, telling him that he knew nothing of the history of the Dutch wars (fought in the seventeenth century!) if he did not appreciate the importance of patrolling the 'Broad Fourteens'. A Court of Enquiry blamed the Admiralty for the loss, as did the Third and Fourth Sea Lords.

Jellicoe's fear of submarines increased and he moved the Grand Fleet out of the North Sea (a considerable victory for the Germans had they but known it) and into Loch Swilly in Ireland. Now came another disaster. On 27 October the battleship *Audacious*, a modern super-dreadnought, was sailing out for firing practice when she struck a German mine. Despite attempts to rescue her she blew up that evening and sank. The loss of life was small but the loss of a major battle unit was considerable. This followed the loss of the ancient cruiser *Hawke* to a torpedo from *U-9* a week earlier, with the death of 524 men.

All of these incidents significantly tarnished the navy's reputation at home; and Kit Cradock would have known this. As Prime Minister Asquith wrote to the king, the cabinet considered the list of setbacks suffered so far was not 'creditable to the officers of the Navy'.[9]

19

The Admiralty in 1914

In 1914, as so it seemed from time immemorial, the navy was run by the Board of Admiralty. The board consisted of four or five senior officers, usually of flag rank or senior captains, called the Sea Lords. The First Sea Lord was the man in overall command and the person who took the strategic decisions. In August 1914 the First Sea Lord was Admiral His Serene Highness Prince Louis of Battenberg. Born a prince of the blood in Graz, Austro-Hungary, he was the son of Prince Alexander of Hesse and Rhine and was a German national who became a naturalised British subject.

As First Sea Lord he was responsible to the First Lord of the Admiralty, a political appointment of cabinet rank, for the readiness of the fleet and for naval strategy – and in August 1914, as he had been from 1911, the First Lord was Winston Spencer Churchill, the man who had appointed Battenberg to his position.

Churchill's reputation and standing now are well known and taken as read. The man who faced down Hitler and led Britain to survival and then success in the Second World War is regarded by many as one of the greatest Britons of all time. In truth Churchill was, like many great men, deeply flawed, and in 1914 he was neither particularly liked nor trusted by the king, his cabinet colleagues or by the navy high command. He had originally opposed the expansion of the battleship navy, siding with Lloyd George and the 'little Englanders' in 1909. Lord Stamfordham, King Edward's Private Secretary wrote of him, 'What are Winston's reasons for acting as he does. Of course it cannot be from conviction or principle. The very idea of him having either is enough to make anyone laugh.'[1]

On Churchill's appointment to the Admiralty the *Navy League Annual* stated that his arrival was not regarded with much favour; the *National Review* went one better calling him a 'self-advertising mountebank'.[2] The *Globe* of 21 December 1912 stated that 'the methods of Mr Churchill are wholly unfitted for the great Service of which he is the responsible head'. Churchill was seen as a grand-stander, a bully, a man of fixed ideas, someone who gave advice but did not take it, an amateur strategist and a back seat driver. He wanted, nay needed, to be in charge and to be in the limelight. He took strong positions and held to them in the teeth of opposition. A good example was his sponsorship of a plan to take the island of Borkum, off the mouth of the Ems river – a plan he pressed hard on the War Office – described by Captain Herbert Richmond, then Assistant Director of Operations, as 'quite mad ... I have never read such an idiotic, amateur piece of work as this outline in my life'.[3] So also was Churchill's later proposal and sponsorship of the whole Gallipoli debacle and consequent destruction of the British and ANZAC forces (a decision which saw him forced out of the Admiralty and eventually the cabinet).

Future First Sea Lord John Jellicoe, recalling the time he had joined the Admiralty as Second Sea Lord, said, 'It did not take me very long to find out that Mr Churchill, the First Lord, was very apt to express strong opinions upon purely technical matters; moreover, not satisfied with expressing his opinions, he tried to force his views upon the board ... his wonderful argumentative powers enabled him to make a weak case exceedingly strong.'[4] In later times Admiral Sir Andrew Cunningham wrote to a relative that Churchill was 'a bad strategist but doesn't know it and nobody has the courage to stand up to him'.[5]

Churchill's appointment of Battenberg to be his First Sea Lord reflected his need for power. A prominent historian thought that 'not the least of his attractions ... was his malleability'.[6] As an admiral, a colleague described him as 'more cerebral than the average, although somewhat lazy'.[7] In Admiralty House he was known as 'I concur', owing to his habit of writing this on any memorandum or suggestion sent to him by Churchill. Battenberg was diplomatic, courteous, a capable administrator and well liked by the rank and file; but he was Churchill's glove puppet ('Churchill's dupe' to Fisher), as his predecessor, Admiral Sir Francis Bridgeman, had not been – leading Churchill to engineer Bridgeman's resignation on health grounds.

In fact, as the transcriptions of many WT signals show, Churchill was involved in the detail of everything and Battenberg was often just a rubber stamp. Doveton Sturdee, Chief of Staff at the Admiralty, said to Jellicoe that there was very little united decision making (indeed by 1915 Churchill was sending operational signals to commanders in the field as 'from the First Lord' or 'from the First Lord, copy First Sea Lord after despatch', completely overturning the chain of command). The navy was under the control of a man who had briefly been a naval cadet at Osborne and a lieutenant in the 4th Hussars.

Churchill's vehicle for controlling the day to day decisions in the navy was the Admiralty War Staff Group. This met each morning under his chairmanship and comprised Churchill, First and Second Sea Lords, Chief of the War Staff and a secretary. This group took all important decisions and minuted or telegraphed them to those who had to carry them out. Sturdee wrote that 'there was very little united decision making'.[8] Churchill himself, in his book *The World Crisis*, admitted as much and demonstrated that it was he himself who ran the show: 'I exercised a close supervision over everything that was done or proposed and I claimed and exercised an unlimited power of suggestion and initiative,'[9] he wrote.

Battenberg was under attack for his original nationality before war broke out, and on the outbreak of war things grew worse. He felt it deeply and also felt it to be unfair. In parliament and in the press he was reviled, particularly after some early naval reverses. He was suffering from gout and the naval staff he had created failed to function properly, throwing more burden on him. He did at least take the decision not to disperse the fleet and fleet reserve after the annual manoeuvres and test mobilisation held in July. On the weekend of 25–27 July the fleet was planned to disperse following the completion of the test. With Churchill away from his office and at the seaside building sandcastles with his wife and children, Battenberg issued the instruction that 'no ship to leave harbour until further orders' to the CinC Home Fleet (the famous signal 'stand the fleet fast', for which Churchill later tried to take credit, despite having been out of communication at the time of its issue). Hence by 1600 on 3 August the fleet was fully ready.

That signal, incidentally, had the side effect of ensuring that the ships sent out to Kit to replace those being assigned elsewhere, *Monmouth* and the *Good Hope*, were crewed almost entirely by coastguardsmen and boys, reservists and trainees, and very inexperienced in their duties when they set sail for their date with destiny.

Churchill's position was anything but secure. His flamboyance, excessive self-belief and overweening ambition inspired a profound mistrust in him amongst his cabinet colleagues and few were prepared to lift a finger to sustain him in office. The navy's performance had been poor – a sacrifice was required and Churchill was determined it would not be him. Utilising as his reason a rising tide of anti-Battenberg public opinion, Churchill asked him to resign on 27 October 1914. He wanted to replace him with Lord Fisher, now retired and not all that willing to work with Churchill but prepared to try; but Fisher was unacceptable to the king and the change of personnel dragged on, with Battenberg condemned to stay on in a role he no longer wanted and saw as a burden. He wrote to Churchill, 'I beg you release me, I am on the verge of breaking down and I cannot use my brain for anything.'[10] Finally his resignation was announced on 13 November after Fisher had replaced him.

So, from (at least) the beginning of October (and probably before then) to early November the most senior decision taker in the navy was preoccupied by his resignation, gout, and the lack of confidence shown in him by the public and his political masters. It is easy to imagine that Churchill stepped willingly into this vacuum; and this, of course, is the very time that Cradock was trying to decide his strategic options and fathom what the Admiralty wanted him to do. The navy was leaderless professionally and in the hands of an amateur.

20

Cradock versus Churchill, August to October 1914

Like the rest of the fleet, Kit received the order to place his squadron on a war footing on 27 July. At the outbreak of war, Kit's initial responsibilities were for an area of ocean extending from the St Lawrence in Canada to Brazil. Strategically he needed to protect British trade but also disrupt German commerce – for Germany's only source of ammonia, essential for the manufacture of explosives, was Chilean nitrates (the navy's ultimate success in preventing this trade led directly to the invention of synthesising of ammonia by the Haber process). In the early weeks of the war he achieved some success, driving the German cruiser *Karlsruhe* (on a mission to disrupt and sink British trade) out of his area of operation after nearly forcing an action (he could not catch her due to the speed difference) and preventing interdiction of trade by armed merchant cruisers. He was able to report 'the passage across the Atlantic is safe. British trade is running as usual'.[1] But there were two German light cruisers reported on the southern edge of his command and he was not a man to shirk a fight. He requested and obtained permission to leave his area of operation, transferred his flag to the *Good Hope* for its greater speed and set off south, reaching St Lucia on 23 August. The next few days were spent hunting the enemy without success. With pressing problems to attend to, the admiral responsible for the southern waters (Stoddart) had too much on his plate, so Kit was ordered to permanently extend his responsibilities into the south and towards Coronel and the Falklands.

He did not know it yet, but his nemesis was on the move. Admiral Graf von Spee had been based at Germany's naval base on the coast of China, Tsingtao. Correctly perceiving this base to be incapable of defence when Japan entered the lists he set sail with his two modern armoured cruisers, intending to link up with the four light cruisers of the squadron and make his way back to Germany, causing maximum disruption to British trade and shipping on the way. The Admiralty were uncertain where he was or the routes he would sail; but they knew of the danger of his modern ships and the damage to *materiel* and prestige they could cause.

In the fog of war, communication between commanders, field commanders and units is critical; and is often confused, distorted by egos and prejudices and lacking in clarity. Thousands of miles away from London, Kit carried out a dialogue of the deaf with the Admiralty, each assuming and presuming too much. Admiralty minutes show that Churchill was deeply involved in the decision taking and strategy, overruling the views of the Admiralty staff. That Kit thought Churchill disliked him, both over the *Delhi* affair and as a member of the Beresfordite faction, has already been noted. Did this animus inform the tenor of the signals between them?

On 3 September Kit signalled the Admiralty his intentions and dispositions; his primary concern, reflected in the dispositions, was to protect trade and find the German light cruisers which he knew to be in the area. Both he and the Admiralty were concerned that German raiders might disrupt the vital trade in grain and, particularly, nitrates. Of the *Scharnhorst* and *Gneisenau* he had as yet no knowledge, but on 5 September he reported intelligence that they had been sighted in the Caroline Islands and asked for information; he was understandably concerned that they might come his way. The Admiralty were unable to help but suggested that von Spee might seek to use the Falklands anchorages. Kit refined his planning and on the 14th he had a palpable hit when the armed merchant cruiser *Carmania* found its German equivalent, the *Cap Trafalg*ar, and sank her. For this and driving off the *Karlsruhe* he was later acclaimed a hero by the Uruguayans when he put into Montevideo, and he and his Flag Lieutenant, Cummings, were pictured in the Montevideo press[2] – to the chagrin of the officers of the *Karlsruhe* who later saw these papers on a captured vessel.

Finally, also on 14 September the Admiralty signalled Cradock further instructions. They had finally decided that von Spee was heading his way. Kit and his small force would be the tool to stop him. The orders are worth reading in full, for the kernel of the deafening dialogue is within them.

> There is a strong probability of Scharnhorst and Gneisenau arriving in the Magellan Straits or on the west coast of South America ... Leave sufficient force to deal with [light cruisers]. Concentrate a squadron strong enough to meet Scharnhorst and Gneisenau making Falklands Islands your coaling base. *Canopus* now on route to Albrohos, *Defence* is joining you from Mediterranean. Until *Defence* joins, keep at least *Canopus* and one 'county' class with your flagship. As soon as you have superior force, search the Magellan Straits with squadron, being ready to return and cover River Plate or, according to information as far north as Valparaiso. Break up the German trade and destroy the German cruisers.[3]

This was about as badly drafted as you can get; swooping in scope and light on detail, Churchillian in tone. It is easy to imagine Kit puzzling over it in his admiral's cabin, trying to understand the Admiralty's wishes. Good news, he was to get HMS *Defence*, an armoured cruiser to match one of von Spee's; bad news, he was specifically being told that his two obsolete cruisers and the antique *Canopus*, an old battleship built in 1897, were a sufficient force to deal with the German threat. Indeed Churchill later wrote that the *Canopus* was 'a citadel around which our cruisers would find absolute security'.[4] Kit was an experienced seaman. He knew that this was tosh and that his force was inadequate for that task. What was he to do?

It was also poor man management. Instead of defining the objective or mission to be achieved, the signal told Cradock specifically what to do. Advances in communications technology had facilitated this sort of instruction, which had been impossible in Nelson's time, and Churchill had a reputation for back seat driving in both world wars. It stands in stark contrast to the latitude given to von Spee.

Actually, Kit was not alone in thinking his forces insufficient. The admiralty staff had, on 7 September, recommended reinforcing him with three armoured cruisers and a light cruiser. Overruled by Battenberg, Doveton Sturdee (Chief of Staff, a Beresfordite and a particular bête noir of Fisher's) suggested sending battle cruisers, and HMS *Indomitable* was readied for the task. But in the face of objection from Jellicoe, Churchill would not agree to it. As a sop, *Defence* and *Canopus* were ordered to Kit but one was a liability and one would never arrive.

Churchill had form in the sending of badly drafted signals. At the start of the hunt for von Spee a signal was sent to Admiral Jerram, in East Asiatic waters, as follows: 'How is China squadron disposed? Destruction of Scharnhorst and Gneisenau is of first importance. Proceed on this service as soon as possible with Minotaur, Hampshire and Dupleix, keeping in communication with RA Australia who together with Montcalm is engaged on the same service. They are at present searching for them in Samoa.'[5] This signal is, first, startling for its lack of knowledge of what Jerram was up to; second, for the complete lack of information on where he should 'proceed on this service'; and third, by the delusion that RA Australia (Admiral Patey) was in Samoa – he wasn't, he was busy escorting convoys from Australasia; and the phrasing is more Churchillian than naval; 'proceed on this service' indeed. He then followed this up by radically altering Jerrram's agreed plans of concentration by ordering him to position his forces 900 miles away from his chosen geography and close to Hong Kong, allowing von Spee free passage into the southern Pacific. This was because Churchill felt that Jerram should concentrate on the old battleship, *Triumph*, a poorly armed ship (four 10-inch, fourteen 7.5-inch guns) which had been placed in reserve in Hong Kong and was in the process of being re-commissioned. In this there are echoes of Churchill's insistence to Cradock that the equally obsolete battleship *Canopus* would provide him with a 'citadel'. Jerram was outraged at the interference. He later wrote to his wife, 'to my horror the Admiralty ordered me to concentrate on Hong Kong. I was reluctant to do so as it placed me 900 miles from what I conceived to be my correct strategical position ... I was so upset I very nearly disobeyed the order entirely. I now wish that I had done so'.[6] If he had, he might well have intercepted von Spee.

Even more culpably, Australian naval forces were deployed at the First Lord's request covering expeditionary forces sent to capture the German possessions of Samoa and New Guinea – which were of limited strategic value and could have been taken at any time – rather than hunting for the German armoured cruisers. An officer of von Spee's squadron commented that 'we had in the First Lord of the Admiralty an involuntary ally'.[7]

On 16 September Cradock received a further signal: on the basis of what turned out to be faulty intelligence the Admiralty told him that von Spee was steering away from South America and that he should attack German trade on the SW coast without the need for concentration. Kit might have been puzzled by this (why would von Spee steer away from his logical course for the Atlantic and, eventually, home?), but he could be forgiven for assuming that their intelligence was better than his. As a result he signalled his intentions to sweep south with his squadron and then send *Monmouth* and *Glasgow* west to attack trade.

At the Admiralty, on the basis of their new, and false, appreciation, they ordered *Defence* to remain at Malta – and they didn't tell Kit.

Cradock decides

Meanwhile, von Spee was steadily making his way to the west coast of South America, by way of remote islands and atolls, sinking a

French warship and desperately – and largely unsuccessfully – looking for coal. By the end of September he had reached the French Marquesas (where it was not known that the world was at war) and coaled. Von Spee paid a courtesy call on the Catholic Mission. Discovering, by way of their radio signals, his light cruisers, he began to concentrate his fleet.

Cradock was looking for the *Dresden* specifically and German light cruisers in general; on 28 September he gained information from the British consul at Punta Arenas (Chile) that she was hiding in Orange Bay. He set sail with darkened ships and after midnight to avoid detection, but the bird had flown and Cradock now needed to coal so he ordered his cruisers back to the Falklands. On 3 October *Glasgow* and *Monmouth* sailed to meet *Otranto* and comply with the orders to attack German trade. *Good Hope*, and Cradock, remained in Port Stanley against the *Dresden* coming east, no news having been received as to Spee's whereabouts. After another fruitless swoop on Orange Bay the flagship returned to port where, on 7 October he received a message sent two days earlier in which the Admiralty informed him that *Scharnhorst* and *Gneisenau* 'appeared to be working across to South America'[8] and telling him he should be prepared to meet them together. Again the message implied that *Canopus* and a cruiser was a sufficient encounter force. Cradock responded the following day, correctly identifying that there were three light cruisers in company with *Scharnhorst* and *Gneisenau* and that he 'intended to concentrate and avoid division of forces'.[9] He requested the release of HMS *Cornwall* to join him (a sister to *Monmouth* and of little utility) and enquired after the whereabouts of *Defence* and when it would join his flag. He also wanted to know if von Spee would be permitted by the Americans to use the Panama Canal (if he could he could fall on the West Indian colonies with ease). And Kit went further, suggesting to the Admiralty, openly and for the first time, that his force was insufficient and that there should be reinforcements to provide a strong presence on either coast. With the current dispositions, von Spee was stronger than either Cradock or Stoddart individually and might defeat both of them *in seria*.

123

In reply he was told that *Defence* had been assigned to Stoddart on the east coast and that his proposed concentration of his forces for combined operations had been agreed.

Finally, *Canopus* arrived at Port Stanley, only for Cradock to be told she needed five days' engine room work and could not exceed 12 knots. On 18 October Kit signalled the Admiralty, '... I fear strategically the speed of my squadron cannot exceed 12 knots, owing to the *Canopus*, but trust circumstances will enable me to force an action'.[10] Of course even at the old battleship's full speed of 16 knots this would also have been true, a fact consistently ignored by Churchill and the admiralty.

And so, in mid-October, Cradock sat in the admiral's day cabin and reflected. It was clear that the Admiralty wanted him to engage and destroy von Spee, as had been made obvious in the orders sent to him on 14 September. It was clear they believed that he had sufficient force. It was clear that, if the *Canopus* was in company, his fleet speed would never force an action. He had asked for reinforcements and been declined twice. Indeed there was a later rumour (reported in the *Morning Post*) that he had been told he would be recalled if he asked again. Orders were to be obeyed and there was no further room for debate.

But at the Admiralty Churchill's comprehension of Cradock's final signal was that he understood the Admiralty's intention that he should concentrate on the Falklands and that he would act only with *Canopus* in company. All seemed well, if you believed that *Canopus* balanced the odds – and no professional sailor, as opposed to amateur strategist, did believe that.

21

Arms and the Men

To understand Kit's concerns and his desire for better reinforcement, it is necessary to understand the comparative forces at the disposal of the two converging admirals, Cradock and von Spee.

The British squadron of ships at Coronel comprised the obsolete, the inadequate and the risible. The tactical thinking behind ship design in the Victorian era had not evolved beyond the wooden walls of Trafalgar, despite the advances in armaments, protection and *materiel*. In the days of Nelson, ships were designed to fight a close-range, broadside to broadside, battle. If possible a captain would try to cross an opponent's bow and fire a broadside along the length of the enemy ship causing massive devastation. This required ships that possessed a large number of guns, ranged along the side of the vessel and mounted in the decks (hence the classic three-decker ship of the line).

Amazingly, during the Victorian period the admirals still thought that this was the way warfare would be fought and commissioned ship designs that reflected such thinking. Large numbers of mixed calibre guns were fitted, mainly mounted along the side decks. In response to the growth of armour plate, a small number (generally two) of larger calibre weapons were specified fore and aft, called 'hull crackers'. The idea was that they would 'crack' the enemy's armour plate in order that the smaller side-mounted guns could pour in a broadside. Mixed calibre guns made spotting accuracy difficult (shell splashes could not be distinguished), and only two large calibre weapons made salvo fire and 'bracketing' impossible. Target practice range was, in any case, often 2,000 yards (at the beginning of the twentieth century, the gunnery prize was awarded for shooting at 1400 yards) for weapons which could easily reach 10,000. The whole battle doctrine was backward looking and officers such as Percy Scott who tried to revolutionise gunnery methods and tactics were largely ostracised (Charlie B famously had a very public row with Scott when commanding in the Med – see Chapter 24). The lessons of the Russo Japanese war and the Battle of Tsushima in 1905 (the Japanese opened fire at around 7,000 yards, the Russians at 18,000) were slow to be learned. In any case they came too late to influence the design of Cradock's major units and the paradigm was not broken until Jackie Fisher's *Dreadnought* in 1906.

Additionally, the accuracy of shooting was poor, as gun laying was largely manual and based on human intuition. Hence the rate of fire of a gun was important, for the more shells one got away the better chance that one of them might find its mark. Large calibre weapons had a low rate of fire whereas the British 6-inch quick firer had, for the time, a rapid one. Hence batteries of quick-firing weapons continued to be fitted even as big gun technology improved.

At the outbreak of war Kit had his flag in HMS *Suffolk*; but he deemed her too slow and transferred to HMS *Good Hope* on 17 August on the basis that she was a faster ship (their design speeds were identical so this must have been down to actual performance). On 1 November 1914 his squadron comprised His Majesty's Ships *Good Hope*, *Monmouth*, *Glasgow* and *Otranto* (and 300 miles away the *Canopus*).

Kit's flagship, the *Good Hope*, had been commissioned in 1898 and launched four weeks after Queen Victoria died in 1901. This vessel's original name was *Africa*, but it was changed to *Good Hope* before launching, in honour of the Cape Colony government who had decided to present the imperial government with a sum equivalent to the interest on her capital value. She was a Drake class armoured cruiser, designed for trade protection, keeping trade routes free and, if in company with the fleet, as its fast or scouting arm. She carried two 9.2-inch guns, sixteen 6-inch mounted in the decks (eight either

side), and twelve 12-pounders, and had 6-inch armour amidships; with forty-three coal-fired boilers, her best recorded speed was 25 knots – but she was an old lady now. She had been decommissioned into the reserve fleet in 1913 but was plucked off the harbour wall on the outbreak of war and sailed to join Cradock on 2 August with a crew, ninety per cent of whom were reservists, under Captain Philip Francklin.

Good Hope was an antique, a design 16 years old but obsolescent when launched and obsolete now. Her engines were unreliable and indeed she was to suffer a failure in the port engine during September which took a week to repair. On board, apart from Francklin, Kit had his admiral's staff; his secretary, Paymaster G.B. Owens, Flag Lieutenant, Commander G.E. Cumming and two clerks, John Egremont and E.C. Webber.

Kit's second armoured cruiser was the *Monmouth*, a county class ship, also launched in 1901. Fisher said of this class, 'Sir William White designed the County Class but he forgot to put the guns in.'[1]

She mounted fourteen 6-inch guns (one at bow and stern, the rest in two ranks along the sides) and four 12-pounders. Her amidships armour was 4 inches. Her casemate 6-inch guns were sited so close to the waterline that they were unusable in any kind of seaway. Decommissioned into the reserve fleet in January 1914, she too was quickly despatched to Cradock with a reserve crew under the command of Captain Frank Brandt.

In the *Navy* magazine of 1915 one Hector Bywater wrote, 'The *Monmouth* deserved to be called a tin-clad, rather than armoured, cruiser. She had a narrow 4-inch belt, quite inadequate to keep out even 6-inch projectiles. Her casements were of the same thickness and must have been death-traps. But to crown it all, the armament of this cruiser, displacing as she did nearly 10,000 tons, included guns no more powerful than 6 inch quick firers. Fourteen of them were carried – six mounted in the main deck casements so near the water that they could not be used in dirty weather and four mounted in twin turrets which were so close that the utmost difficulty was experienced in working them. It is difficult to understand how such ships came to be designed. In every respect they violated the fundamental cannons of naval architecture and costing three-quarters of a million each they possessed not half the battle value of cruisers with considerably less displacement and of much smaller initial cost.[2] Clearly everyone in the navy knew this; but *Monmouth* was still sent to South America. She was an antique too – and basically useless.

Captain Brandt is worth a moment's reflection. Brandt joined the navy in *Britannia* aged thirteen. He was a slightly unconventional character and unusually intelligent, getting first- or second-class certificates in his seamanship and board exams. He specialised in torpedoes, and this and submarines became his metier. Submarines were a new and mistrusted naval development and definitely not a specialism which would necessarily bring social and professional advancement in the Edwardian navy. The branch attracted misfits and Frank – unconventional in dress, firm of opinion, volatile, explosive and enquiring, unwilling to accept orders without question – was an exception amongst his fellow officers. In 1906 he took command of the Portsmouth Submarine Flotilla of twelve vessels, was promoted captain in 1909 and in 1912 became the first captain of HMS *Maidstone* (depot ship) and of the 8th Submarine Flotilla. Brandt had served eight years with torpedoes and subs by 1914 and was one of the most modern captains in the navy – and yet he was thrust into command of an old scow instead of deploying his expertise where it could matter. *Monmouth* was not a prestigious command, far from it. Had his abrasive and questioning manner upset his career path and caused this backward-looking posting? Given the admiralty of the time it could well have happened. Brandt fought bravely at Coronel. Sources at the time suggested that he turned his crippled cruiser towards the enemy to enable *Glasgow* to escape. Certainly the ship refused to strike its flag before being pummelled to death by the *Nurnberg*.

HMS *Glasgow* was a modern ship, launched in 1909, with a full-time crew and an able commander. She was a town class light cruiser, designed for scouting, the eyes of the fleet and for patrolling trade routes – roles fulfilled by Nelson's frigates 100 years before. But she was never intended to fight in a line of battle against heavy ships. Lightly armoured (nowhere more than 2 inches) and armed (two 6-inch, ten 4-inch) *Glasgow* was out of her depth in an exchange with the German heavy ships. Nonetheless she did inflict some damage on the enemy and must have been a lucky ship, for an estimated 600 shells were aimed at her during the battle without fatally wounding her.

The last member of the squadron was the *Otranto*. A converted liner, formally with the Orient Steam Navigation company, she was commandeered by the navy on the outbreak of war and fitted with six 4.6-inch guns. Standing massively high from the water (she was nicknamed 'The Floating Haystack'), completely unarmoured, and capable of only 18 knots she should never have been there. Fisher believed this type of ship was useful for scouting ('large mercantile vessels are the best scouts'[3]) and information gathering but they were only ever intended to fight their own kind; such armed merchantmen were the result of the Admiralty believing that there were German liners and cargo boats in American harbours capable of being fitted with guns and interfering with Atlantic trade. That they could fight bravely was not in doubt, for the RMS *Carmania* had sunk the SMS *Cap Trafalgar* in September, but to fight heavy cruisers was suicide.

Three hundred miles away, battling through the heaving seas, was the old battleship HMS *Canopus*. Launched in 1897 she carried four 12-inch and twelve 6-inch guns. She and her sisters were smaller than other designs of the time as they were intended for Far Eastern service to counteract the growth of the Japanese fleet and thus had to be able to transit the Suez Canal. As a result she was more lightly armoured than her predecessors and, indeed, than von Spee's large cruisers. Placed into reserve in 1912 (and intended for scrapping in 1915) she was reactivated on the outbreak of war and eventually sent out to join Cradock under the command of Captain Heathcote Grant, who had been rushed into his new appointment on 1 August 1914 hot foot from the position of Naval Attaché in Washington D.C. and was a 'great friend' of Kit's.

Whilst in C&M (care and maintenance) at Milford Haven, her

engineer commander had been one William Denbow. He had kept the old engines in decent condition, despite the planned scrapping, and remained with the ship when she sailed. Possibly worried about his fate, or from concern over his ability to drive this old ship with a largely reserve crew through the Atlantic, he remained in his cabin all voyage, never once communicating with his subordinates. He informed Captain Grant that there was a major problem with her condensers and she was only capable of making 12 knots, which Grant passed onto Cradock. At such speed she was no use to him and so Kit relegated her to convoying his colliers. Grant then realised that his engineer was a sick man and had had some sort of nervous breakdown; the problems were minor and the ship could do 16 knots. He set out in pursuit, despite the fact he had carried out no practice shoots with his main weapons (whose turrets were commanded by RNVR lieutenants who had never been in a turret before or fired her big guns) and that their range was severely restricted by the age and past usage. At the time of the battle *Canopus* was still a day's steaming away; and probably just as well for the old, untrained and obsolete ship would have merely added further to the British losses that day. She survived to play a part in the subsequent Battle of the Falklands and later in another of Churchill's debacles at the Dardenelles, and was scrapped in 1920.

As for Denbow he was watched over by three naval doctors who decided that he 'was in a bad mental state'. He was sent home before Coronel, invalided out of the service and disappeared into obscurity.

The enemy

In 1912 Vice-Admiral Maximilian Graf von Spee was appointed to command the East Asiatic Squadron, based at Tsingtao (a little bit of Berlin in Asia, ceded to the fatherland in 1898 and equipped with efficient German electric lighting, a school and a pilsner brewery). The now famous Tsingtao beer is still brewed there. A tall, well-made man with jerky movements, flashing eyes and a quick intelligence, he exuded energy and aggression mixed with occasional outbursts of temper, probably not helped by the rheumatism to which he was a martyr. Not a stereotypical Junker (and born in Denmark) he was a Catholic, happily married and was capable of great warmth and affability at times. Both his sons were serving with him in his squadron. Like Cradock he came from a land-owning family. Kit had met von Spee on the China station, and liked him.[4]

Von Spee's journey since leaving Tsingtao (rightly for it could not be defended against the Japanese and fell to them in November) had taken him through the Pacific Ocean and its islands and he was now half a world away from Germany, with no bases and an increasing number of his enemies searching for him; but he had caused chaos on the way.

At the outbreak of war the British Admiralty had three priorities. Safe conveyance of the BEF to France, blockade of the German navy and ports, and preventing disruption to merchant shipping thus protecting the British supply chain. (The latter point was evident even in Elizabethan times as Sir Walter Raleigh noted, 'There are two ways in which England may be afflicted. The one is by invasion ... the other by impeachment of our trades.'[5]) To prevent such 'impeachment' the Admiralty had to protect against U-boats and commerce raiders; and commerce raiding was von Spee's mission. Simply by existing he posed a threat which caused valuable naval resource to be tied up in looking for him.

An example of the disruption a determined commerce raider can cause came when von Spee detached the light cruiser SMS *Emden* for independent action in the Indian Ocean. In the subsequent operation, *Emden* sank two Allied warships and captured thirty merchant vessels. Trade was virtually shut down as owners panicked and the vital Singapore–Colombo route stopped running. Eventually hunted down by HMAS *Sidney*, *Emden* had, single-handedly, brought shipping, to a key part of the Empire, to a halt; and the Admiralty were terrified that von Spee and his ships could do the same to the critical North Atlantic trade routes if they got there.

Von Spee flew his flag in *Scharnhorst*, which with her sister ship

Gneisenau (both named for Prussian army reformers) provided the attacking punch of his squadron. Of identical design and heavily armed they were launched in 1904 and carried eight 8.2-inch guns (with a maximum range of 17,800 yards) and six 5.9-inch. With 6 inches of armour plate amidships and a top speed of 23 knots they were formidable units and both outgunned and outranged Cradock's armoured cruisers.

In company he had three light cruisers: SMS *Dresden* (launched 1908), *Leipzig* (1905) and *Nürnberg* (1908). Although of three different classes, they each mounted ten 4.1-inch guns and had maximum speeds of 23–25 knots. Each one individually was a pretty good match for *Glasgow* and they were designed to perform the same roles. Together, the German ships could deliver a broadside of 4,010 pounds, compared with the 2,815 pounds of Cradock's four ships. If *Canopus* had been present, and able to range, it would have added another 4,000 pounds to the fusillade but it could not have reached von Spee's vessels unless the German had chosen to close, which he would never have done. His heavy cruisers could have despatched *Canopus* without ever being in her fire arc.

They formed a modern, experienced group; the squadron had won accolades for gunnery, the officers were handpicked by Grand Admiral Tirpitz for detached duty. On the loose in the Atlantic they could cause major disruption to commerce. This was Kit's enemy. Against whom, to quote Hickling, 'Their Lordships saw fit to concentrate some of their best museum pieces.'[6]

The two admirals who now sought each other in the southern wastes were experientially different as well as in temperament and *materiel*. Kit Cradock was fifty-two when war broke out. He had joined the navy at age twelve and a half. Up until 1896 his whole career had been on old-fashioned sailing ships or ships powered by sail, with back-up steam engines. The only purely steam powered vessel he served on was the Royal Yacht *Victoria and Albert* in 1894–6 which was a paddle steamer.

Following this appointment he became second in command of

the training ship *Britannia* and was then posted to command HMS *Alacrity* on the China station in 1900. *Alacrity* was a third rate cruiser used as a despatch boat for ferrying messages round the fleet or ashore and, because of its luxurious accommodation fit, as the admiral's barge. It was unarmoured, carried only four 5-inch guns plus four 6-pounders and made only 18 knots. *Alacrity* was the sort of vessel Fisher had in mind when describing ships that were too weak to fight and too slow to run away. Cradock commanded her for 18 months but for much of that time was ashore leading the naval brigade in the Boxer Rebellion to great effect and with considerable courage. He was then posted to HMS *Duke of Wellington*, another sailing ship with steam assistance built in 1852 and used as a training ship at the time, permanently moored in harbour at Portsmouth where he directed transport operations for the Boer War. Cradock held a commander's rank for five years; but he was only in command of a ship for 18 months and some of that was spent fighting on land.

Awarded the four gold stripes of a full captain in 1901 he was immediately put on half pay for eight months as no suitable appointment was to hand, a not uncommon eventuality for newly promoted captains. In March 1902 he took command of HMS *Andromeda* and, later that year, of the *Bacchante*, both based with the Mediterranean fleet at Malta. *Andromeda* was a Diadem class protected cruiser built in 1895 and very similar to the *Monmouth*, carrying sixteen 6-inch guns and having the same design flaws (and designer, Sir William White) as the later ship did. *Bacchante* was a Cressy class armoured cruiser launched in 1901 and equipped very similarly to the *Good Hope* with two 9.2-inch and twelve 6-inch guns. Her sisters were to form the 'live bait squadron' so disastrously lost in the channel in the early days of the war. After two years in *Bacchante* he took charge of *Leviathan*, a Drake class cruiser, sister ship to HMS *Good Hope* and identically fitted out. Incidentally *Canopus* was based with the fleet at Malta in 1902 as well, so Kit would know her capability.

In 1905 he was on sick leave and then half pay before taking over the battleship *Swiftsure* (of a design similar to *Canopus* and obsolete by the time Kit took over) between 1906 and 1908, serving in the channel fleet, before going on half pay for a year whilst he served as naval ADC to King Edward VII. Finally he was promoted Commodore in July 1909 to a shore based appointment.

In eight years as a captain Kit had been at sea for five of them, primarily in cruisers of a design which was rapidly becoming antiquated. They were, in fact, the very type of ship which he would take over as Rear Admiral in 1913 and lead into battle at Coronel a year later. In a naval career of 40 years Cradock had only directly commanded anything remotely resembling a modern warship for five of them. His experience was tide and sail, rope and mast, wind and warp. Modern gunnery, cruiser tactics and battle plans were things of which he had limited experience. A fierce and warlike warrior on land he had little but personal courage to fall back on in the conduct of a modern war at sea. Moreover, his experiences in the Med with his cruiser commands would surely have familiarised him with the self-evident weaknesses of the class of ships he was to lead in the battle of All Saints Day.

His adversary had followed a different career path and had developed a very different skill set. Maximilian Johannes Maria Hubertus Reichgraf von Spee, born 1861 and a year older than Cradock, was the fifth son in a family whose lineage could be traced back to the twelfth century. He was educated at the family's castle in the Rhineland and joined the navy at the age of sixteen. As a lieutenant he served in training establishments in Kiel and in ships on the African station, becoming Port Commander in the Cameroons, from where he was invalided home with rheumatic fever. By 1893 he was considered a gunnery specialist and served in the battleship *Bayern* and as assistant to the Superintendent of Coastal Artillery. In 1897 he was flag lieutenant on the cruiser *Deutschland* and was promoted to Commander in 1899, serving in the battleship *Brandenberg* and then in the weapons department of the German admiralty. Appointed Captain, he commanded the battleship *Weisbaden* and was Chief of staff to the Admiral, North Sea station. He saw action on the Yangtse during the Boxer rebellion, and in 1910, at the early age of 49, was made Rear Admiral, flying his flag in the *Yorck* as second in command High Seas Fleet Scouting Group. Finally he was promoted Vice-Admiral and put in charge of the German East Asiatic squadron.

Von Spee was a technician, a good staff officer, a man who understood gunnery and tactics, experienced in commanding modern ships. His achievement in sailing from Tsingtao to the Pacific undetected and the chaos his captains had caused was testament to his command skills. Furthermore he was unhampered by back seat driving from the German admiralty which had a very realistic view of the likely eventual outcomes for their commerce raiders. The conclusion of a long appreciation written by the German Naval Staff was that 'we are ignorant of the commanding officer's dispositions regarding coal supplies ... it may be taken for granted that he will attempt to bring the enemy to action ... he must have complete freedom of action ... it would be wrong of us to interfere ... In view of the above it is better to send no instruction to the Commander-in-Chief.'[7] They did not, in fact, expect him to return.

A tactical appreciation

It is perverse that, in the action off Coronel, both German and British squadrons were acting against their tactical interests. Von Spee's orders from his masters in Berlin defined the goals he should achieve and gave him considerable latitude in how to achieve them. Indeed, the German naval staff wrote, in their appreciation of the situation, that 'any interference on our part could be disastrous'.[8] He was a long way from home with limited coaling opportunities and a finite supply of ammunition that would be difficult, if not impossible, to replace. His tactical goals were to cause as much disruption to Allied trade and communications as possible, in both the Pacific and Atlantic Oceans, whilst attempting to bring his fleet eventually safe home to Germany. To do so he could wage war on merchant ships using his fast light cruisers whilst using his bigger ships to ensure that these aggressors did not meet a similar enemy on equal terms. If forced into action against Allied light cruisers or armed merchantmen, his big guns would ensure that they could not get into range to damage his heavy ships with their gunfire.

For this was his Achilles' heel. He had no port or dock facilities within thousands of miles. If forced into an action where he sustained damage his mission could be irretrievably crippled. If either of his heavy ships were to be wounded he would have to put into a neutral port with the near certainty of interment of ships and men for the duration of the war. It was therefore in his best interest to avoid action with anything like an equal or superior force and to adopt a conservative, risk averse, approach to his dispositions; but this was not in von Spee's personality. By nature aggressive, he was predisposed to seek battle, despite the tactical risks.

Cradock's mission was different. He had to keep trade moving by protecting the freedom of the seas over an enormous area of ocean. To do so he had to deploy his ships widely, seeking to 'keep the head down' of any enemy units and if possible fix and destroy them *in seria*. He knew that his scrapyard flotilla was unfit for action with heavy enemy units and that, if he encountered any, his mission should be to maintain contact with the enemy whilst awaiting the arrival of more capable, heavy ships. This is in the best tradition of cruiser warfare, as exemplified by, *inter alia*, Howard Kelly and the *Goeben* or, in a later war, Wake-Walker and the *Bismarck*.

As has been seen, Cradock's orders were to seek and destroy the enemy cruisers. The Admiralty had seemingly told him that he had a sufficient force to do so. He had seen the debacle of the *Goeben* affair and the vilification heaped on Berkley-Milne and Troubridge for their want of aggressive action. He had been stung by the damage to the reputation of his beloved navy; and Cradock was a brave man. He would not decline battle if it came.

So the Battle of Coronel would come to be fought between two opponents both acting against their tactical interest; one driven by his own aggressive nature and one driven by the desire to fulfil orders and avoid the acid sting of accusations of cowardice which had destroyed the reputations of Milne, Troubridge and – in Kit's mind perhaps – the navy which, by implication, accused him of cowardice if he were to avoid action.

22

On the Falkland Islands, October 1914

Between the beginning of October and the 22nd, Kit was harboured in Port Stanley, awaiting *Canopus* and fretting over his orders, the lack of information from the Admiralty and the composition of his fleet. He was a regular visitor to Government House and frequently dined there, inviting the governor, William Lamond Allardyce (known locally as 'The King of the Penguins') to dine on board *Good Hope* in return. Cradock and his terrier dog were frequently spotted walking up to the mansion. His diplomatic and open personality no doubt helped him become friendly with the governor and his staff. Allardyce wrote that he saw a great deal of Kit and that they became great friends, taking long walks round the island together, examining how to strengthen the defences of, *inter alia*, the radio power house. Hence, and for the first time in this story, we have eye witness evidence as to Kit's mood and thinking.

One such confidant was the future Wing Commander H.M. Stanley Turner. Turner was a doctor but also an adventurer, and as such a man after Kit's own heart. He studied medicine at Durham and Guys, qualifying in 1899 and becoming an ear nose and throat specialist. Whilst still a student he took part in the Greco-Turkish wars and was made a Knight of the Royal Order of Saviour of Greece for his pains. In 1910 he went out to the Falklands as an assistant surgeon and within a short time was taking a leading role in government. He became a local JP, President of the Board of Health and Deputy Governor. In addition he joined the West Falkland mounted infantry and rose to command the Falkland Islands Defence Force by the outbreak of war with the rank of major. For his work on the defence of the islands he was made an MBE. After service on the Western Front he joined the RAF in 1918 and retired into private practice with the rank of Wing Commander in 1930. His experience is detailed here at length to reinforce that he is a credible witness, a professional medical man and serving officer who understood martial life.

In April 1924 Turner wrote to Admiral Sir Francis Bridgeman from Cairo where he was based with the RAF. In the letter he stated, 'I well remember that after Cradock's signal asking for reinforcements, he finally received a definitive order. I cannot pretend after this period to remember what the exact wording was but ... it was to the effect that he was to proceed to sea forthwith, seek out the enemy and engage him ... Cradock stayed the night at Government House and was in my opinion worried, although he largely concealed it under his usual cheerful manner. I remember that he wrote two letters; one to Admiral Meux, and the other ... to a relative. These letters were put on the governor's mantelpiece and they were to be posted when the news came that the *Good Hope* had been sunk. I also remember that morning at breakfast Cradock said "Winston has always borne a grudge against me ever since the ... affair" (I forget the name of the ship, but it was I think, a P&O – the one which was wrecked with the Duchess of Fife on board). He then said "this is Winston's doing" – referring apparently to the order I have mentioned above. He seemed very worried'.[1] The P&O could only be the *Delhi*. Kit thought Churchill was acting out of spite.

Turner added a further observation. Just before departure the crew were allowed a run ashore. 'It was common talk amongst them that this was the last chance they would have and they proceeded to drink Port Stanley dry and smash up the public houses. I well remember the trouble we had gathering them up and getting them into their launches ... a number of them (eight I think) fell into the water and were picked out half drowned.'[2] (The beer in the Falklands Arms and Rose and Crown was unusually strong as it had to be fortified to survive the journey from the UK.) Turner also noted that the *Good Hope*'s gunnery range finder was defective.

Allardyce later wrote that he felt they had a premonition of what was to come. He too gave witness to Kit's frame of mind and also added his own views as to Kit's predicament. The governor formed the view, after checking the size and speed of Cradock's opponents in a reference book, that Kit's squadron was both outgunned and outrun, and he pointed this out to Kit. Apparently Kit 'hesitatingly' admitted it. Allardyce also readily spotted the uselessness of the *Canopus*, so beloved of Churchill, describing her as 'an old battleship, very slow and with 12 inch guns which were not of a modern type'.[3] At a subsequent discussion Allardyce raised the issue of the squadron strength again and Kit responded that he had asked for the *Defence* but that he had been refused by the Admiralty. Indeed he told Allardyce that he had asked twice for her, adding that, 'I should be willing to engage them with the ships I have and I don't care a d..n if we all go to the bottom.'[4] The governor was impressed. He formed the view that Kit was a 'very brave man'; but he was also concerned, for he believed that the result of a meeting between the two squadrons would be a foregone conclusion and 'our gallant fellows'[5] had no chance of success. Allardyce decided to telegraph his masters at the Colonial Office explaining his views, but showed the draft to Kit first out of courtesy. Kit did not want it sent. He was worried that the Admiralty would think he was 'squeaking'[6] – and through a third party to boot. The governor did eventually send his message in a modified form but it had no effect, although his assessment was spot on.

Allardyce noted that Kit's ships had been sent to his icy kingdom with only tropical kit and very little in the way of rations and provisions. On his own initiative he let Kit have the islands' gold reserves of around £3,000 in exchange for a draft on the Admiralty, and this Kit spent at the Falkland Islands Company's shop to reclothe and reprovision his men and ships. Finally, Allardyce gave a dinner at Government House on 21 October for Kit and his officers and his team and their wives – it must have been a sombre affair.

Before leaving the Falklands for the last time, Kit wrote to the governor thanking him for his hospitality. The letter is worth reproducing in full as it gives a clear picture as to Kit's state of mind. The underlinings are his own.

Cradock to Allardyce 22 Oct 1914

My Dear Governor

Thank you very much for your hospitality. Thank you very much for your kindness. I will return the books as I may miss the Falklands on my way back? Suez?

I shall not fail to let them know at home officially what I have seen and think of your gallant precautions and plans for upholding our honour and would that all dependencies were the same.

I will write the Admiralty re the present and near future dispositions of all colliers etc that come here and leave the later reports to you. Rear Admiral Stoddart is the new Admiral on the SE coast. Montevideo will reach him.

I will give all warning I can if the squadron 'from Germany' eludes us; and only in case of my 'disappearance' will you send the letter to Meux. I mean to say if my squadron disappears and me too – completely.

I have no intention after 40 years at sea of being an unheard victim.

Au revoir and all good luck to you and your great responsibilities.

Yours ever sincerely

Christo Cradock

Somehow I think we shall say how d'ye do to these Teutonic gentlemen. I am generally pretty lucky and we don't want any more disappointments.[7]

The shadow of Troubridge and the *Goeben* affair clearly hung over him. 'Deplorable and contrary to the traditions of the British navy'[8] – so Troubridge's Court of Inquiry had said. Kit would never have wanted that said of him.

But the letter Kit left has not been found. Although we cannot be certain, it is probable that in the letter Kit said he believed it to be his orders and duty to seek out von Spee in the Pacific even though he had an inadequate force to achieve a victory. The letter 'to a relative' is also untraced.

We have another witness in T.N. Goddard, ADC to Allardyce and Clerk to the Council. He later wrote, 'He knew what he was up against and asked for a fast cruiser with big guns to be added to his squadron for he had nothing very powerful and nothing very fast; but the Admiralty said he'd have to do without, so old Cradock slipped off quietly one morning ...'[9]

Goddard added further testimony as to Kit's frame of mind. He wrote, 'The Admiral was a brave old man; he knew he was going to almost certain death in fighting these new and powerful ships and it seemed quite all right as far as he was concerned ... I was dining with him one night and about the only thing I could find in his cabin was a piece of old Cloisonné with the top knocked off. I asked him how it got broken and he said "I got that in China when I was a lieutenant and I have carried it with me ever since and it has always bought me luck, but last month when we changed over from the *Suffolk* at half an hours' notice, I managed to get on board with my dog in one fist and this vase in the other ... and knocked its head off".'[10]

According to Glasgow's gunnery officer Lieutenant-Commander Charles Backhouse's later account, Kit buried his medals and sword on the island before he sailed.[11] This has the tang of truth about it, for Allardyce and his staff were busily burying their confidential papers. In a letter to J.C.C. Davidson (PPS to Harcourt, Secretary of State for the Colonies) of 12 September Allardyce first notes this activity ('buried documents and our Lares and Penates') and later records that three inches of rain then washed them up again.[12] Lieutenant Harold Hicking noted that Kit asked Allardyce to keep his medals and decorations and 'send them to my people'.[13]

So Kit took his ships to their joust with destiny. Why? Did he still believe that he could encounter the German ships in detail and overwhelm them individually? Did he think that von Spee would refuse contact for fear of damage? Was he fed up with Churchill and a supposed animus that he felt was setting him and his command up for disaster? It has been noted that Cradock was quick to resent and bear a grudge. Did he sail in a bate, to prove he was right? Or did the concept of disobeying or ignoring orders with which he disagreed simply not cross his mind? His whole training, his naval beliefs, his tradition all compelled him to accept the chain of command without question. And his pride in the Service would drive him to ensure its reputation was not tarnished by accusations of cowardice. He would have seriously disciplined anyone who disobeyed his own orders; and would expect nothing less from his own superiors. So, he sailed.

23

The Battle of Coronel and its Aftermath, 22 October to 8 December 1914

A Forlorn Hope

On 22 October Kit walked up from the admiral's stateroom, having blanked out the Royal Order Crown of Prussia from his medal bar in blue ink, and stood tall and quietly on the open bridge. It was the Falklands summer, the temperature a balmy 48°F. He was coatless, enjoying the feel of the wind on his face. It reminded him of the hunting field. He reflected on those at home, one person in particular. Then Cradock looked up at his personal flag – two red balls on a cross of St George – as if in a reverie. 'We are sailing to our doom unless help arrives,' he muttered to no one in particular; then he briskly ordered Captain Francklin to get under way. Good Hope *slipped quietly out of Port Stanley and left* Canopus *to look after the colliers and transports; she picked up* Glasgow *and* Monmouth *and went to seek von Spee. Many officers had written last letters home before sailing in a state of foreboding that sweethearts, wives and families would not be seen again. Kit had too.*

There was a witness to the state of mind of both Kit and the ship's company as they departed Port Stanley. Sub-Lieutenant Charles W. Gould was a radio officer on *Good Hope* – he kept a diary of the period, which has survived. He was to be landed on Achilu Veshupi on 27 October to set up a radio station and thus both he and his diary survived the carnage of Coronel. On 20 October he still believed that *Defence* was joining them. Kit knew that she would not, and seemed, according to Gould, 'angry and bitter'. Gould records

Kit telling Captain Francklin that the mission was 'suicide' – a belief shared by the crew, for Gould relates that on the 25th, at divine service, the chaplain aboard *Good Hope* broke down in tears and by the time the service had ended the entire crew were weeping.[1]

This seems a little far-fetched. Hardened sailors crying at sea? Except they were not hardened sailors. They were reservists, coastguards, boys; Gould himself was RNVR. They had expected to spend two weeks at sea on exercises and go home to their loved ones. Instead they were thousands of miles away from their jobs and beds preparing to fight a much superior foe. They were frightened.

What did Kit make of this? He *was* a hardened sailor, forty years at sea and a man of great personal courage. He knew that potentially he was taking these amateur sailors to their deaths. From his writings we know he had a sensitive streak, a romantic vision running all the way through him. He would have felt conflicted, angry and yet bound by the iron fetters of duty, orders and tradition. Kit would feel their pain.

He had no one to share his feelings with. He and his flag captain, Francklin, were 'estranged' and seldom spoke. Francklin had been an instructor at the War College immediately before the war. Perhaps there was a difference of opinion between the technocratic captain and his romantic, old navy admiral? Luce, who was an admirer of Kit and regarded him as a friend, said of him at this time, 'Cradock at times was very difficult and tended to regard any difference of views as obstruction.' Luce also commented that 'Cradock had not seemed a bit like his old dynamic self'.[2]

There was one more important exchange of signals between Churchill and Cradock before battle was joined. On 27 October Kit sent as follows: 'With reference to orders to search for enemy and our great desire for early success, consider it impractical on account of *Canopus* slow speed to find and destroy enemy's squadron. Consequently have ordered *Defence* to join me after calling at Montevideo for orders. *Canopus* will be employed in necessary convoying of colliers ...'[3]

Churchill, much preoccupied at the time (he was firing Battenberg and fighting with the king to get Fisher appointed) minuted, 'this telegram obscure'. What Kit meant – and what the naval staff could have told Churchill – was that if he was tied to *Canopus* they could not fix the enemy, but with *Defence* he had the speed and the arms to do so. In fact the signal angered Churchill. It seemed to him that Kit was flaunting Admiralty orders and relegating the *Canopus* – in which Churchill reposed much hope as a 'citadel' around which Kit could build his force – to menial duties.

On 29 October Kit established a coaling station in the Vallenar Roads. He still had no definite information regarding the whereabouts of his enemy and had had no further assistance from the Admiralty since the first week of October when he was informed that *Scharnhorst* was near Easter Island. He had been to Orange Bay and seen that the *Dresden* had been there, but he didn't know whether von Spee was making for Cape Horn or the Panama Canal – and 4000 miles of water separated them.

When *Glasgow* went into Coronel to receive and send messages, she heard wireless transmissions no more than 150 miles away and seemingly from a single ship. Receiving this news on the 30th, Kit sailed immediately with his two armoured cruisers, leaving orders for the *Canopus*, shortly expected at the roadstead with his colliers, to follow when able. On the 31st *Glasgow* reported hearing further German radio signals indicating a warship communicating with a merchant ship. Kit told Luce to hasten his visit to Coronel and rendezvous with the flagship, which he did on the 1st of November. Kit also asked Luce for four dozen oranges ('good for the guts you know'[4]). Luce brought with him the reply to Kit's signal to Churchill of the 27th. The seas were so rough that transfer of messages and provisions was impossible by boat and they were instead shipped across by barricoe, earning Luce the congratulatory signal 'manoeuvre well executed'.

Any hopes Kit might have entertained of strengthening his forces were dashed when he read Churchill's response: '*Defence* to remain on east coast with Stoddart ... this will leave sufficient force on each side [of the Cape].'[5] Churchill later argued that Cradock did not receive this signal – but he did, and we have the evidence of *Glasgow*'s Paymaster Commander, Lloyd Hirst, and Hickling,[6] as confirmation. And 'sufficient force' is the sort of phrase which could only mean one thing to a brave and impetuous admiral such as Kit. Cradock was out looking for his enemy off the coast of Coronel. Now he had been told again that he had appropriate resources. No doubt weary of protesting his views to an uncomprehending admiralty, when further transmissions were heard that afternoon and Kit formed the opinion, shared by Luce, that they were from a single light cruiser, probably the *Leipzig*, he signalled to his squadron by flags 'spread out twenty miles apart and look for the enemy'.

Forming the squadron into a line of search, and at 15 knots, the squadron steamed to find the foe. In gale force winds, Luce sighted smoke at 1620 and altered course towards it. They had found the *Leipzig* – and were the victims of a simple trick.

Radio telegraphy was still a primitive technology and the 'arc and spark' sets used gave a distinctive signal bloom which could be picked up by suitably equipped ships other than those intended. In order to conceal the presence of his whole squadron, von Spee passed all wireless messages through and to the *Leipzig*. To anyone listening in, there was only one ship within range. Kit thought that he had achieved the tactical superiority he sought and was about to fight a single ship – and perhaps be able to destroy the enemy one by one.

Von Spee had been alerted by a German merchantman to the presence of *Glasgow* at Coronel and immediately disposed his force to catch her as she left, not knowing that he was already too late. But now he was searching for a single light cruiser too. Shortly after 1630 the *Leipzig* sighted smoke and hauled out to investigate. Thus, when the two squadrons made contact, each was looking for a single ship and both found one. That which people prefer to believe, they prefer to be true.

At 1640 Luce sighted and identified the enemy. He turned around and hared back to Cradock and radioed the news that the *Leipzig* was there for sure; but in company with the *Scharnhorst* and *Gneisenau.*

Kit could still have avoided battle. An immediate alteration of course to the south would have taken his ships to safety; he had plenty of sea room, his speed (with the exception of the *Otranto* which would have had to take pot luck) gave him an advantage and the Germans, who did not know he was so close, had steam up for only a cruising speed of 14 knots. He could fall back onto the *Canopus* as the Admiralty had expected. The signal brought out by Luce from Coronel that day also told him that his orders to the *Defence* to join his fleet had been countermanded and she was nowhere near him. In all probability he could have escaped.

Kit could not do this. He believed his orders were to seek and destroy the enemy and that he had been told his resources were appropriate to the job. He obeyed orders, he maintained traditions. British admirals did not run away; they stood and fought like Greville or Drake. It was not his reputation at stake, it was the navy's and everything she stood for, everything he had lived his life believing. He would show Churchill and his ridiculous attitude. He gave the order to raise the Battle Ensigns and with the huge cross of St George flying at the masthead he sought his foe.

Likewise, von Spee had no hesitation. Knowing nothing of the *Canopus* (and had he known, caring less, for with his superior speed he could evade her) his aggressive nature would impel him into an action with a force clearly inferior to his own. That was exactly in line with his orders, and with his massive advantage in weaponry he hesitated not at all.

Engagement

There was not much daylight left when the two squadrons sighted each other and Cradock's ships were not trained to fight at night, unlike the Germans. So Kit needed to force an action quickly – and that meant getting into range for his 6-inch guns. Consequently he ordered his ships to concentrate on *Glasgow*, nearest the enemy, and formed into line ahead with *Good Hope* and *Monmouth* in the van and *Otranto* to the rear. This generated two problems. First it meant sailing into a heavy sea, which made the majority of the deck-mounted guns unusable, and second von Spee, with his preponderance of longer-range armament, could choose not to play.

At 1804 Cradock altered four points towards the enemy, trying to place himself between them and the setting sun which would thus be in the eyes of von Spee's gunlayers; but von Spee knew the game and turned away. If he was to force an action, Kit had to be more aggressive. At 1818 he signalled *Canopus*, 'I am now going to attack the enemy'. The distance between the two fleets was still some two miles beyond the range of their heaviest guns. Von Spee waited. At 1900 the sun slipped under the horizon and von Spee accepted action – with Cradock's ships silhouetted against the sunset and von Spee's lost in the murk to Kit.

Scharnhorst and *Gneisenau* opened fire at a range of 12,300 yards. At this range the British had two guns that could reach (the 9.2s on *Good Hope*), whereas the Germans had twelve. In the words of a German source, 'disaster broke over Admiral Cradock's squadron'.[7]

In Churchill's words, 'thus began the saddest action of the war'.[8]

Cradock had included the *Otranto* in his line, which made sense when searching for the enemy but not when in a line of battle engagement. *Otranto* was clearly worrying him; at 1850 he had signalled, 'I cannot go down and attack the enemy at present leaving *Otranto*', but he seems to have issued no instructions as to how he wanted to deploy her. Captain Edwards, on her bridge, made his own decision and edged out of the line to stay beyond range. At 1845 he had signalled Cradock that, given he could play no useful part in the action, he should stay out of range; he only received an unfinished reply 'there is danger; proceed at your best speed ...'. Edwards had thought Kit wanted him close to protect his vulnerable ship; but when the *Gneisenau* bracketed the ship he knew that he had to act independently, and turned for the open sea as fast as he could.

Scharnhorst engaged the flagship and with her third salvo blew up

Good Hope's forward 9.2-inch gun. *Gneisenau* struck the *Monmouth* on the forecastle and forward gun turret, setting her alight. Despite that, Brandt maintained an initial rapid, but useless, rate of fire, the range being too great for his guns.

An officer on the *Glasgow* later wrote of the battle, 'A continuous sheet of flame appeared along the sides of the *Good Hope* and *Monmouth* on which the heavy seas seemed to have no effect. Both ships however continued to fight their guns and were rewarded with a few hit's ...'[9]

Kit continued to close the range, trying to get his 6-inch guns into action or perhaps considering a torpedo attack. At 1935 it was down to 5500 yards and his ships were taking terrible punishment. Lieutenant Kloop, a spotting officer on the *Scharnhorst*, recorded, 'The *Monmouth* was hit on her 6 inch turret ... the shell blew off the roof ... a terrific explosion of charges blew the whole turret off the forecastle ... a huge column of fire, almost as high as the mast and sixty to ninety feet across, suddenly shot up the starboard side. Between 30 and 40 hits were counted in all ... at times three or four fires were burning.'[10]

Glasgow's gunnery officer further recorded, 'by 1945 ... *Good Hope* and *Monmouth* were obviously in distress. *Monmouth* yawed off to starboard burning furiously and heeling ... *Good Hope* was firing only a few of her guns. The fires on board were increasing their brilliance. At 1950 there was a terrible explosion between her mainmast and her after funnel; the gust of flames reached a height of over 200 feet.' Lieutenant Hickling of the *Glasgow* thought it looked like a giant firework.[11] The fires or a shell had found *Good Hope*'s magazine and she blew herself and her crew of 926 officers and men to pieces. Kit Cradock died with her.

Luce had been benefiting from the German light cruisers' inability to properly fight their guns in the bad weather, but nonetheless he had taken damage. Now he had the whole German squadron to deal with and he could not fight that particular battle. He turned to see if he could help the burning and sinking *Monmouth* and at 2015 signalled, 'are you all right' (which must count as one of the most fatuous signals in naval history, given the state of Brandt's vessel). Brandt responded, 'I want to get stern to the sea, am making water badly forward'. Luce tried again. 'Can you steer NW, the enemy are following us astern'. There was no reply.

Luce could see that *Monmouth* was finished and someone had to reach and warn the *Canopus*, which was making best possible speed to join up and, if surprised by von Spee, would be sunk in minutes. He considered launching a torpedo attack, which would surely have been futile, but was talked out of it by his first lieutenant. *Glasgow*'s paymaster, Hirst, later told Allardyce that those on board the *Monmouth* recognised their hopeless position but 'with the greatest nonchalance' stood about on deck smoking. A friend of his signalled him, 'please go and see my people and tell them'.[12]

Luce turned away and left the *Monmouth* to her fate. Found as a burning hulk by the *Nurnberg* she refused to strike her flag, recalled her men to the guns from fire-fighting, and was sunk by a 75-shell fusillade of gunfire. At 2145 *Nurnberg* reported, 'have sunk enemy cruiser', to which von Spee replied, 'Bravo *Nurnberg*'.

By then, 1660 British sailors were dead.

Too late

On 3 November, and before the result of the Battle of Coronel was known in Britain, a further signal was sent to Cradock. At last Fisher had taken up the reins and decisive action was ordered: '*Defence* to join your flag with all despatch. *Glasgow* should keep in touch with enemy. You should keep in touch with *Glasgow*, concentrating the rest of your squadron, including the *Canopus*. It is important that you should effect your junction with *Defence* at earliest possible moment ...'[13] It was what Kit had wanted. But it was too late. As Churchill later wrote, 'We were already talking to the void.'[14]

Aftermath

Nurnberg did not stay to look for survivors from the shattered *Monmouth*. Sighting smoke and thinking it British ships, she hauled off and made her way back to Spee. In fact the ships on the horizon were her own comrades and the *Monmouth*'s crew were left to drown. Von Spee meanwhile did not know that the *Good Hope* had sunk. He imagined her wounded and limping to the Chilean coast and did not search for survivors. Assembling his ships, he sailed round the fleet congratulating his brood on their success. Then he sailed for the Valparaiso Roads where, under international law, he would be permitted to remain for two days and where he could pick up stores.

The seemingly pro-German *South Pacific Mail*, published in Valparaiso on 5 November 1914, reported von Spee's success: '*Good Hope* was put out of action and escaped into the darkness. A large explosion was observed and her guns were silenced. The *Monmouth* in a similar position tried to escape but was chased by a small German cruiser who sank her. Unfortunately heavy seas prevented the lowering of boats. The *Glasgow* and *Otranto* were heavily damaged but were able to escape owing to their speed. The German ships suffered no damage ...'

Welcomed ashore to a banquet by the considerable local German community, von Spee and his men were warmly congratulated. A civilian proposed a toast damning the British navy, but von Spee refused to drink to it. 'They were a gallant enemy and fought bravely, and I would rather drink to that.' A small girl presented him with a bunch of flowers. 'Thank you,' he responded, 'they will do nicely for my bier.'[15]

Von Spee was a realist, possibly a fatalist. He knew that the British would not take this loss of prestige and power lightly. To get home safely he had to sail round the Horn and then cross the Atlantic, with the Allies looking for him all the time, and somehow force an entry into a German port. He had expended half his ammunition in fighting the battle and had little hope of obtaining any more. He had limited access to coal. The best he could envisage was a fighting death, taking as many enemies with him as he could.

In London, seventy-three years old, Jackie Fisher marched back in to the Admiralty on 30 October, too late to affect Kit's destiny. The signal of 3 November, with its decisive orders and deployments, shows a new and sharper mind at work. When news of the disaster reached him, he immediately planned retribution. This was the type of work he had designed his beloved battlecruisers for; his 'new testament' ships, his 'greyhounds of the fleet'. Battlecruisers – fast enough to run away from ships they could not fight, big enough to catch and kill ships of smaller armament, all big-gun, terrible weapons of vengeance. Fisher selected HMS *Inflexible* and HMS *Invincible*, sister ships each mounting eight 12-inch guns with a range of 16,400 yards, massively stronger (and faster – 25 knots) than von Spee's big ships, and backed up by four armoured cruisers (including the much ordered about *Defence*) and two light cruisers.

As his Chief of Staff Fisher inherited Doveton Sturdee, a man he cordially hated. Sturdee owed his position to Beresford and had testified against Fisher in the parliamentary hearing that eventually caused him to retire. Not very bright, inflexible of mind and unable to take advice from his subordinates, Sturdee enjoyed the power of the role without really understanding how to perform it. The fleet depositions which led to the early disasters of the war were recommended to Churchill by Sturdee. He continued to press for the channel patrol even after the loss of *Aboukir*, *Cressy* and *Hogue*. Fisher thought him a pedantic ass and an idiot, and wanted rid of him. Sturdee refused to resign and Fisher threatened to walk out if he didn't. Churchill, faced with the prospect of losing his new Sea Lord before he had really started, stumbled on a compromise. Why not let Sturdee lead the avenging fleet? With some qualms, Fisher agreed.

Flying his flag in *Invincible*, Sturdee sailed south from Devonport at the leisurely pace of 10 knots. On 26 November he reached Albrolhos Rocks, met up with his fleet and announced that he intended to remain there three days to coal. Luce, who had sailed from Port Stanley to meet him, was appalled. With some trepidation he visited the flagship and urged his admiral to leave for the Falklands immediately, to pre-empt von Spee arriving before them. Sturdee did not like to be argued with but in the end, rather grumpily, he consented. The squadron sailed the next day.

Meanwhile, the old *Canopus* had picked up Gould and his men and was running for her life. Gould recorded in his diary, 'It's a bit rough, old scrap iron to fight three up-to-date ships. They had no chance ... we are running away, our turn [the *Canopus* he meant] if they catch us, not a gun with anything like the range of theirs and the old crock steaming 14 knots, the enemy 22 knots ... a disgrace to the navy ... well, we will take our chance, only got to die once.'[16]

Finally succumbing to her rude awakening from Care and Maintenance and the flight back to the Falklands, *Canopus*'s engines really did break down. Reduced to a crawl, she limped into Port Stanley. Her officers all admitted to Allardyce that they had suffered from 'cold feet' during the previous six hours. An experienced captain, Grant immediately established defensive preparations – and was no doubt annoyed to receive a signal from the Admiralty on 10 November telling him to do what he had already done. He grounded the ship in mud, camouflaged her, sent ashore his 12-pounders and set them up in protected batteries, filled old barrels with explosives and strung them across the harbour, and readied his 12-inch guns. 'We were determined to give von Spee a dose of his own medicine,'[17] one of her officers later wrote. Churchill had changed his tune regarding the *Canopus* now. She was no longer his 'citadel'. He had ordered that Grant avoid being brought to action by a superior force and 'if attacked the Admiralty is confident that the ship will in all circumstances be fought to the last'.[18] Another suicide note in the making.

On 7 December Sturdee's ships sailed into view. Once again Sturdee had shown no sense of urgency, giving shore leave, ordering a captains' conference and beginning to coal the fleet. He still had no intelligence as to von Spee's whereabouts and yet he posted no ships as scouts or pickets.

The next day disaster almost struck the British; and it was the old *Canopus* that prevented it. Von Spee had determined on a raid on the Falklands, destroying coal stocks and smashing communications equipment; and at 0500 the *Gneisenau* and the *Nurnberg* were sent off on this mission. At 0730 the lookout on the Falklands, who happened to be Swedish, saw smoke and raised the alarm. The British ships were coaling. Both battlecruisers had a collier alongside; two armoured cruisers were coaling and undergoing repairs. The *Bristol* had its engines opened up. It took two hours to get underway. If von Spee had pressed his attack he could have wrought mayhem in the crowded harbour.

That he didn't was down to the *Canopus*. The *Gneisenau* reported smoke and some masts. Unsure what she was seeing and thinking it the burning of coal stocks she pressed on, then two huge water splashes erupted around her without exploding – big splashes; big guns, 12-inch at least. She was under attack by capital ships, superior ships! Captain Maerker turned his ship round and fled.

In fact *Canopus* had seen the lookout's signal and immediately opened fire. Her barrels were loaded with practice shells ahead of a competition planned by Grant for that day; it would take too long to replace them so they fired anyway and got creditably close to their target. The old *Canopus*, the ship that Churchill thought would sustain Cradock and that Kit believed would result in his failure to find the enemy, had saved the day. She fired five shots in total; one ricocheted killing five men on the *Gneisenau* and wounding seven more.

Luce and the *Glasgow* had finished coaling and were moored in a position that put them in visual contact with both *Canopus* and *Invincible*. His officer of the watch tried fruitlessly to pass on the news of the sighting to the flagship but the dust of coaling was too dense for a signal lamp to be seen. Hearing of this Luce, frustrated by Sturdee's lethargy, and fearful that Cradock's nemesis was again upon them, snapped, 'Well, for God's sake, do something about it – fire a gun, send a boat, don't just stand there like a stuffed dummy.'[19] A combination of a saluting gun and a 24-inch searchlight eventually did the job.

From then on, von Spee's fate was sealed. If only he had pressed home he could have won a famous victory, but somehow he lost his nerve. Concern about ammunition? Exaggerated fear of British gunnery? Or just tiredness and bad luck? Everyone is human in the end and perhaps von Spee, after a brilliant voyage halfway round the world, with little succour or comfort ahead or behind him, just ran out of decision-making capacity. It happens.

The Battle of the Falklands started when Sturdee eventually sailed at 1000 and began a long stern chase that had only one end. Eventually catching the two big German ships, he sank them both and destroyed the light cruisers in detail, although *Dresden* survived until March 1915 when she scuttled off Robinson Crusoe Island under the attentions of HMS *Kent* and the *Glasgow.*

Scharnhorst sank with all hands after being hit by over forty 12-inch shells. Admiral Maximilian Graf von Spee died with his crew, and joined Cradock in a sailor's grave. The *Gneisenau* succumbed shortly afterwards, although she had to be assisted by her crew who, when no longer able to fight, opened the sea cocks and exploded charges against her hull. Two hundred men were rescued.

The spotting top officer in *Invincible* was Lieutenant H.E. Dannreuther. He was the son of Edward, an eminent Victorian music critic, the man who had popularised Wagner in the UK and organised a concert of Wagner's music at the Albert Hall in 1877. Lieutenant Dannreuther was Wagner's godson. He witnessed the dying moments of the German flagship: 'She was being torn apart and was blazing and it seemed impossible that anyone could still be alive,'[20] he wrote. 'Gotterdammerung', surely.

24

Gunnery and Coal

Gunnery

In Kit's whole battle with von Spee, only six British shells struck the German heavy cruisers. Two hit the *Scharnhorst* and failed to explode; four hit the *Gneisenau* but caused minimal, repairable, damage and wounded only two sailors. No German seaman died on either ship. In the subsequent retaliation off the Falklands, HMS *Invincible* and *Inflexible* scored hits with only five per cent of the shells fired (a fact that Fisher used to berate the hated Sturdee after the Battle of the Falklands). There were three problems: *materiel*, culture and ship design.

The navy had two principal dependencies: gunnery as its means of offence and defence, and coal as its means of propulsion. Kit was not a gunnery expert, so damned by his own hand in his books. In this he was not alone for the British navy of the pre-war period struggled to take gunnery and gunnery tactics seriously.

British naval armour-piercing shells proved to be inferior to those of the Germans. The British shells were brittle and frequently disintegrated on contact without penetration. When the explosive content did ignite it proved to be too weak to ensure an effective impact explosion. At the Battle of Jutland, for example, large British shell fragments were found strewn on the decks of the German warships and could be fitted together to reform the complete casing, thus demonstrating the inefficacy of the explosive content. The German shells also often had delayed-action fuses that considerably improved their efficacy. Additionally, British shells were tested by firing at an angle of 90 degrees to the target, i.e. a broadside from close range. In practice the ranges at which ships engaged meant that the shells came plunging down on the decks, causing on impact a completely different set of forces upon them to those which had been assumed and tested. And to cap it all, the propellant used was less stable than the German equivalent. The British used four cordite quarter charges to make a full charge, bags of propellant with a gunpowder igniter at each end which was quite unprotected, and twice as many as was necessary. The Germans used two bags of charges, the front one protected by a light metal container and the rear charge in a brass container ejected on firing. It was intrinsically a safer system.

The efficacy of British shell design, production, quality and quantity was a national disgrace, especially on land in the last days of 1914 and during the 'shell crisis' of 1915. Consumption of shells was massively higher than predicted and production was unable to keep pace. At the First Battle of Ypres in Oct 1914, for example, Haig had to withdraw a third of his artillery to the rear as he had no ammunition for them. Eventually Lloyd George was appointed Minister of Munitions in May 1915 to sort it out – that he succeeded in raising output (by amongst other things bringing women into the workforce for the first time and nationalising the pubs in certain ammunition-producing areas, for example Carlisle) is testament to his energy, but quality issues persisted to the end.

A greater problem was the whole Victorian and Edwardian navy's approach to gunfire and tactics. Von Spee opened fire at a range of some 12,300 yards. That is almost seven miles. Throughout the late nineteenth century British gunnery prize shooting had been at 2,000 yards and battle practice was only 3,000 yards in 1904 – the year that the Russian fleet opened an accurate fire at 18,000 yards during the Russo-Japanese war. British admirals still expected to close the enemy and pepper them with quick-firing weapons. Cradock had only two guns in his fleet that could range that far and one was knocked out by *Scharnhorst*'s third salvo. *Monmouth*'s 6-inch quick-firers were useless at that range, even in a calm sea, hence the need to close the enemy.

Accurate gunnery was not in the British naval tradition. As captain your job was to get as close to the enemy as possible and smash him with broadsides. If you could cross his bow and rake him, so much the better. This was the Nelsonian tradition and it remained embedded in naval thinking long after explosive shell had replaced round shot and gunnery ranges had opened up to 20,000 yards. HMS *Warrior*, the first British ironclad, was recognisably a Nelsonian vessel despite her armour and steam engines, and relied upon a traditional broadside. The first 'sail-less' British ocean-going battleship was HMS *Devastation* of 1873. She had an armoured citadel with huge (muzzle loading) guns at either end and was recognisable as a forerunner of the twentieth-century navy. Turrets were experimented with as a mean of moving away from the need for all-broadside armaments. The early advocate of turrets, Captain Coles, designed the first turret ship (HMS *Captain*) in 1870, but she was unstable and sank, taking him to an early grave.

Ships carried mixed armament of all calibres. This made range finding impossible as no one could tell the splashes apart at distance. Gun smoke made it worse. Individual gun captains were expected to sight and fire their own guns and each gun fired when ready, exacerbating the aiming and ranging problems. *Dreadnought* solved this problem, having no smaller calibre weapons, although later ships mounted anti torpedo boat armament. Fisher actively promoted improvements in gunnery, including centralisation of gunnery control in director towers, high above the ship (and giving British warships a distinctive profile with their tripod masts), but at the outbreak of war only eight battleships had been fitted with director control.

Fisher also promoted early forms of gunnery control 'computers' such as Pollen's and Scott's. But in this, as in so much else, he was obstructed by Beresford and the traditionalists who disliked the removal of responsibility from the Nelsonian sailor at each gun, and by the admiralty who baulked at the cost.

In 1907 Charlie B had a public spat with Rear Admiral Percy Scott – an officer renowned for his understanding of, and developments in, gunnery – while Scott (coincidentally flying his flag in *Good Hope*) was serving under him. Beresford ordered the whole fleet to Portland to be painted and cleaned for a visit by Kaiser Wilhelm and this stopped Scott's squadron carrying out gunnery practice. Scott had signalled to his command 'painting appears to be in more demand than gunnery so you had better come in and make yourself look pretty'.[1]

This was not all that unusual. Sometimes captains ordered practice rounds thrown over the side, as the smoke would spoil the paintwork and the recoil shake dust loose on the ship. More points were awarded for smartness of ship than for a small improvement in accuracy of gunfire. Scott wrote in his book *Fifty Years in the Royal Navy* that when he took command of the *Scylla* in 1896 'the state of the paintwork was the only idea. To be the cleanest ship in the fleet was the only objective'.[2]

A commander's (i.e. second in command on a large ship) promotion could depend on the smart turnout of their ship. Those with a large purse were advantaged in this regard as they could afford to buy enamel paint, gold leaf, steel fittings etc. to the detriment of their less well-off fellows. An illustration of the need to keep a 'smart ship' can be seen in the inspection technique of Admiral 'Pompo' Heneage, CinC Pacific and then Nore between 1887 and 1894. He liked nothing better than to carry out his investigations, especially of the engine room or heads, wearing a pair of lavender-scented white kid gloves which he would run over or behind pipework. Woe betide the commander if dirt should show on them. Behind him his coxswain carried a silver tray with a dozen or so spare pairs. Once when told that a mark on a lavatory pan was a fault in the glaze, he responded in his affected drawl, 'Ven de Admiral says de pan's dirty, de pan is dirty'.[3]

Kit's official naval record shows the priorities of reviewing officers. In 1892 Rear Admiral Markham inspected the *Dolphin* where Cradock was second in command. He reported 'smart looking ship's company, ship efficient and clean'. Jellicoe, reviewing Cradock's command *Alacrity* as Flag Captain in 1900, had similar criteria: 'ship clean, well turned out and in a creditable condition'.[4]

Sir Arthur Knyvet Wilson V.C. was First Sea Lord in succession to Fisher in 1910. He was against systems for long-range gunnery as he could only imagine that naval actions would take place at medium ranges of around 5000 yards, for which sophisticated gunnery control systems were not required. This despite the fact that it was only in 1908 that Fisher had managed to get gunnery practice ranges upped to 9000 yards. Wilson also resisted attempts to improve the quality of armour piercing shell, which had proved inadequate at long range, in the belief that HE (high explosive) shells would be more effective. As a consequence reformers like Scott, Dreyer and civilians like Pollen found it hard work to make progress. The highly effective Pollen system for fire control (the Argo Clock) was ignored (not least because Pollen was a civilian) in favour of an inferior design, the Dreyer Table, which was unable to deal with the high change of range rate in battle conditions but had the important recommendation of having been invented by a serving naval officer. It would not do to admit that the 'club' could not solve its own problems.

In their neglect of gunnery science the Admiralty reflected the prejudices of their class. Science was not seen as an important part of the educational curriculum and its practitioners were somehow not 'gentlemen'. Classics were the only thing to study and the source of all useful knowledge. Science, modern languages, even history were all seen as ancillary and ranked well below the study of Greek and Latin and their associated literature. The education provided by the public (i.e. private) schools – the growth of which was a phenomenon of the 1840s and 50s – was based on these precepts. Middle-class families, avid to turn out sons who were gentlemen, flocked to the new schools. Hence a cadre of the best of society was produced to whom science was an alien concept; its use and investigation considered infra-dig. In 1913 in England and Wales, for all branches of science including technology, mathematics and physics, only 350 students graduated with first- or second-class honours; in Germany 3,000 so graduated in engineering alone. As in society so in the navy – and gunnery science and engineering officers alike found it hard to gain acceptance.

This was the milieu in which Kit grew up. These were the values he treasured. *Canopus* had never test-fired her big guns on voyage. Neither armoured cruiser had conducted test shoots. On mobilisation 200 trainee gunnery lieutenants had been ripped away from gunnery school (HMS *Excellent*) so quickly that they left their kit behind. Some of these men would be directing Cradock's guns with the untrained reservists. He had made no provision for gunnery practice – culturally and technically Kit Cradock was not equipped for a modern war.

Coal

The British navy of 1914 was powered, like the industrial revolution of a century earlier, by coal. Vast amounts of it. Coal produced steam, and steam drove huge reciprocating engines the like of which still dominated the machinery used by the fleet.

The first coal fired navy ship, HMS *Congo*, had been launched as early as 1816. She proved a failure and eventually the engines were removed and she sailed under canvas. However, from the 1850s steam came increasingly to be used, often in combination with sail, for all warships. The French *La Gloire* of 1860 was the first ocean-going ironclad and was powered by steam and sail (1,100 square metres of canvas and 2,500 horsepower of steam), triggering a mini arms race to which the British replied with HMS *Warrior* in 1861, the largest, fastest and most heavily armed warship ever built at that time. She could make 13 knots under sail, 14.5 knots under steam and 17.5 knots combined. As engine technology developed, steam replaced sail, but never in the affections of traditionalists like Cradock.

The navy was slow to innovate. Only when Charles Algernon Parsons hijacked the 1897 Spithead Review, and outpaced the fastest ships in his revolutionary turbine powered *Turbania*, did the navy start to consider the steam turbine. The first turbine powered warship was Fisher's iconoclastic *Dreadnought* of 1906. Oil was even slower to be adopted, although Fisher had been pushing for it since 1901. The first oil fired warships were the Queen Elizabeths of 1915, four of which were under Evan-Thomas at Jutland. There was an understandable reluctance to adopt oil (which had twice the thermal value of coal, and was much less manpower intensive) as Britain had lots of coal and little or no oil. As a consequence Fisher pushed government to expand the British presence in the Middle East, especially Persia. The acquisition of new oilfields and facilities followed, as did the construction of new tankers under the aegis of the Anglo Persian oil company, the forerunner of BP, which the British government purchased for £2M.

So Cradock and von Spee depended on coal and hence on coaling at regular intervals. Cradock had his collier train and pre-existing coaling stations under British control. Von Spee depended on capture of stocks or on agents in neutral countries procuring coal and colliers to meet him at secret locations.

Coaling ship was an all hands job. Cradock devotes a chapter to it in *Whispers from the Fleet*. With a collier alongside all available officers and men went over into the collier to dig the coal into 2-cwt bags. Each bag was then hoisted into the coaling vessel and emptied into the coal bunkers (Kit recommends 150 bags and 50 shovels per hold of the collier). It was a backbreaking and filthy business, and was universally detested. Once coaling was complete, men and ship would be covered in coal dust which would require a full clean down of both – the ship first. In 1908 the record rate of coaling was 174 tons an hour, and the process created clouds of dust which, in a busy harbour, could settle like a fog or rise up into the air like smoke from a raging fire. It was this 'smoke' that the *Gneisenau* had spotted on 8 December.

25

Recrimination and Blame, 1914

'Kit Cradock is gone at Coronel … His death and the loss of the ships and the gallant lives in them can be laid to the door of the incompetency of the Admiralty. They have as much idea of strategy as the board school boy and have broken over and over again the first principles.'[1] So wrote Admiral David Beatty to his wife from his command on HMS *Lion*.

Who was to blame for Coronel? Many people blamed the Admiralty, which meant in particular the staff and Sturdee. Others, especially in the navy, blamed Churchill for his back seat driving. Some, including Churchill, blamed Kit.

Immediately upon receiving the news of the disaster, Churchill attempted to exculpate the Admiralty from blame, expressing disbelief that Kit should not have concentrated his force on the 'citadel' (as he called it) of the *Canopus*. He also presented his cabinet colleagues with a wholly misleading version of events and of the signals sent. Cradock, he stated, was 'insubordinate' and at fault in disobeying 'his instructions, which were express to the effect that he must concentrate his whole squadron'.[2] The reliance Churchill placed on the *Canopus*, the presence of which actually made Kit's mission impossible due to its slow speed, shows the worst of his amateur strategising. As one officer commented, had the *Canopus* met with von Spee it could only have increased the British casualty numbers.

Prime Minister Asquith swallowed Churchill's version hook, line and sinker: 'I'm afraid the poor man has gone to the bottom; otherwise he richly deserves to be court martialled,'[3] he wrote to his amorata, Venitia Stanley. To the king he reported, 'the mishap is the more regrettable as it would appear that the Admiral was acting in disobedience to his instructions'.[4]

Others knew better. Allardyce, writing to Davidson on 1 December 1914 stated, 'all on board [the *Good Hope*] had a premonition of trouble ahead of them. The vessels at Sir Christopher Cradock's disposal were not, in my opinion, sufficiently powerful to contend with such modern vessels as the *Scharnhorst* and *Gneisenau*, apart from the fact that our own squadron was several knots slower that the Germans.'[5]

When, a decade later, Churchill published his magisterial book *The World Crisis*, he once again attempted to pin the responsibility solely on Kit. 'I cannot accept for the Admiralty any share in the responsibility for this disaster,'[6] he wrote. In other words, it was Kit's fault. The impact of this publication will be examined later in Chapter 28.

According to the *South Pacific Mail*, von Spee attributed his victory to the 'bad tactics and bad shooting of the English'. He also commented that attacking him as they did was a tactical error as 'their ships rolled in the heavy seas from the South and could not fire half their guns'. [7]

In defence of Churchill, von Spee had stated that 'against the *Canopus* we can do nothing'.[8] But this is the statement of a weary man after a successful battle. He did not know that *Canopus'* gunnery lieutenant had never been in a turret before, that her big gun barrels, worn smooth with age, could only range 9000 yards, much less than his own weapons, and that her maximum speed was significantly less than his. But the risk of damage from her big guns when he was thousands of miles from repair and friends might just have dissuaded him from pressing an action had he met Kit in her company.

The Admiralty staff – under Churchill's direction and with the titular naval head, Battenberg, seemingly suffering some sort of nervous collapse – is certainly culpable. The day-to-day work fell to Sturdee who, although possessing a reputation for unflappability, did not possess an equally generous standing for intelligence. His initial dispositions of the fleet, sending some old and obsolete cruisers previously mothballed for eventual scrapping and then tasking them with a search and destroy mission against superior forces, lacks any sort of strategic thought and smacks of desperation. The loose drafting of signals and misapprehension of Kit's responses is simply negligent. Admiral Bridgeman, writing to Sheldon in 1917, stated, 'to send three old crocks to meet von Spee was the highth [sic] of folly'.[9]

It is worth revisiting and reviewing some of these signals in more detail. Kit's original orders, dated 14 September, were to find and destroy enemy cruisers. These orders were never countermanded and, as far as he was concerned, remained the task the Admiralty expected him to fulfil. On 14 October Churchill and Battenberg agreed that Cradock should concentrate on the Falklands and that pending the arrival of reinforcements he might have to limit his ambitions to locating and shadowing – but they didn't tell Kit this. Their signal only approved his proposed concentration, which they assumed to be at the Falklands – which was not what Kit meant or intended. Moreover, the Admiralty signal of 7 October implicitly told him that he had sufficient force to meet von Spee (thought to be two heavy and one light cruiser at that time) with only his two armoured ships. When he replied that he expected to find von Spee with three light cruisers and again requested when he would receive the support of the *Defence* he was not told of the negation of his request. Furthermore in this telegram Kit added, 'I recommend two forces, individually strong enough to defeat the German squadron, to operate on each coast.'[10] Churchill and the staff ignored his suggestion.

On 18 October Kit sent his signal explaining that, in company with *Canopus*, his speed would be restricted to 12 knots, but that 'he trusted that circumstances would allow him to force an action'.[11] In other words, four days after Churchill and Battenberg had assumed he would avoid an action and shadow the enemy, he was still following the un-countermanded orders of 14 September and looking for a fight.

Finally, Kit signalled that he had ordered *Defence* to join him and that *Canopus* was to convoy the colliers owing to her slow speed – but did not say that he was dispensing with *Canopus* before *Defence* arrived. This was the signal that Churchill called 'obscure'. In response the Admiralty told him that his orders to *Defence* had been countermanded and that there was 'sufficient force on each side [of South America]'.[12] Once again he was implicitly being told that he had sufficient force – and given he had already told the Admiralty that he was dropping *Canopus* this could only mean that they believed his cruisers were 'sufficient force'. These were the orders that reached him on 1 November when he was off Coronel seeking *Leipzig*. Confused? We might be forgiven for thinking that Kit would have been.

And then there is Kit. How much blame attaches to him? He could have avoided the action at Coronel – and in falling back on the *Canopus* he would have been obeying the orders the Admiralty thought they had given him, to concentrate and make *Canopus* his 'citadel'. But Kit could no more do this than a religious believer could renounce his credo. For Kit, the navy, its tradition and its reputation were his religion. The navy was a church, a congregation bound together by a set of shared values, a belief system forged in the Med and in a century of unchallenged naval domination. Orders were the same as revealed scripture. He had been told to seek and destroy the enemy. He had been told that he had sufficient force. He knew of the damage to the reputation of the Service of recent events and the whiff of cowardice that hung over Troubridge. Indeed, Troubridge later wrote to Bridgeman, 'Good God what a cruel shame. They say in the fleet that Cradock lost his squadron because Churchill court marshalled Troubridge for not losing his.'[13]

A fellow officer said of him, 'Cradock was incapable of refusing or postponing action if there was the smallest chance of success.'[14] Luce later wrote that he felt the admiral 'had no clear plan or doctrine in his head, but was always inclined to act on the impulse of the moment'.[15] Just as on the hunting field he could not baulk at a high fence, or when charging an enemy on land do other than lead from the front, so Kit could not turn aside from battle when the time came. His orders were to 'destroy enemy cruisers'. If he damaged one of them enough they might seek internment and that would be a victory of sorts. On the bridge of the *Good Hope*, alone with his thoughts and his responsibilities, feeling the weight of tradition pressing down on his shoulders, surely there was only one decision that he was permitted, by his upbringing and his beliefs, to take. He altered course towards the enemy ships and offered combat.

In the end, it was the Navy itself that allowed Kit to be killed; the accumulated history of a lifetime's duty in which he had been indoctrinated with the religion of the Service. The Navy was a cult and Churchill had elected himself its high priest. Kit could only do what zealots do and follow his canon orders. It was that system of beliefs that killed Kit and his men on 1 November 1914.

Of course, Kit's frame of mind at the time of his departure from the Falklands would be known if his last personal letters had survived. If this were a novel, Kit's final letter from Port Stanley to Admiral Meux would be the key plot point. Here Kit's motives would be explained and Churchill possibly excoriated. In a novel, Meux would have received and kept the letter, producing it at some suitably dramatic juncture.

The letter has never been found. Indeed it may never have been sent by Governor Allardyce. If it was sent, then Meux is the key. If it wasn't, we need to consider Allardyce's character.

Meux has already featured in these pages. Born Hedworth Lampton in 1856, son of the Earl of Durham, he attended *Britannia* from the age of 14. He was well connected with royalty and Lord Charles Beresford. In 1899, Captain of HMS *Powerful* and returning from a posting in Chinese waters, Lambton was ordered to South Africa during the second Boer War. On his own initiative he stopped en route at Mauritius and picked up a battalion of soldiers there. Knowing of the siege of Ladysmith, he and Captain Percy Scott designed carriages for naval guns, and Lampton led a naval brigade to the rescue. The relief of Ladysmith made heroes of all involved. Queen Victoria sent a congratulatory telegram to the naval brigade and Lambton was awarded the CB.

The beautiful socialite Valerie, Lady Meux, on hearing of Lambton's escapades, had ordered six 12-pounder cannons to be sent to South Africa at her own expense and Lambton called on her to thank her. A relationship was established between the forty-four-year-old naval captain and the fifty-three-year-old widow. In 1900 Lady Meux became fabulously wealthy on the death of her husband, Sir Henry Bruce Meux Bt. whose family owned the Meux Brewery. Valerie had married Henry in secret. She was an actress – a word synonymous with prostitute or mistress in those times – and from a poor background, and polite society never accepted her. She took to playing the socialite, spending huge sums of money on entertainments and even driving herself round London in a carriage pulled by two zebras. Known as a beauty, she was painted no less than three times by James Abbot McNeil Whistler.

After meeting Lambton she left her entire estate to him in her will, on condition that he changed his name to Meux. On Valerie's death in 1910, Lambton/Meux became an extremely wealthy man.

Meux stayed in the navy until 1916 when, as an admiral of the fleet, he retired aged sixty and succeeded Beresford as Conservative MP for Portsmouth. This was young for a senior admiral to leave the service (sixty-five was the official retirement age) and in time of war too. One might ask why. He retired from public service in 1918 and devoted the rest of his life to breeding and racing horses (his horse had won the Grand Military Gold Cup in 1895). According to the DNB the navy had been an 'interest not a profession'. He was called an aristocrat and court favourite. He was 'not a typical naval officer'.[16]

This was the man – Commander in Chief, Portsmouth at the time, a fellow huntsman, polo player and devotee of the turf – to whom Kit chose to entrust his final thoughts. We can only surmise the reasons – possibly because he was a fellow Beresfordite, independent and no lover of Churchill; or because Meux was one of the two admirals who had comprised Troubridge's Court of Enquiry, finding his actions 'deplorable and contrary to the tradition of the British navy'.

To return to Kit's letters, what of the one left on the Falklands 'to a relative'? A relative, or someone more intimate? In either case, it has never been discovered.

So to the governor. Sir William Lamond Allardyce was a career Colonial Office civil servant who served abroad for all of his adult life. He was a professional administrator of Empire. Born in India, he served as governor of Fiji, The Falklands, Bahamas, Tasmania and Newfoundland. He was knighted in 1916 and died only two years after retiring, in 1930, aged sixty-nine. In his time governing Newfoundland he was recognised as one of the most competent administrators ever in that post.

At the moment of Cradock's arrival at the Falkland Islands, Allardyce was slated for a new posting to the Bahamas. We can imagine that this held rather more attraction than the cold and lonely islands he currently controlled and which he had served since 1904. He was a man imbued by training and experience with the spirit of service and of loyalty to the crown and its ministers. He and Cradock were almost the same age and it is clear that they 'got on' socially and respected each other during their brief acquaintance. Cradock entrusted his last letters to this man and, apparently, left them on the mantelpiece at the governor's mansion.

So, did the governor mail the letters and did Meux receive them? As we have seen, Kit's instruction was to send the letters if the whole of his squadron were lost, a point he underlined in his last letter to Allardyce – but that was not the case, for *Glasgow*, *Otranto* and *Canopus* were safe. Did Allardyce take that to mean he should not mail the letters and possibly should destroy them? Or did he believe, as a servant of the crown in a time of war, that the publicity resulting from the letters becoming public would be detrimental to the cause, and so destroyed them anyway?

If the letters were sent and received, Meux, as a serving officer in a position of authority, might also have thought that no good could come from mentioning them at that point and so kept them to himself. But in the furore surrounding Churchill's vilification of Kit, resulting from the publication of the first volume of *The World Crisis* in 1923, would Meux have kept quiet? He was a very wealthy man with no public role to fulfil and protect. He was a Beresfordite (he had been a leader of the 'syndicate of discontent') and loathed Fisher and Churchill for preventing him getting the post of First Sea Lord. It is inconceivable that he would not have spoken out and joined forces with his friend Bridgeman in defence of the man whose memorial service he had attended in 1916.

It seems extremely likely that he never received Kit's last missive and neither did a relative or other intimate. William Allardyce, Governor of the Falklands Islands and His Majesty's representative there for ten years, almost certainly decided that the greater good of the British Empire would not be served by allowing Kit to speak from beyond the grave, and destroyed the letter to Meux.

26

Memories, 1916

The church of St Agatha was (and is) the parish church of Gilling with Hartforth and Sedbury; here generations of Cradocks were baptised, worshipped and were buried. It lay off the High (indeed virtually the only) Street in West Gilling, set back from the road and easy to miss. The village had two public houses. Farms lined the High Street; there was a blacksmith's and a humpback bridge crossing the River Gilling. In the seventh century it was the seat of Saxon Earls and had a castle, visible even in 1823 but no more. The church, supposedly built on the site of a Saxon monastery, is of Norman heritage with an eleventh-century tower largely untouched. Squat and much added to over the years, it sat prettily at the end of a short lane surrounded by its churchyard and with rolling fields beyond.

Old Sheldon Cradock, Kit's great-great grandfather, his family and staff came here. In 1742 he constructed private pews in the gallery for his family and servants. The interior reflects the three families who came to dominate the area; Cradocks, Gilpin-Browns and the largest landowners in the district, the Whartons, who also held the advowson for the parish. Younger sons of the family benefited from this right of presentation as three different Whartons held the office of Rector between 1801 and 1899. One of them, John Thomas, rebuilt the church between 1843 and 1847 at his own expense. His predecessor William demolished the houses leading up to the church and built himself a very pleasant rectory in their place

The Cradocks do not appear to have contributed substantially to the rebuilding. Their religion would be of the traditional Anglican kind. Church attendance was as much social as religious. Religion supported the gentry's view that there was an established order and that they, the gentry, were at the top of it. Pews were generally personal and paid for – the poor stood or sat at the back. The clergy were just the gentry in a different suit; they hunted and shot with the rest of their kind.

Memorials to the land-owning families abound in the church but there is no doubt as to the most dominant ones. The Cradocks, proud of their family achievements, are commemorated in splendour in the north aisle of the nave. At its east end is a magnificent Victorian stained glass window celebrating the life of Kit's mother, Georgina, who died on 31 March 1865, aged only thirty-five. The window dominates the church, glowing red and purple in the morning sunlight and would not be out of place in a cathedral.

Today Cradock memorial windows occupy three of the four north wall lancets. They are essays in Arthurian, chivalric art. Knights straight out of Malory or Tennyson; figures drawn from Alfred Gilbert's sculptures or the paintings of Burne-Jones and his followers. This is how the Cradocks saw themselves, Knights errant on a quest to protect England and Empire.

The westernmost window commemorates Kit's brother Sheldon. It depicts an armoured knight from about the fifteenth century and an idealised archer, both mounted on horseback. Beneath is an inscription: 'For God and the King, a mighty hunter before the Lord'. This Old Testament invocation of Nimrod is altogether apt for such a hunt-obsessed family. 'Very pleasant hast thou been to me my brother.' The misquote from Samuel would have been a tribute from Montagu to his elder sibling.

The easternmost window is dedicated to both Montagu and his sister Gwendoline. It was commissioned in 1933, a year after Gwendoline's death by her daughter, by then Lady Barnard, and manufactured by the prestigious firm of Clayton and Bell. For her there is an angel holding a wheatsheaf with a small child at its feet. For him a dismounted kneeling soldier, sword reversed, receiving an Arthurian chalice (the holy grail?) from another angel, straight out of a Burne-Jones copy book. In the topmost quatrefoil is the Cradock coat of arms.

But in 1916 the visitor to St Agatha's would first see Georgina's magnificent stained glass and beneath it Kit's own memorial, which dominated the church. Set beneath his mother's window was a large white marble plaque, with side panels in rosso antico marble, in relief a ceremonial sword and an anchor within a wreath made of gun-metal. The tablet records his rank and titles:

In memory of Rear Admiral Sir Christopher Cradock
Knight Commander of the Victorian Order
Commander of the Bath
Knight of the Royal Order Crown of Prussia
Knight of the Royal Spanish Order of Naval Merit
Member of the Imperial Ottoman Order of the Medjideh
Aide de Camp to King Edward VII 1909–10

4th son of Christopher Cradock of Hartforth
Born 1862 – killed in action 1914
'The day thou gavest Lord is ended, the darkness falls at thy
behest'

John Ellerton's words, meant for missionary work and chosen by Queen Victoria for the service to mark the Golden Jubilee year of her reign, seem appropriate for a man who died in the gloaming and did not live to see the death of everything he held to be dear. Flanking this tablet the two pink marble plaques record his naval achievements. In front of the memorial are two crossed naval ensigns, one his Admiral's flag, red balls on a St George's cross, one a simple white ensign. The memorial was erected and paid for by elder brother Sheldon.

Then, on the north wall, the visitor's eye would be drawn to Kit's window, also by Clayton and Bell. Sunset and Evening Star are depicted as two drapery-clad angelic figures, Evening Star is blind-folded, Sunset exposing a shapely breast whilst a miniature *Good Hope* sinks into the waves beneath her feet. The inscription reads, 'In memory of Rear Admiral Sir Christopher Cradock, 1 November 1914'. In gothic script is added 'from MF'. Who was MF? There are no such initials in the Cradock lineage.

Here in St Agatha's church, Kit's memory was kept alive – a fitting dedicatee perhaps, for Agatha is patron saint of Malta where Kit enjoyed his polo and horse racing so much. In the churchyard, to the north, lies the Cradock vault, originally an altar tomb with a chain fence and where Kit hoped to be laid.

So who was the MF who so wished Kit to be remembered? According to the parish records the MF inscribed on Kit's memorial window was Maud Frances Elizabeth, 7th Countess Fitzwilliam, and at the time of Coronel, as previously noted, married to – but largely estranged from – one of the richest men in Britain. Born Lady Maud Elizabeth Frederica Dundas in 1877 she was the daughter of Lawrence Dundas, 1st Marquess Zetland, Master of the Zetland Hunt for 35 years and with whom Kit and his father hunted.

In 1915 she petitioned the church authorities for permission to erect a memorial window to Kit at St Agatha's. She specified 'stained glass, the light on the left containing a figure "Hope" as illustrated by the well-known painting by G.F. Watts RA and the light on the right containing a figure representing "peace". Also to place on the said window the following inscription, "In memory of Rear Admiral Sir Christopher Cradock, KCVO, CB. To Kit from Maud. There was a great calm. 1 Nov 1914".[1]

Maud didn't quite get what she wanted. The figure to the left does indeed resemble Watt's 'Hope', although it is entitled 'Sunset'. The inscription reads not 'to Kit from Maud' but 'from MF'. 'There was a great calm' was also omitted.

So what was their relationship? Kit was her senior by some 15 years. His father and her father had hunted together and been friends. Her father was still alive and could have made his own gesture if it was family friendship that caused the commission of the window. Childhood friendship would be unlikely given the age gap and as Kit was often away at sea. Or was there something more intimate to their relationship? Kit had much service abroad but did return to the family seat on occasions and had had a small bungalow built into the stonework of the walled garden, to serve as a pied-a-terre. Maud was living at Wentworth Woodhouse, near Rotherham, but her family lived at Aske Hall between West Gilling and Richmond, a literal stone's throw from Hartforth. She had married young and had been wed for 14 years when she had her last child.

Kit had frequent extended periods of half pay in 1901–2, 1905–6 and again between October 1910 and August 1911, and would have spent all or much of the time in Yorkshire. He was a Rear Admiral and a hero of the Chinese wars. Hunting and riding could have brought them together. Would Kit's sense of chivalry have prevented an intimate relationship or would it have furthered it, the inaccessible Venus, the Guinevere attainable? The unusual naming of Maud's third child has already been noted.

And then there is the nature of the intended inscription. Personal, affectionate, on first name terms; but in the execution redacted and more veiled. An objection from Maud's husband? She could hardly have spent the money without his say-so. Did he know something but not care – at least, care only enough not to want too public an exposure?

Described variously as lonely, warm, kind, and possessed of a sense of fun and mischievousness, Maud sought solace with other men and had a number of affairs, including a long-term relationship with the Earl's land agent, John Diggle (in modern terms, Billy's managing director for the Fitzwilliam estate) and there were certainly others.[2] Maud's granddaughter has said she was made to promise that she would not tell anyone of the private things that happened at Wentworth; and indeed in 1972 the 10th Earl destroyed by burning sixteen tons of documents and family letters relating to the period.

In Kit's will he left a letter for Maud and a memento of value, such that Montagu's probate lawyer told him to 'register it'.

Only an intimate would have specified such a memorial to Kit as did Maud. And only an intimate would leave a valuable memento. It seems clear there was something between them; she cared enough to want him remembered, and he cared enough to want her to remember him. He had been special to her. Like his brothers Montagu and Sheldon, Kit had at least one mistress. I believe Maud had been Kit's lover and he was the father of her daughter Donatia.

27

In Memoriam, 1916 and Later

On 16 June 1916 a group of naval men, uniformed and bemedalled, epaulettes and swords sparkling in the sunshine, gathered at York Minster, the mother church of the diocese in which Kit had been born. Mixed in amongst them were severe-looking men and women in civilian dress, including the quondam prime minister and now First Lord of the Admiralty, A.J. Balfour, resplendent in a black top hat. They had come to honour Kit Cradock. The Princess Royal was represented. Beresford was there. Meux was there. Bridgeman and Warrender were there. Fisher and Churchill's enemies, Cradock's friends.

Soldiers lined the road to the Minster for Balfour to inspect, their rifles at the 'present'. A file of sailors quick marched into the nave, a dog running barking alongside them. As they crossed the threshold they removed their hats. Sword-carrying officers accompanied them.

The order of ceremony was reverential. As the Archbishop of York entered a band played Chopin's funeral march. The choir sang 'The Lord is my Shepherd'. A priest read Revelations Chapter 20 verse 11–13, 'and the sea gave up the dead that were in it; and death and hell delivered up the dead which were in them; and they were judged every man according to their works'.

Then the Marquess of Zetland, Lawrence Dundas, ex MP for Richmond and Master of the Zetland Hunt, Maud's father, unveiled a memorial tablet in Derbyshire alabaster, designed by the sculptor F.W. Pomeroy, who had created the figure of Justice on the dome of the Old Bailey. On it is inscribed:

To the glory of God
And
In memory of
REAR ADMIRAL
SIR CHRISTOPHER CRADOCK,
Who gallantly upholding
the high tradition of the British Navy
led his squadron
Against an overwhelming force of the Enemy
Off Coronel, on the coast of Chile
And fell gloriously in action
On All Saints' Day, 1914
'God forbid that I should do this thing, To flee away from
them:
If our time be come, let us die manfully for our brethren
And let us not stain our honour.'
I. Maccabeas ix 10
This monument is erected by his
grateful countrymen

After unveiling the memorial by pulling aside an oversized Union Flag, Lord Zetland made a speech. He noted that when Kit had been offered his last command (in 1913) he made representations to the First Lord (Churchill) as to the fitness and qualifications of his ships.[1] Zetland continued, 'Sir Christopher Cradock was not a man to shirk his duty. He accepted his command and went to America with the vessels placed under him and we know what happened. The moment war broke out Admiral Cradock went in search of the enemy. He did not employ such tactics as sheltering under cover of darkness. He upheld the best traditions of the British navy.'[2]

The committal of the monument to the cathedral was made by Admiral Francis Bridgeman. Lady Maud Warrender sang 'O rest in the Lord' and the choir responded with Mendelssohn's 'He that shall endure to the end shall be saved'. Reveille rang out round the cathedral's ancient stones.

As the bugles sounding the last post faded into silence, Balfour rose to give his oration to the congregation. He concluded it by saying, 'We do not know, we never shall know, what were the thoughts of Admiral Cradock when it became evident that, out-gunned and outranged, success was an impossibility. We shall never know what he felt when the setting sun on that evening threw his own ships up clearly against the bright western sky, a mark for his enemies, and at the same time rendered his own fire difficult and ineffective by placing them in the shade. He must have realised then that his hopes were dashed for ever to the ground, that his plan had failed. In the face of death, certain and imminent, I doubt not that he thought, if only for a moment, of how his friends and his countrymen would judge his action. If he did I feel sure that he realised, what is the truth, that he could safely leave his fame to the admiring justice of his countrymen. He lies beneath the ocean – no more fitting resting-place for men of our race – his body is sepa-rated from us by half the world, and he and his gallant comrades lie far from the pleasant homes of England, yet they have their reward, and we, looking at what they attempted and judging what they did in the light of what they attempted, are surely right in saying that theirs' is an immortal place in the great roll of naval heroes whose work has built up the Empire and secured the freedom of mankind, and whose work, at the very moment I am speaking, is preserving that Empire and maintaining that freedom, and who, God willing, will have successors who will preserve and maintain it until the end of time.'[3]

The service ended with a benediction by Cosmo Lang, the Lord Archbishop of York. Then bugles sounded Reveille and the sonorous sounds of the 'dead march' from Handel's 'Saul' echoed round the ancient Minster, the anthem to Saul and Jonathan pro-viding a sombre accompaniment to the soft marching steps of the exiting sailors.

Admiral Sir Francis Bridgeman, now retired from the navy but once First Sea Lord and engineered out of office by Churchill, had acted as Chair of the Cradock memorial fund-raising committee and at a reception held afterwards at the Mansion House he proposed a toast to Balfour's health and, no doubt, to the memory of Kit and his men. Like Kit he was a Yorkshireman, having his estate, Cop-grove Hall, at Burton Leonard near Harrogate. He was first cousin once removed to Billy Fitzbilly through his mother and thus knew Maud. Indeed he was very close to the family for on 8 July 1912, when King George V stayed and dined at Wentworth as part of his tour of the north of England, the dinner guests invited by Billy included Bridgeman and his wife, and Charlie B too. Excluding the hosts and the king and queen there were only 34 guests. Anna Pavlova danced for the guests in the Marble Hall. Bridgeman was a family intimate. Perhaps Maud persuaded him to act on Kit's behalf.

The plaque is still in the Minster at the entrance to the North Choir, overlooked now by the majority of the visitors; perhaps puzzled over by those who do notice it and ponder what drives a man to such sacrifice.

This formal service of remembrance followed a hasty one on 13 November 1914 held in Kit's memory at Christ Church, Mayfair, London. The Rev. E. Hilliard conducted it, The Princess Royal, remembering her rescuer, sent a wreath of lilies and palms, and Sir Lionel Cust attended for the king.

In the port of Hull the firm of Pickering and Haldane named trawler H103 *Admiral Cradock* out of respect for Kit's memory. There were other memorials. We have already noted the stone and glass commemoratives to Cradock in St Agatha's Church, West Gilling. At All Saints Church, Catherington there is another mem-orial. Catherington sits on the top of the Hampshire downs, not far from Portsmouth and surrounded by wonderful hunting country. Approaching from the road through the lych gate, one passes along a grassy path and finds, standing between the gate and the church west door, a stone pillar in the style of an Eleanor Cross. Inscribed on the east face of the plinth are the words, 'In loving memory of Rear Admiral Sir Christopher Cradock killed in action off Coronel All Saints Day 1914. His body rests in the Pacific Ocean. Of Keith H. Barnes Rector of Cattistock by whose inspiration the East

Window and Reredos were erected. And of Albert W.S. Barnes with whom many happy years were spent at St Catherine's. Mary C. Barnes 1925.'

The Barnes family were prominent locals but were also connected to Kit by blood. Albert and Mary's aunt, Janet Barnes, was Kit's grandmother; they were Cradock's first cousins once removed. Neither brother nor sister married and they lived together for many years at the Barnes ancestral home, St Catherine's in Catherington, a large Georgian house situated handily opposite the church and the village inn. Albert, who died in 1905, was a military man (2nd West Yorks Light Infantry) and a JP. It does not take a wild leap of imagination to see the urbane and heroic Kit visiting his relatives and making a big impression on his spinster relative, his death causing her much grief. Certainly Albert liked Kit, for he left him £3,500 in his will, although there seems to have been some difficulty raising the money from the residual estate. Kit reciprocated in his will, leaving a letter and 'little thing' to Mary.

At the foot of the cross there is a second plaque. It reads, 'Sacred also to all who lost their lives in the Battle of Coronel 1914, The Falklands 1914 and The River Plate 1939. May they rest in peace'.

Cradock's memorial shares the churchyard with a perhaps more famous sailor, as Admiral Sir Charles Napier (Black Charlie), who died in 1860 after a long career as a fighting admiral and member of parliament, is buried there. Admiral Samuel Hood, 1st Viscount Hood, mentor of Nelson, was another distinguished local resident. His great-great grandson, Rear Admiral Horace Hood was to die at Jutland in 1916; like Kit's, his body would not be recovered.

Kit would have got to know the area in his time in command of RN barracks Portsmouth and no doubt hunted with the local gentry. The Hambledon Hunt covered the Portsmouth area and horses could be hired from, for example, Clarke's of Cosham, with transport boxes if necessary. Certainly Kit was well enough known for his distant relatives to want to share a memorial with him. And interesting that the memory was still alive in 1925, two years after Churchill had published his attack on Kit's reputation.

In 1921 Sir Arthur Stockdale Cope painted 'Naval Officers of World War I', now in the National Portrait Gallery collection. It shows a group of some twenty-two officers, Beatty and Keyes prominent in the front, Kit a spectral presence standing at the very back. Perhaps he was already drifting out of memory.

There is a rather splendid railing, in the form of a silhouette of HMS *Good Hope*, outside 'Cradock Block' RN Portsmouth, erected as late as 2001. Further afield, there is a memorial in the cathedral at

Port Stanley, paid for by donations received at a commemorative service held on 29 November 1914; the Falklanders were duly grateful for their deliverance. Dedicated at a service in July 1916 the tablets read, 'In Memory of Rear Admiral Sir Christopher Cradock K.C.V.O., C.B.; Captain Philip Franklin [sic] M.V.O. Captain Frank Brandt. The Officers, Warrant Officers and men of the HMS Good Hope and HMS Monmouth who laid down their lives for King and Empire in a naval engagement off Coronel on 1st November 1914.

'This tablet was erected from offertories given at a Memorial Service held in the cathedral on 29th November 1914, which was attended by His Excellency the Governor, the Captain, Officers and men of HMS Canopus and by other officers and men of the Falkland Islands Volunteers.'

In Coronel, at the 'Plaza de 21 de Mayo', a memorial to all the lost sailors was erected in 1989; puzzlingly late, at a time when no one alive could remember the action.

In Monmouth town there is a tribute to the crew of the *Monmouth* in St Mary's Church; and, of course, the names of the lost were recognised on the war memorials that sprang up all over the land in the years following the end of the war. Cheltenham had eight men in the battle, five of whom were on the *Monmouth* and included Brandt, who had Cheltenham connections. His name and theirs can be seen at All Saints and St Matthew's Churches as well as on the town war memorial. The *Cheltenham Looker-On* recorded a memorial service for Brandt (son of Mr F. Brandt JP of Cheltenham) at St Dunstan's chapel, St Paul Cathedral, London. Mrs Brandt and her four children attended. Brandt is also remembered at St Johns, Torquay, near where he lived. Captain Philip Francklin is commemorated in the Church of Gonalston St Lawrence, Nottinghamshire.

There are also somewhat more esoteric memorials. In British Columbia, Canada. Cradock Ridge was named in 1919. In 1923 Richard Preston Bishop, a land surveyor for the state climbed and then named Mount Good Hope and Mount Monmouth. In the 1950s these were renamed as Good Hope Mountain and Monmouth Mountain, and the Alpine Club of Canada then continued the nomenclature system on hitherto unnamed peaks during the 1950s and 60s. Hence came Admiral Mountain, Canopus Mountain, Coronel Mountain, Cradock Glacier, Glasgow Mountain, Mount Cradock and Otranto Mountain. Kit, with his punctiliousness over decorations and honours, would no doubt be pleased to be the only Great War admiral to have both a glacier and a mountain named after him. British Columbia is also home to the Coronel Memorial Library at Royal Roads University.

After the war the Admiralty wrote to Kit's sister, Gwendoline, to tell her that in America it was proposed to name a new town (a 'government built planned community') in Virginia after him.[4] It was developed to house the shipyard workers of nearby Portsmouth, VA, and still thrives. And at Boodles Club, in St James's Street, London, where Kit and Montagu were both members, an annual naval dinner is held which is named the Cradock Dinner in memory of Kit.[5]

The First World War killed very many people. Some one million British and Commonwealth servicemen lost their lives and another two million were wounded. In total 10 million soldiers and civilians died and an additional 21 million were wounded. Against that scale, the loss at Coronel might seem small, but I think something else died there too. Cradock was a representative of a previous age; he was a Victorian in word, deed and belief. He represented a privileged, closed, complacent coterie that had been blown apart by the guns of August. His was a cleaner, nobler, more certain world, where self-sacrifice and chivalry still had a place; a world that died on the battlefields of the Western Front. The values that he represented – honour, loyalty, certainty, obedience, bravery, sacrifice – came to be derided; now they are fading in many ways and it makes it difficult for us in the twenty-first century to understand his actions. But to Kit there was never any doubt. He knew that he would die and he knew that he had been compromised by Churchill and the Admiralty. He also knew that it didn't matter because the navy was bigger than him or them, and he would sacrifice himself and his men to protect it.

28

Churchill's Attack on Cradock's Reputation, 1923–1924

The need for self-exculpation and promotion lay deep in Churchill's psyche. In 1923 he published the first of his four-volume history of the war *The World Crisis*. Journalistically written, flowing and resonant in prose, it was not so much a history more a justification and promotion of one Winston S. Churchill. So much so that the *Dundee Advertiser* (a more important newspaper then than now, as it was at the centre of the D.C. Thompson empire – and Churchill had been MP for Dundee between 1908 and 1922) was moved to comment: 'Mr Churchill is a very great egotist and in placing himself on the cosmic stage his egotism attains to an amusing quality ... the reader has exhibited to him the titanic events of the war happening around and in no small way controlled by Mr Churchill. We see him teaching the great sailors at the Admiralty, which perhaps was to be expected. But we also see him offering guidance to the Foreign office, to the Minister of War and the Commanders in the field. He has a policy for everybody ... Mr Churchill's narrative is really a determined laying down of the proposition that whoever made mistakes, he made none'.[1]

And when Churchill wrote about Coronel he did not scruple to defend himself by attacking Kit's shade, dead those nine years. In the navy there was considerable outrage, the more so for the way in which Churchill traduced Kit's reputation. With regard to Coronel, Churchill laid two main charges at Kit's door.

His key contention was that Cradock did not concentrate his

ships around the 'citadel' of *Canopus* and divided his forces: 'It ought not to be necessary to tell an experienced Admiral to concentrate his forces,' he wrote. In so writing he ignored the facts that *Canopus* was a battleship in name only and that the Admiralty themselves had divided Kit's forces in setting Stoddart's little squadron up on the east coast, thus ensuring that neither Cradock nor Stoddart was appropriately equipped to deal with von Spee. Churchill also insisted that, in the absence of *Canopus*, Kit should have trailed von Spee until other forces could join, ignoring the fact that only *Glasgow* had the speed to do this. In effect he accused Kit of incompetence and failure to obey orders, and stated, 'I cannot accept any share on behalf of the Admiralty in the responsibility for what followed.'[2]

This assault on the memory of a sailor unable to defend himself touched off a firestorm of protest in the press. The man who started it was Admiral (rtd) Sir Francis Bridgeman, First Sea Lord 1911–12, pushed out of office by Churchill. Bridgeman had been the chairman of Kit's memorial fund in 1916. Springing to Cradock's defence, on 19 April 1923 Bridgeman wrote to the *Morning Post* and the *Daily Telegraph*. In his letter he carefully demolished the fragile edifice of half-truth that Churchill had erected. He ridiculed Churchill's contention that the *Canopus* was a 'citadel' and clearly showed that her guns, speed and armour were inferior to von Spee's and indeed hardly on a par with *Good Hope*. He pointed out that the Admiralty themselves had divided the ships available, creating two inferior forces. He pointed up the mediocre nature of Kit's squadron and the conflicting nature of his orders. Bridgeman also quoted from a letter written 'by a brother officer of [Cradock's] after the battle' which is worth reproducing here in full:

I happen to know that Cradock wired to the Admiralty for the *Defence* to be allowed to join him and was told his present force was sufficient but personally I have no desire to run up against them unless we have some later class than the *Good Hope*.

Poor Cradock, when the Admiralty refused to let him have the *Defence*, he knew he would never get back, and buried all his medals and decorations in the Governor's garden in the Falklands and left a large sealed packet with the Governor to send home when his death was confirmed. Perhaps his people might like to know this ... it does seem hard luck on Cradock to give him inferior ships off the dock wall, manned by coastguards, boys straight from the training ships, reserve men, bandsmen and naval cadets and putting them up against ships manned by the pick of the German Navy and a long time in commission; it will be horrible if the blame is put on Cradock for the disasters. We all feel out here that any brave man would have done exactly the same as him.[3]

The press seized on Bridgeman's letter with glee and editorial pens started to fly. For example: 'Mr Churchill is much more concerned to absolve the Admiralty from blame than to give due honour to the heroic Cradock.'[4] 'We are given what was in Mr Churchill's mind not the impression conveyed to Cradock's mind by the orders he received.'[5] 'Mr Churchill is not endearing himself to the Navy by his literary performances.'[6]

Churchill fought back with a letter to the *Morning Post* on 28 April. It is an odd document, a good half of it being taken up with an attack on Bridgeman for decisions taken in 1911 and not addressed in Bridgeman's original letter at all. On *Canopus* Churchill weaselled and admitted that there might be more than one view of its effectiveness, accusing Bridgeman of selective quotation. He advanced that he only acted on advice from Battenberg (then also dead) and his staff and signed off with an attempt to show that he thought Kit a brave man (if a mistaken one). It was a shabby performance.

Meanwhile letter writers were sharpening their quills. Gwendolyn, Kit's sister, wrote to Bridgeman thanking him for his support. He replied on 25 April:

Dear Mrs Straker

Thank you for your letter. Naturally I was not going to let Churchill defame Kit's good name without protest. I don't

190

know that I ever enjoyed writing a letter more than I did this one; to be able to state facts in contradiction of what he says in his book was a real delight. I have got many letters of appreciation from people one has never even heard of which describe the view taken by the public not only of Kit's personal character in the handling of his squadron but also the disgraceful behaviour of the ex-First Lord in his attempt to save his own reputation at the expense of a noble and patriotic soul, who he had sent to his doom.

With the kindest wishes to yourself and all of yours.
Believe me,
Francis Bridgeman[7]

The quondam radio officer, Lieutenant Charles Gould, sent this missive to Gwen on April 25th:

Rodney House
Sophia Place
Portsmouth

Dear Madam

Many thanks for sending Mr W Churchill's account of the battle of Coronel and Falklands. However clever and weighty his pen may be he cannot explain away the awful fact that a mistake was made by the authorities at home and not by Admiral Cradock.

The cry about the Canopus only condemns Mr Churchill. For he should have known that the range of her guns were nothing compared with the Scharnhorst and her sister ship. Her speed was also against success too. The Admiral received orders he obeyed and did his duty.

Every soul aboard knew about the enemy and we expected the Defence on Oct 20th. On October 22nd I was on the bridge with the Admiral and Capt. Francklin. The Admiral was really angry and his words to the Captain will for ever condemn Mr Churchill. I can hear them now. I shall never forget. 'We knew we were going to our doom unless help arrived'. Yes, I have no objection to Sir Francis Bridgeman seeing my diary "he will understand". I honour and will defend the name of Admiral Sir C Cradock at all times. Every officer and man was a credit to our own gallant Navy.

Yours faithfully
Chas W P Gould[8]

Bridgeman responded to Churchill's letter with a resigned air. In a missive to the *Yorkshire Post* on the 30th he makes a measured and reasoned response, rebutting both the attack on him personally and the view advanced by Churchill that Cradock himself suggested dividing the forces between east and west coast (he did not; he suggested a force either side appropriate to deal with von Spee).

The media firestorm continued to rage. Following up on Bridgeman's letter, the *Yorkshire Post* published a long editorial the same day which gives a balanced view of the controversy but makes the point that Churchill has a tendency to 'widen the field of controversy by including Prince Louis Battenberg, now also dead, and whose friends may seek to put a different interpretation on matters'.[9] The *Morning Post* in a long editorial seeks to refute many of Churchill's original points, reminding readers that it prophesied, when reviewing *The World Crisis*, that, 'In seeking self-justification in connection with naval misfortunes ... his imputations, implied and otherwise, against naval commanders concerned are likely to rebound on his own head.' It remarks on the dangers of allowing a civilian amateur to exercise executive control, as Churchill (perhaps inadvertently) demonstrates in his remarks that he did. The paper added, '... attacking the memory of an heroic martyr to his duty (and his orders)' and casting the blame 'upon the principal victim of his (Churchill's) own error of judgement ... he would have been wiser to have left the reputation of the dead sailor alone.'[10]

Now the cabinet entered the fray, for Churchill in his writings had demonstrated that he had in his possession very many papers which should rightly be in the Admiralty vaults and which he obviously took with him when removed from office. A newspaper report stated that 'the cabinet is apprehensive and not a few of its members have reached the conclusion that the whole business has gone too far and that something must be done to restore Ministerial secretiveness and sense of responsibility'.[11] The *Morning Post*, bit firmly between its teeth published another editorial and adduced that 'if blame is attached to anybody it should be to the Admiralty because of the contradictory nature of their orders. There is certainly no occasion for attacking, as Mr Churchill has done in a manner that was bound to stir resentment, the reputation of a distinguished naval officer who laid down his life in devotion to duty. As he has provoked the controversy he cannot complain if it recoils on his own head and naval critics tell him that the responsibility for the destruction of Admiral Cradock's squadron at Coronel rests with the ex-First Lord of the Admiralty himself. But the real gravamen of the offence is that an ex-Minister should use his access to secret documents for the purpose of criticising and discrediting officers who, even if alive, have no opportunity for defending themselves by reference to the official archives.'[12]

There was much more in similar vein. The mood of the press was anti-Churchill, pro-Cradock. And so were the letter writers. The Dean of Port Stanley cathedral, J. Stanley Smith, wrote to Bridgeman on 27 July: 'We are full of admiration for the able manner in which you defend Admiral Cradock from the charge of responsibility for the disaster at Coronel. That portion of Mr Churchill's book ... caused intense indignation here amongst the people who knew the truth. We felt that some protest ought to be made.' He continued, 'We regard Admiral Cradock as a hero and we wish to our utmost to make Falkland Islanders of all generations realise the service he rendered to the colony.'[13] And in November Captain Alfred Carpenter V.C., the man who commanded HMS *Vindictive* in the Zeebrugge raid, wrote, 'his example of gallantry, intensity of purpose, and sportsmanship will for ever remain invaluable to the British race'.[14] (At Zeebrugge, Keyes and Carpenter's signal exchange before the attack was another genuflection to the chivalric. Keyes 'St George for England' drew the response 'may we give the dragon's tail a good twist.)

Perhaps the last word should be left to L.J. Maxse, editor of the *National Review*: 'When men like Cradock die, let us look to it that their memories are preserved, because they are among the treasures of our history. Those guilty of providing them with inferior weapons shall at any rate not be allowed to besmirch their unsullied fame. Non-combatants demand justice for all combatants. But they must do more. They must see that justice is done to the living and to the dead. Every sailor and soldier must feel that he is not merely serving a department with no body to kick or soul to save – but a nation worthy of supreme sacrifice, a jealous guardian of their name and fame.'[15]

29

Cradock the Movie, 1926–1927

In 1926 it was announced that a film was to be made of the Battles of Coronel and The Falklands. It was to be financed by one A.E. Bundy, made by British Instructional Films, produced by Bruce Woolfe and directed by Captain Summers M.M, M.C., and D.C.M. The latter two were the same team who had earlier made the movies 'Ypres', 'Mons' and 'Nelson'. The permission and help of the Admiralty had been enlisted and they had undertaken to supply ships, men and advice for the shooting. A total budget of £30,000 had been allocated.

Montagu, now the sole surviving brother and the guardian of Kit's reputation swung into action. Given the positions taken by Churchill and the Admiralty during the *Morning Post* correspondence following the publication of *The World Crisis* he was concerned that Kit's role in the battle would be further traduced. On 21 October 1926 he fired off a coruscating letter to the editor of the *Morning Post*, Cope-Cornford, from his address at 90 Piccadilly. It is worth reproducing completely for it conveys the full bile of the family's disdain for Churchill.

My Dear Mr Cope-Cornford

I am much disturbed by seeing in the newspapers that they are going to 'film' both the Coronel and Falklands Islands battles, and that the Admiralty has given full sanction to it. Of course I can see no harm in initiating the public into the glories of a successful Naval engagement – that is if Sturdee's can be called an engagement when only one side was within range of the others guns – but why rake up our only unsuccessful one, why not leave the dead in peace, why not let them rest.

I can visualise the theatrical banalities of flares and flames and big drum guns – then Sturdee's face on the film to super patriotic airs on the band – then possibly Beatty's – more cheers from the audience – and then as an ultra crescendo the smug face of that arch malefactor Winston – the prime cause of the disaster, and with no part whatever in the caste [sic] of the revenge.

I write strongly – I feel strongly – the more that I am powerless to prevent it – forgive me.

Yours sincerely[1]

The letter was published the next day and a furore broke out. Monty followed this up with a letter to the First Lord of the Admiralty, the thrust of which was that the depiction of the tragic events at Coronel would be distressing to the relatives of all those who had lost loved ones in the carnage. The Admiralty backtracked quickly. Montagu was offered a full discussion with Admiralty representatives which had been completed by 26 October, for the First Lord (William Bridgeman) replied to him, confirming in the final paragraph of the letter that 'it is the Admiralty's intention that nothing shall be included to which exception could be taken on the grounds you mention, and I think you can rest assured that the matter will have full consideration'.[2]

Press coverage of the controversy was widespread from *The Times* to the *Edinburgh Evening Despatch* and various opinions were aired, some in support of Monty and some against. The pro view was exemplified by a leader in the *Eastern Daily Press* of 28 October in which the writer suggested that no good could come from 'the reproduction of the actual scenes of death and disaster in all their dreadful reality'. The con position, taken by the film company and others was that no one had objected to the films of Mons, Ypres and

Zeebrugge where many more men died and named batteries and battalions were shown in action. The Admiralty and the production company were anxious to conciliate. The *Western Herald* of 27 October carried the report that Montagu had withdrawn his objections after discussion with the Admiralty and Mr Bruce Woolfe of British Instructional Films, and that there would be 'no close ups of British ships sinking and the only suggestion that ships have blown will be conveyed by an impression of a glare of light on the horizon. All the scenes of the actual fight at Coronel will be reproduced as if they had been witnessed from the deck of *Scharnhorst*.'

A committee to advise the film makers had been formed and Admiral John Luce, former captain of the *Glasgow*, was appointed its chairman. On 4 November he presided over a dinner at the Savoy to celebrate the commencement of filming. In his speech he emphasised the chivalric behaviour of both sides, exculpated von Spee from failing to pick up survivors and told how *Glasgow*'s crew had cheered the survivors of the *Leipzig* after sinking her. The producer announced that Provincial Cinematograph Pictures had entered into a contract to show the film and that 'the financial success of the picture is therefore assured'.[3]

But now there came a twist. It was rumoured that Churchill himself would appear in the film. The script scenario read: 'Mr Churchill at his desk in the Admiralty receives a telegram. Have just heard from Chilean Admiral that German Admiral states that on 1 November at sunset and wicked weather etc. Churchill looks very grave. Fade into First Sea Lord's room. Fisher, Churchill and Sturdee in consultation. Fisher says we take *Inflexible* and *Invincible* from the Grand Fleet. You, Sturdee, will hoist your flag in *Invincible*'.[4] Monty's concerns about the veracity of the script were justified!

Further uproar followed when it was alleged that the German navy had also been approached for help and that German sailors would be aboard British ships for the filming. The Admiralty and the producers vigorously denied this and that Churchill would personally appear, but the claims and counter claims rumbled on in the press.

Questions were now asked in the House of Commons. The *Sheffield Independent* reported that on 24 November Col. Day MP quizzed the First Lord of the Admiralty as to what facilities were being given to the producers of the film. He reported that no navy ships or men would be used (which was at variance with earlier comments), that no extra costs would be incurred and that a proportion of the profits would be given to the Admiralty. And here the matter rested, fading from the public consciousness as the film crew headed for the Scilly Isles which were to do service as the Falklands

The film was released in 1927, black and white, silent, 8,300 feet long. The script, written by Harry Engholm, Fred C. Bowen and the celebrated author John Buchan (*The Thirty-Nine Steps* etc.) was written 'in co-operation with the British Admiralty, The Navy League and an advisory committee'. Kit was depicted as attacking 'acting on standing orders' so Montagu got his way after all. Intriguingly, and despite the answer given to Col. Day above, the Admiralty did supply battleships for the filming.

30

Envoi

The British navy of 1914 was almost completely unprepared for the war it would have to fight. Tactically it had advanced little from the time of Nelson. A close blockade was the default assumption in the channel (still being advocated in 1911); in fact the war required distant blockade with the fleet based hundreds of miles from its originally assumed positions. No consideration had been given to the possibility that the enemy might decline fleet to fleet conflict and rely on the threat of a 'fleet in being'. Apart from a few voices in the wilderness such as Fisher and Keyes, the submarine menace was ignored (it was seen as unsportsmanlike; Arthur Wilson, when First Sea Lord, said that captured submariners should be hung like pirates), an omission which nearly cost Britain the war. The Admiralty assumed that the war would be settled by big-gun ship to ship conflict at short range, and built and trained on that basis – in fact ranges of over 15,000 yards were commonplace. This is not dissimilar to the generals on the Western Front who assumed that horse cavalry would be a deciding factor.

Staff work was virtually non-existent and the Admiralty staff, such as it was, barely worth the name. Churchill effectively ran it as a fiefdom. The command and control system allowed his amateur meddling to take control of the professional levers of power. Initiative was stymied by the centralisation of authority brought about by improvements to radio communication, the rule and procedure orientation of naval training and obedience to orders. Away from the Admiralty, admirals' personal staffs were there to implement, not to consult and advise – and father always knew best. Cleverness and flexibility of thought was discouraged. The *materiel* was of widely differing value; outside the Grand Fleet the ships were largely obsolete or inadequate for the tasks required.

Commanders and men were undoubtedly brave and fought courageously when called upon, but they fought yesterday's war and were prisoners of an ethic which had no place in modern warfare: cruiser captains stopping *in seria* to pick up survivors and allowing a single submarine to pick them off (the *Bacchantes* in the Channel in 1914); the denigration of submariners and air power; the unwillingness to take calculated risks (the *Goeben* affair); the lack of understanding of the power of collective decision taking and of intelligence gathering (Fisher and just about every other admiral in the fleet); the unwillingness to recognise that new thinking and people from the 'lower orders' might have something to offer.

The Vicwardian navy was a private members' club, exclusive and blessed with privilege. The price of membership was high – conformity, physical danger on occasion, absolute faith in, and adherence to, the rules of the club, often long spells away from loved ones – but the benefits were superb. Admirals and captains were media celebrities with fan clubs and dedicated followers. The Navy League, founded in 1894 to aid recruitment and act as a pro-naval pressure group, had 2.5 million members. Naval commanders' exploits were front page news. They had servants at taxpayers' expense and travelled the world in luxury. The navy was sexy and made you famous. On or before retirement, knighthoods, company directorships and wealth were virtually assured.

As a result, thinking and innovation were discouraged and the rules of the club ensured that the navy entered the war with a command group who shared the same background, class, identity and adherence to the glories of the club's past achievements and members.

It is difficult, perhaps, to envisage this from our modern standpoint. Our references have changed so dramatically. The components that went to make up the Vicwardian world – a subservient proletariat, land based wealth, respect for status and authority, the place of women in the work force and in society, chivalry as the ethical basis for behaviour, a restricted electoral franchise – were swept away in the maelstrom of the First World War. The world that Kit knew, loved and grew up in has been lost for ever. The survivors of his generation never again knew the Edenic existence that the pre-war years had brought, as death duties, income tax, the cost of labour and the demise of deference ruined their world. And if they survived to 1939 they discovered it had all been for naught anyway.

Much that is good has been gained since Cradock's time, but things of value have been lost too. In Kit's world physical and moral courage, respect and obedience to properly constituted authority, manners and polite behaviour and well developed social skills were all important personal assets and respected as such. Now they are all too often objects of scorn and derision. And another important asset has been taken from us – certainty. Kit was *sure* he was right, he *knew* what he should do, he had *confidence* in his beliefs, he had no anxiety as to his role in life and the actions that were required of him. Kit was at peace with himself; and very few people of today's society have that boon it seems.

Kit represents a forgotten England, one recalled now only through the prism of a literature which harks back to that Vicwardian paradise. A.G. Macdonell's *England their England*; Jerome K. Jerome and *Three Men in a Boat*; Hugh De Selincourt's 'The Cricket Match'; the works of P.G. Wodehouse; and a thousand memoires of the blessed prelapsarian Edwardian era.

Perhaps Kit Cradock and his kind were already an anachronism by the time war began – but they were *our* anachronism and their bravery and values sustained the country through its darkest hours.

Rest in peace, Kit.

31

Postscript

This story has many participants, human and mechanical, some of whom prospered and some not.

Cradock has had no ship named after him. The standard practice in the British navy was not to name ships after admirals until they had been dead 100 years. There is still time!

No ship has subsequently been named *Good Hope*. However there have been *Monmouth*s and *Glasgow*s down the years. In 1982 a modern HMS *Glasgow* served in the Falklands campaign and was badly damaged by bombs. She was a Type 42 destroyer, almost as big – at 4,100 tons, as Luce's original ship. Serving alongside her was an HMS *Invincible*.

Von Spee and both his sons died in the Falklands battle but the German people respected his gallantry. A ship bearing his name was laid down in 1917 but never finished and the keel was subsequently scrapped. A second ship of the name was commissioned in 1934 and was designed as a long range commerce raider. Positioned in the south Atlantic at the outbreak of the Second World War she was briefly a menace until attacked and outmanoeuvred by an inferior British cruiser force under Commodore Harwood – an example of what Troubridge should have done with the *Goeben*. Bottled up in Montevideo harbour she was scuttled and her captain committed suicide.

The *Scharnhorst* and the *Gneisenau* were resurrected as 11-inch-gunned battleships by the Third Reich in the late 1930s. Known in the British navy as Salmon and Gluckstein, they met with limited success, sinking only one warship of any size. In 1942 *Gneisenau* was so badly damaged by bombing that it was decided not to repair her and her guns were removed for coastal defence. In 1943 the *Scharnhorst*, in an uncanny replay of her namesake's fate, was taken under attack by the battleship HMS *Duke of York* whose 15-inch weapons damaged her so badly that she sank unseen, taking all but 36 of her 2000 crew to the ocean bottom.

The brief honeymoon between Churchill and Fisher did not last. Fisher rightly believed it was his job to run the Admiralty. He ran it from his desk as he had run a ship or a fleet, rising between four and five, often commencing work 'before the cleaners' and finishing around six in the evening before retiring at nine. He lived an austere life and dedicated himself to his work. Churchill rarely rose before noon and would work late into the night in his office until one in the morning or lying in bed with his boxes following a decent dinner and fortifying himself with a bottle of brandy and an imperial of champagne (his favourite brand was Pol Roger; an imperial was an obsolete measure of around half a litre). Fisher would arrive at his desk to find peremptory memos from Churchill demanding courses of action that wasted many days of Fisher's time. He grew weary of this ('Winston has monopolised all initiative in the admiralty'[1]). The flashpoint was over the Dardenelles campaign, in which Fisher had never totally believed. Churchill, whose initiative it was, first fired off direct orders to the admiral commanding the operation and then later instructed Fisher by memo as to the dispositions of ships and material that he wanted, including ships built and earmarked for Fisher's beloved 'Baltic' plan. Jackie went, in modern parlance, 'ballistic'. He resigned on 17 May 1915, stormed out of the Admiralty, refused to return to his post (ignoring even a direct instruction from Asquith, the Prime Minister: 'Lord Fisher. In the King's name return to your post'), and holed up in the Charing Cross Hotel and then in Scotland with the Duchess of Hamilton. The affair lit the touch-paper which led to Churchill's dismissal from his post and eventually the cabinet, and his exile from government during which he wrote the self-exculpatory *The World Crisis* – which was once thought of as a history, but now can be seen for what it was – self justification. Fisher died in 1920, still fulminating and bitter.

Beresford continued to pursue his feud with Fisher, and many other officers and cabinet members, regularly writing to Asquith, and subsequently Lloyd George to complain about his conduct of the war. To many people he became a rather comic figure, an extinct volcano of bile perpetuating a vendetta that had no relevance in a time of mass slaughter. He died in 1919 aged seventy-three.

Sturdee was given honours and plaudits on his return. He was made a baron in 1916 and parliament voted him a grant of £10,000 – a small fortune at the time (perhaps the equivalent of £800,000 today) – which made him financially secure forever. This must have particularly galled Fisher who had struggled to live on his pay most of his life. When Fisher resigned as First Sea Lord for the second time in 1915 Sturdee was an obvious candidate, but was passed over as he was again when a new commander for the Grand Fleet was sought. Promoted full Admiral in 1917 and given the CinC Nore post, he retired in 1921 and involved himself in the restoration of the *Victory* at Portsmouth dock, dying in 1925 aged sixty-six.

Meux resigned from the navy in 1916 and from parliament in 1918 and devoted himself to horse breeding at Stapleford Park in Yorkshire and then at Theobalds Park, part of his Meux inheritance. It was said of him that he 'would have been even more successful [as a horse breeder] if he had not been too fond of his horses to sell them'.[2] He died in 1929, leaving the vast sum of £910,000 gross in his estate, which after his wife's consideration was left to her godson, Ian Hedworth John Little Gilmour, later to be Secretary for Defence in the Heath administration and Margaret Thatcher's Lord Privy Seal.

Jellicoe and Beatty found that their lives continued to be entwined and not for the best. After the failure to inflict a Trafalgar on the Germans at Jutland, and the lack-lustre performance of Beatty's command, public recriminations grew loud. Some favoured Jellicoe, others Beatty, and a *sotto voce* feud began to blossom. When Jellicoe was appointed First Sea Lord in 1916, Beatty took control of the

Grand Fleet and the tensions between the two grew worse. Jellicoe was a poor First Sea Lord, being unable either to delegate or to see the need for a convoy system to stem the growing losses of cargo ships to submarines (Lloyd George, by now Prime Minister, had to forcibly instruct him to introduce convoys). Jellicoe found the new First Lord, Geddes, appointed by Lloyd George to put a fire under the Admiralty, uncongenial to work with and the same was true in reverse for Geddes. He determined to fire Jellicoe and did so by letter on Christmas Eve 1917. In 1919 Jellicoe was sent to tour the commonwealth and make recommendation regarding the development of their navies, and was then appointed Governor General of New Zealand. Beatty, appointed First Sea Lord in 1919, used his position and Jellicoe's absence to rewrite history with regard to the conduct of the Battle of Jutland. When the official report of the battle was published his role was much enhanced and Jellicoe's implicitly criticised. This worsened the feud between them, and public spats between Jellicoites and Beattyites resembled the Fisher–Beresford schism of ten years earlier. Jellicoe died in 1935, bitter at the criticism he had endured (and largely ignored) particularly from Churchill who used *The World Crisis* to further the Beatty legend (Beatty had once been Churchill's naval secretary). On hearing of Jellicoe's death, Admiral Raeder, the German navy CinC who had served at Jutland, ordered all German warships to fly their flags at half-mast. Beatty held office for eight years whereupon he left the navy and died aged only sixty-five in 1936, his latter years darkened by his wealthy American wife's multiple infidelities.

Luce made Admiral, fathered an admiral and has his memorial in Malmesbury Abbey. He played an active role in the development of naval aviation, was Admiral Commanding Malta in 1921 and High Sheriff of Wiltshire 1930–31, dying a year later.

Heathcote Grant was appointed Rear Admiral in 1916 and became Senior Officer Naval Establishments Gibraltar in 1917, seeing out the war there and retiring in 1923.

Dannreuther, who had seen one Gotterdammerung, saw another two years later. Still gunnery officer of the *Invincible* he was at his post in the gunnery control position, high up in the foretop at the Battle of Jutland. *Invincible* was hit by a full salvo from SMS *Derfflinger* and blew up, breaking in half. Out of a crew of 1032 only six survived – and he was one. He went on to command in Australia, captain an aircraft carrier and, like Cradock, be officer in charge of RN Barracks Portsmouth. He was appointed Rear Admiral in 1932, placed on the retired list and died having lived a very full (and rather lucky) life aged ninety-seven.

Battenberg never served again after resigning as First Sea Lord. During the war he wrote the definitive book on naval medals and in 1917 changed his name to Mountbatten at the king's urging (as did George V, to Windsor) and was raised to the UK peerage as Marquess of Milford Haven. He fell on hard times financially, having to sell a castle in Germany and his house in England (and his collection of medals) and died in 1921. His second son, Louis Mountbatten, was to emulate him, becoming First Sea Lord himself and serving with (somewhat self-promoting) honour in the Second World War, eventually taking the title Earl Mountbatten of Burma.

Bridgeman had been placed on the retired list in 1913 and busied himself with the life of a country gentleman at his seat near Harrogate. At Fisher's funeral he was one of the pallbearers and had given the same service to Charlie B, who he had served under as a second in command, a year earlier. He held the (honorary) title of Vice-Admiral of the United Kingdom between 1920 and his death in the Bahamas in 1929, and is commemorated in the tiny church of St Michael and All Angels in Copgrove.

Milne's and Troubridge's careers never recovered from the *Goeben* debacle. Milne was on half pay for the rest of the war. He was briefly offered Command of the Nore in 1916 but the offer was withdrawn and he retired at his own request in 1919 to write a book to clear his name. It was not a best seller. He died in 1938 aged eighty-three, leaving his collection of rare shrubs and orchids to the Edinburgh botanic garden.

Troubridge never had another seagoing command but in 1915 was posted to command naval forces on the river Danube in the naval campaign to support Serbia, a motley collection of old monitors and river launches. Post war he briefly chaired the Danube Commission before being evicted by the Foreign Office in favour of their nominee, although he was later recalled and was president until 1924. His second wife Margot left him in 1915 to live in a lesbian relationship with the writer Marguerite Radclyffe Hall, author of the shocking (for the time) lesbian novel *The Well of Loneliness.*

Roger Keyes became one of the naval heroes of the Empire in a career that spanned both world wars. In 1914 he was appointed commander of the Harwich submarine force, and served as Chief of Staff in the Dardenelles campaign. He was promoted Rear Admiral, was Sturdee's number two commanding the 4th Battle Squadron, and finished the war commanding the Dover Patrol where he planned and led the Zeebrugge and Ostend raids in which the port of Zeebrugge was denied to the Germans by sinking British blockships across the harbour mouth. In 1925 he gained the plum job of CinC Mediterranean Fleet, eventually hauling down his flag in 1931 and retiring with the rank of Admiral of the Fleet. MP for Portsmouth from 1934, he vigorously opposed appeasement and argued for rearmament. Utilising his friendship with King Leopold of the Belgians he was an important link between government and that country in the early days of the war, and went on to help plan the Norwegian adventure and tour America and Canada drumming up support for the Allies. He was raised to the peerage in 1943 and died two years later aged seventy-three.

Charles Gould survived Coronel and survived the war. In 1918 he was sent on a hydrography course and promoted full Lieutenant later that year. He was demobbed in January 1919, but the scenes he had witnessed did not put him off the service for he re-enrolled in June 1921 in the new Royal Fleet Reserve.

Captain Francklin's widow, Irene Catherine, was not put off a naval husband by her loss and remarried to Osmond de B. Brock, Beatty's chief of staff and later an admiral himself. Her son by her first marriage continued the naval legacy, serving with distinction through the Second World War in the Fleet Air Arm.

As for the Cradocks, Sheldon William Keith died in 1922 leaving the estate to Montague who died seven years later. Neither Sheldon, Montague nor Kit had married and there was no direct line of inheritance. In his will Montague left the estate to Guy, his nephew, on condition that he (1) marry, (2) obtain his parents' consent to marriage, (3) change his name to Cradock, and (4) apply for, and obtain, a licence to bear the Cradock coat of arms. For the second time in three generations a royal licence had to be obtained. Guy was reportedly reluctant to take the Cradock name and give up his career in the Colonial Service but eventually he fulfilled the terms of the will by marrying Felicity Cecil Marie Micklethwaite in 1930; she was twenty-seven, he thirty-eight. Felicity was a Roman Catholic and an avid gardener. There were no children. We may wonder, from this distance, whether there was an element of convenience about this union. With the death of Guy in 1975, housebound and having sold his guns and horses, the Cradock tradition of service to crown and country died.

To whom did the estate now fall? Gwendoline's daughter, Sylvia Mary Straker, married Sir Christopher William Vane M.C., 10th Lord Barnard and Master of the Raby Hunt, in 1920. He was a descendant of the same Earl of Darlington who had sponsored Sylvia's great-grandfather Sheldon to be an MP. Through the marriage of her daughter Rosemary Myra to Sir Angus Josslyn Gore-Booth (a short-lived affair of only six years) Hartforth Hall and estate passed to Rosemary and her son in 1975 and was sold by her son, also Josslyn, in 1986 to be a hotel.

The Hall still stands, neglected and forlorn, a small country hotel in need of refurbishment. In the 'Black and Gold room' there are two photographs of Kit and a very bad painting of the *Good Hope*. Apart from that, there is nothing to show for over 200 years of Cradock ownership and the self-sacrifice of the brothers.

Maud, Countess Fitzwilliam outlived her husband by twenty-four years after his death in 1943. In 1920 she was made a CBE and became a Commander, Most Venerable Order of the Hospital of St John of Jerusalem, an order of chivalry of the British Crown incorporated by Queen Victoria in 1888. Between 1921 and 1940 she was 'British Scout Commander' South Yorkshire. Her only son, W.H.L. Peter Wentworth Fitzwilliam, a decorated member of the Special Operations Executive during the Second World War, became the 8th Earl but did not enjoy the title for long, dying in an air crash in France with his mistress Kathleen 'Kick' Cavendish, Marchioness of Hartington and sister of future US President J.F. Kennedy. Maud's grand-daughter by Peter, Juliet, married three times, the first being to Victor Hervey, 6th Marquess Bristol, 20 years her senior, divorced, a criminal and bankrupt. Their only son killed himself. Juliet married again, becoming the fourth wife of Somerset Struben de Chair, son of Admiral Dudley de Chair, Cradock's friend who had sailed with Kit on the *Cleopatra* and with whom Kit corresponded from Mexico. Maud lived to see the ruination of the Fitzwilliam family seat, Wentworth Woodhouse, by the 1945 Labour government, who coal mined up to the front door in an act of class war led by Manny Shinwell. She died in 1967 aged eighty-nine. Both she and Kit would no doubt have raised a glass to her fourth daughter Helena who died in an accident on the hunting field aged sixty-three.

And Kit – Kit slid into obscurity and the world forgot him.

Appendices

Appendix 1: List of Articles required for a Naval Cadet on joining Her Majesty's Ship *Britannia*

A Midshipman's Sea Chest complete, with Name in full on top, engraved on plain brass plate:
Length, 3 ft. 6 in.; breadth, 2 ft.; height, 2 ft. 3 in.
(It is requested that the chest may be at Dartmouth 7 days previous to the Cadet's joining.)

3 Pillow Cases.
1 Hair Mattress, 5 ft. 6 in. × 1 ft. 9 in.
1 Hair Pillow.
2 Blankets, 6 ft. 6 in. × 4 ft. 6 in.
1 Counterpane, 6 ft. 6 in. × 4 ft. 6 in.
3 Pair Sheets, 6 ft. 6 in. × 4 ft. 6 in.
1 Uniform Jacket.
1 Uniform Trowsers [sic]. Superfine.
1 Uniform Waistcoat.
1 Uniform Cap, peak ½ turn down.
2 Working Uniform Suits (one of thick flannel; one of pilot cloth).
1 Uniform Working Cap, peak ½ turn down.
12 White Shirts.
12 Collars.
6 Night Shirts.
12 Pair Merino Socks.
4 White Flannel Trowsers, well shrunk.

6 Pair Drawers, Merino.
3 White Flannel Shirts (with collars to turn down)
3 Lambswool Under-vests.
2 White Waistcoats.
12 Towels.
7 Merino Vests.
2 Black Silk Neckties (made up).
2 Pair Braces.
3 Pair Strong laced Boots, with thick soles.
1 Clothes Brush.
1 Sponge.
1 Carpet Bag.
1 Clothes flag
12 Pocket Handkerchiefs.
1 Pair elastic-side Oxford Shoes, with strong soles.
1 Brush and Comb.
1 Tooth Brush.
1 Nail Brush.

Pea Jackets are not to be supplied, as the thick Working Jacket can be worn over the Uniform Jacket, if necessary.

Clothing to be distinctly marked with the Cadet's Name in full.

NOTE – Trowsers to be made without pockets, and only one pocket on the left breast of the Jackets of the two Working Uniform Suits.

School Books and Instruments will be supplied in *Britannia* as required in each Term; but each Cadet on entering the fourth Term, will be required to provide himself with a sextant, of the approximate value of £7, such instrument being obtained under the direction of the Captain of the *Britannia*.

Appendix 2: Kit's legatees

In his will Kit left remembrances and letters to six people: Lady Maud Fitzwilliam, Mrs Slingsby Bethell, Capt. Hugh Sinclair RN, Capt. E.I. Alexander-Sinclair RN, J.M. de Robeck and Mary Barnes.

The first and last of these have been discussed in the main text.

Alexander-Sinclair had played polo with Kit on Malta, as previously noted. He was the 12th Laird of Freswick and like Kit rose to be a KCVO and eventually a full Admiral. During the Battle of Jutland he commanded the 1st Light Cruiser Squadron with inconspicuous success and after the war became principal naval ADC to George V. He was a 'Royal'. Kit left him a gold hunter watch.

Hugh Sinclair rose to be the Director of Naval Intelligence and then Head of the Secret Service (SIS). He was a larger than life character with a penchant for large cigars and a good wine cellar. In appearance he was apparently the antithesis of the smartly dressed Kit. He was naval ADC to George V in 1920 but a messy divorce slowed his progress through the higher ranks. At the beginning of the Second World War he was one of the moving forces behind setting up Bletchley Park.

John de Robeck rose to flag rank and was the admiral who took over the naval command in the Dardenelles after Churchill and Carden's abortive attempts to force the straits. He argued for withdrawal and was violently opposed by Churchill but the cabinet sided with de Robeck and Churchill was forced to resign as First Lord. Kit would no doubt have taken pleasure in his friend bringing about Churchill's downfall.

Mrs Henry Slingsby Bethell was the owner of Villa Garmisch in Bavaria, chiefly known as the place where the Elgars stayed whilst Edward Elgar wrote 'From the Bavarian Highlands'. The Slingsby-Bethells also owned property in Bath and Rome.

Appendix 3: Kit's decorations

Kit was a man obsessed with correct form and dress. It shows in his concern that his decorations and awards were correctly noted. We see this in his will, for example, where he details them out to make sure they are properly recorded on his memorial. A brave, proud and possibly slightly vain man with great concern for the naval formalities, he followed in the footsteps of the monarchs he served, especially Edward VII and George V, who shared his obsession.

Award	Date	Reason
Khedive's Bronze Star, Tokar Clasp, Medjidie of the Fourth Class	1891	Eastern Soudan Field Force, ADC to Governor General and present at Battle of Tokar and occupation of Affafit
Mentioned in Despatches	1892	Rescue of the crew of the *Almirante Barroza*
China Medal, Taku Clasp, Relief of Pekin Clasp	1900	Boxer Rebellion
Royal Order of the Crown of Prussia 2nd class with Swords	1900	Boxer Rebellion
Companion of the Order of the Bath (CB)	1902	
Member of the Victorian Order (MVO)	1903	The occasion of the visit of King Edward VII to Malta, April 1902
Royal Spanish Order of Naval Merit, 2nd class	1906	

Award	Date	Reason
Testimonial of the Royal Humane Society	1904	Rescue of Siamese Crown Prince, Palmas Bay
Knight Commander Royal Victorian Order (KCVO)	1912	'Personal Service' to the Monarch
Silver medal of the Board of Trade for Gallantry	1912	For the *Delhi* rescue

Appendix 4 – Kit's ships

Kit Cradock had a silver napkin ring on which was engraved the names of all the ships that he had sailed in, beginning with 'Harpooned 1874' referring to his entry into HMS *Britannia*. The table below gives the details of his ships and service (abridged to exclude passage ships, minor episodes, periods of half pay etc.)

HMS	Dates	Rank	Other
Britannia	1874–1876	Cadet	Training ship
Pallas	1876–1879	Cadet, Midshipman	
Cleopatra	1880–1882	Midshipman, Sub-Lieutenant	
Duke of Wellington	1882–1883	Sub-Lieutenant	Training ship
Impregnable	1883	Sub-Lieutenant	
Superb	1883–1885	Sub-Lieutenant	

HMS	Dates	Rank	Other
Linnet	1885–1889	Lieutenant	
Duke of Wellington, Howe, Volage	1889	Lieutenant	Various training appointments
Dolphin	1890–1893	Lieutenant	
Excellent, Viceroy, Northampton	1894	Lieutenant	Various training appointments
Victoria and Albert	1894–1896	Lieutenant	Royal Yacht
Brittania	1896–1899	Commander	Second i/c training ship
President	1899	Commander	Transport duties
Alacrity	1900–1901	Commander	
Duke of Wellington	1901	Commander	Training ship/ leave
Andromeda	1902	Captain	
Bacchante	1902–1905	Captain	
Leviathan	1905	Captain	
Swiftsure	1906–1908	Captain	
Victory for RN Portsmouth	1908–1910	Commodore 2nd class	RN shore establishment
	1901–1911	Rear Admiral	Training and half pay

HMS	Dates	Rank	Other
London	1911–1912	Rear Admiral	
Hibernia	1912–1913	Rear Admiral	
Fourth Cruiser Squadron, Donegal, *Suffolk*, *Essex*, *Good Hope*	1913–1914	Rear Admiral	War gratuity £200

Appendix 5: Cradock family tree

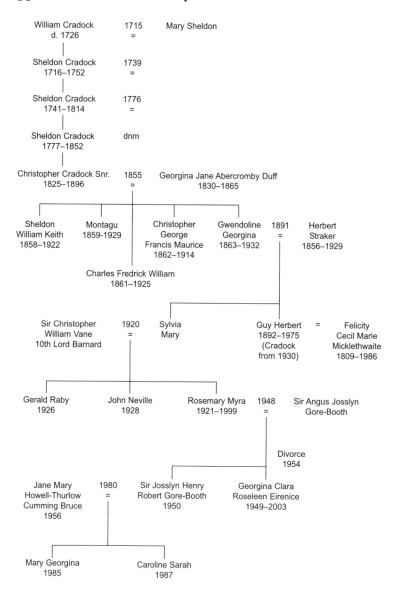

William Cradock
d. 1726
1715 =
Mary Sheldon

Sheldon Cradock
1716–1752
1739 =

Sheldon Cradock
1741–1814
1776 =

Sheldon Cradock
1777–1852
dnm

Christopher Cradock Snr.
1825–1896
1855 =
Georgina Jane Abercromby Duff
1830–1865

Sheldon
William Keith
1858–1922

Montagu
1859-1929

Christopher
George
Francis Maurice
1862–1914

Gwendoline
Georgina
1863–1932
1891 =
Herbert
Straker
1856–1929

Charles Fredrick William
1861–1925

Sir Christopher
William Vane
10th Lord Barnard
1920 =
Sylvia
Mary

Guy Herbert
1892–1975
(Cradock
from 1930)
=
Felicity
Cecil Marie
Micklethwaite
1809–1986

Gerald Raby
1926

John Neville
1928

Rosemary Myra
1921–1999
1948 =
Sir Angus Josslyn
Gore-Booth

Divorce
1954

Jane Mary
Howell-Thurlow
Cumming Bruce
1956
1980 =
Sir Josslyn Henry
Robert Gore-Booth
1950

Georgina Clara
Roseleen Eirenice
1949–2003

Mary Georgina
1985

Caroline Sarah
1987

Appendix 6: Official battle reports of von Spee and Luce

Vice Admiral Graf von Spee's Report

Wind and swell were head on and the vessels had heavy going, especially the small cruisers on both sides. Observation and distance estimation were under a severe handicap because of the seas which washed over the bridges. The swell was so great that it obscured the aim of the gunners at the six inch guns on the middle deck, who could not see the sterns of the enemy ships at all and the bow but seldom. At 6.20 p.m., at a distance of 13,400 yards, I turned one point toward the enemy, and at 6.34 opened fire at a distance of 11,260 yards. The guns of both our armoured cruisers were effective, and by 6.39 already we could note the first hit on the *Good Hope*. I at once resumed a parallel course instead of bearing slightly toward the enemy.

The English opened their fire at this time. I assume that the heavy sea made more trouble for them than it did for us. Their two armoured cruisers remained covered by our fire, while they, so far as could be determined, hit the *Scharnhorst* but twice and the *Gneisenau* only four times.

At 6.53, when 6,500 yards apart, I ordered a course one point away from the enemy. They were firing more slowly at this time, while we were able to count numerous hits. We could see, among other things, that the top of the *Monmouth*'s forward turret had been shot away and that a violent fire was burning in the turret. The *Scharnhorst*, it is thought, hit the *Good Hope* about thirty-five times.

In spite of our altered course the English changed theirs sufficiently so that the distance between us shrunk to 5,300 yards. There was reason to suspect that the enemy despaired of using his artillery effectively and was manoeuvring for a torpedo attack. The position of the moon, which had risen at 6 o'clock, was favourable to this move. Accordingly, I gradually opened up further distance between the squadrons by another deflection of the leading ship at 7.45. In the meantime it had grown dark. The range-finder on the *Scharnhorst* used the fire on the *Monmouth* as a guide for a time, though eventually all range-finding, aiming, and observation became so inexact that firing was stopped at 7.26.

At 7.23 a column of fire from an explosion was noticed between the stacks of the *Good Hope*. The *Monmouth* apparently stopped firing at 7.20. The small cruisers, including the *Nürnberg*, received by wireless at 7.30 the order to follow the enemy and to attack his ships with torpedoes. Vision was somewhat obscured at this time by a rain squall. The light cruisers were not able to find the *Good Hope*, but the *Nürnberg* encountered the *Monmouth*, and at 8.58 was able by shots at closest range to capsize her without a single shot being fired in return. Rescue work in the heavy sea was not to be thought of; especially as the *Nürnberg* immediately afterward believed she had sighted the smoke of another ship and had to prepare for a new attack.

The small cruisers had neither losses nor damage in the battle. On the *Gneisenau* there were two men slightly wounded. The crews of the ships went into the fight with enthusiasm; every one did his duty and played his part in the victory.

The Report of Captain John Luce (HMS Glasgow*)*

Glasgow left Coronel 9 a.m. on November 1 to rejoin *Good Hope* (flagship), *Monmouth* and *Otranto* at rendezvous. At 2 p.m. flagship signalled that apparently from wireless calls there was an enemy ship to northward. Orders were given for squadron to spread N.E. by E. in the following order: *Good Hope, Monmouth, Otranto*, and *Glasgow*, speed to be worked up to 15 knots. 4.20 p.m., saw smoke; proved to be enemy ships, one small cruiser and two armoured cruisers. *Glasgow* reported to admiral, ships in sight were warned, and all concentrated on *Good Hope*. At 5 p.m. *Good Hope* was sighted.

At 5.47 p.m. squadron formed in line-ahead in following order: *Good Hope, Monmouth, Glasgow*, and *Otranto*. Enemy, who had turned south, were now in single line ahead 12 miles off, *Scharnhorst* and *Gneisenau* leading. 6.18 p.m., speed ordered to 17 knots, and flagship signalled *Canopus*, 'I am going to attack enemy now.' Enemy were now 15,000 yards away, and maintained this range, at the same time jamming wireless signals.

By this time sun was getting immediately behind us from enemy position, and while it remained above horizon we had advantage in light, but range too great. 6.55 p.m., sun set, and visibility conditions altered, our ships being silhouetted against afterglow, and failing light made enemy difficult to see. 7.30 p.m., enemy opened fire 12,000 yards, followed in quick succession by *Good Hope*, *Monmouth*, *Glasgow*. Two squadrons were now converging, and each ship engaged opposite number in the line. Growing darkness and heavy spray of head sea made firing difficult, particularly for main deck guns of *Good Hope* and *Monmouth*. Enemy firing salvos got range quickly, and their third salvo caused fire to break out on fore part of both ships, which were constantly on fire till 7.45 p.m. At 7.50 p.m. an immense explosion occurred on *Good Hope* amidships, flames reaching 200 feet high. Total destruction must have followed. It was now quite dark.

Both sides continued firing at flashes of opposing guns. *Monmouth* was badly down by the bow, and turned away to get stern to sea, signalling to *Glasgow* to that effect. 8.30 p.m., *Glasgow* signalled to *Monmouth* 'Enemy following us,' but received no reply. Under rising moon enemy's ships were now seen approaching, and as *Glasgow* could render *Monmouth* no assistance, she proceeded at full speed to avoid destruction. 8.50 p.m., lost sight of enemy. 9.20 p.m., observed 75 flashes of fire, which was no doubt final attack on *Monmouth*.

Nothing could have been more admirable than conduct of officers and men throughout. Though it was most trying to receive great volume of fire without chance of returning it adequately, all kept perfectly cool, there was no wild firing, and discipline was the same as at battle practice. When target ceased to be visible, gun layers spontaneously ceased fire. The serious reverse sustained has entirely failed to impair the spirit of officers and ship's company, and it is our unanimous wish to meet the enemy again as soon as possible.

Appendix 7: The Vane family

Old Sheldon Cradock had been sponsored into parliament by his neighbour the 3rd Earl of Darlington, William Henry Vane, who was made Duke of Cleveland in 1833. His grandfather had been 3rd Lord Barnard and he continued to hold the baronetcy. When the 4th Duke died in 1891 the line of succession to his peerages became unclear and the case was decided by the Committee of Privileges of the House of Lords. They held Henry de Vere Vane to be the Baron Barnard and inheritor of the estates of Raby Castle and Barnard Castle, the estates having been bought in 1626 by the Vane family, although the Committee declared the title of Duke of Cleveland extinct. Henry became the 9th Lord Barnard. His younger son, who succeeded to the title in 1918, married Kit's niece Sylvia. The descendants of Old Sheldon's aristocratic sponsor married his own descendants' offspring.

But the Vane family played a further role in the life of the Cradocks. Another branch of the family, descended from Sir Henry Vane 1st baronet (died 1794) took the name Vane-Tempest. The daughter of Sir Henry Vane-Tempest, 2nd baronet, Lady Frances Ann Vane-Tempest, married the 3rd Marquess of Londonderry who adopted the name Vane as his own by Royal License. Through their daughter, Frances, they were the great-grandparents of Kit's nemesis and the Cradock family's bête-noire, Winston Churchill.

Notes and Sources

I should like to recognise the assistance and hospitality given to me by Sir Josslyn Gore-Booth Bt. and his wife Jane, who not only welcomed me into their home but gave me access to the few remaining Cradock family papers that have survived the ravages of war, dislocation and death. Josslyn and Jane, I hope I have done you proud.

Below are listed sources by chapter, where appropriate; they have informed the book, as has original research and my voracious reading over many years. Admiralty records available at the National Archives clearly inform the battle descriptions. Papers in the collection of Sir Josslyn Gore-Booth are cited as 'JG-B'. Any errors are mine alone and I should be grateful to hear of them. *Humanum est errare.*

Chapter 1

1. J. Hammerton, *The Great War – I Was There* (Amalgamated Press, 1938)
2. Allardyce MS (1916), Scott Polar Research Institute (SPRI), Cambridge; also *Naval Review* and G. Bennett, *Coronel and The Falklands* (Batsford, 1962)

Chapter 2

1. thelibraryofparliament.com
2. JG-B

Chapter 3

1. JG-B
2. National Archives, Kew, Cradock's service record
3. JG-B, Kit's personal journal

Chapter 4

1. National Archives, Kew, Cradock's service record
2. C. Cradock, *Whispers From the Fleet* (Gieve's, 1907)

Chapter 5

1. G. Lowis, *Fabulous Admirals* (Putnam, 1957)
2. Quoted in R. Hough, *Admirals in Collision* (Hamish Hamilton, 1959)

Chapter 6

1. W. Goodenough, *A Rough Record* (Hutchinson, 1943)
2. P. Chrastina, *German Warships Flee British Fleet, Old News*, Dec 1995
3. Quoted in G. Bennett, *Naval Battles of the First World War* (Batsford, 1968)
4. R. Keyes, *Adventures Ashore and Afloat* (Harrap, 1939)
5. A. Marder, *From Dreadnought to Scapa Flow*, volume II (OUP, 1965)
6. Keyes papers, British Library

Chapter 7

1. Quoted in D. J. Silbey, *The Boxer Rebellion* (Hill and Wang, 2012)
2. Keyes, *Adventures Ashore and Afloat*
3. *Ibid.*
4. *Ibid.*
5. Quoted in Silbey, *The Boxer Rebellion*

6. Keyes, *Adventures Ashore and Afloat*
7. JG-B, Cradock unpublished journal; his adventures in China are described in this MS, which informs the whole of this chapter
8. National Archives, Kew, Cradock's service record
9. *Ibid.*
10. *The London Gazette*, 5 October 1900
11. Keyes, *Adventures Ashore and Afloat*
12. JG-B, Cradock's unpublished journal
13. *Ibid.*
14. *Ibid.*
15. *Ibid.*
16. *Ibid.*
17. *Ibid.*
18. *Ibid.*
19. *Ibid.*
20. *Ibid.*
21. *Ibid.*
22. *Ibid.*
23. *Ibid.*
24. *Ibid.*
25. Keyes MSS, Cradock's letters to Keyes, British Library
26. *Ibid.*
27. *Ibid.*
28. *Ibid.*
29. National Archives, Kew, Cradock's service record

Chapter 8

1. C. Dundas, *An Admiral's Yarns* (Jenkins, 1922)
2. Quoted in F. MacCarthy, *William Morris* (Faber and Faber, 2010)
3. W. Thackeray, *On The Hanoverians* (lecture tour)
4. N. Annan, *Our Age* (Weidenfeld and Nicolson, 1990)
5. T. Roosevelt, speech to the American Naval War College, 1897
6. *Dictionary of National Biography*
7. C. P. Scott, *The Political Diaries* (Collins, 1970)

Chapter 9

1. E. Bulwer-Lytton, *England and the English* (Routledge, 1876)

Chapter 10

1. C. Penrose-Fitzgerald, *From Steam to Sail* (E. Arnold, 1922)
2. N. Machiavelli, *The Prince* (Antonio Blado d'Asola, 1532)
3. National Archives, Kew, log book of HMS *Bacchante*
4. National Archives, Kew, Cradock's naval record
5. *Ibid.*

Chapter 11

1. Quoted in J. Winton, 'Life and education in a technically evolving navy', *Oxford History of the Royal Navy,* ed. J. Hill (OUP, 1998)
2. *The Times,* 27 June 1897
3. Admiralty circular no 36, 24 June 1869
4. Cradock, *Whispers from the Fleet*
5. Keyes, *Adventures Ashore and Afloat*
6. *The London Gazette,* 26 March 1907

Chapter 12

1. JG-B
2. Keyes papers, British Library
3. Cradock, *Whispers from the Fleet*

Chapter 13

1. A. Cunningham, *A Sailor's Odyssey* (Hutchinson, 1951)
2. *Dictionary of National Biography*

3. Scott, *The Political Diaries*
4. *Dictionary of National Biography*
5. *National Review,* April 1923
6. JG-B, Jellicoe letter to Gwendoline, 1923
7. JG-B, Carpenter letter to Gwendoline, October 1923
8. Allardyce MS, SPRI
9. Cradock, *Whispers from the Fleet*
10. *Ibid.*
11. *Ibid.*
12. *Ibid.*
13. Quoted in, *inter alia, Front Forum, discussing the Great War,* The Western Front Association
14. JG-B
15. Cradock, *Whispers from the Fleet*
16. For example, R. Massie in *Castles of Steel* (Jonathan Cape, 2004)

Chapter 14

1. Quoted in, *inter alia,* R. K. Massie, *Dreadnought* (Random House, 1991)
2. Quoted in, *inter alia,* R. Freeman, *The Great Naval Feud* (Pen and Sword, 2009)
3. Author's notes, *ipse dixit*
4. *Dictionary of National Biography*
5. Cradock, *Whispers from the Fleet*

Chapter 15

1. National Archives MSS
2. Obituary, *The Times,* 8 December 1911

Chapter 16

1. National Archives, Kew, Cradock's service record
2. Keyes papers, British Library

3. JG-B
4. *Ibid.*
5. *Ibid.*

Chapter 17

1. Keyes papers, British Library
2. JG-B, Cradock's unpublished journal of his time in Mexico plus his copies of correspondence with the Admiralty and the King
3. *Ibid.*
4. *Ibid.*
5. *Ibid.*
6. *Ibid.*
7. *Ibid.*
8. *Ibid.*
9. *Ibid.*
10. *Ibid.*
11. *Ibid.*
12. *Ibid.*
13. JG-B, letter from the German Ambassador

Chapter 18

1. BBC.co.uk/history, John Redmond
2. Letter to his brother August 1914; *Letters of Thomas Mann*, ed. Richard and Clara Winston (Knopf, 1971)
3. Quoted in E. Chatfield, The Navy and Defence', (Heinemann 1942).
4. Battenberg, quoted in, *inter alia*, G. Miller, *Superior Force* (Hull University Press, 1996)
5. Admiralty court of enquiry September 1914, quoted ibid.
6. Admiralty court martial, HMS *Bulwark*, November 1914, quoted ibid.
7. Troubridge papers, National Maritime Museum, Greenwich
8. Quoted in, *inter alia*, R. Hough, *The Great War at Sea* (OUP, 1983)
9. Quoted in, *inter alia*, Miller, *Superior Force*

Chapter 19

1. Hough, *The Great War at Sea*
2. *National Review* 1911
3. Richmond, Diary 19 January 1915
4. J. Winton, *Jellicoe* (Michael Joseph, 1981)
5. A. Cunningham, letter to his mother
6. H. Strachan, *The First World War*, volume 1 (OUP, 2003)
7. A. Lambert, *Admirals* (Faber and Faber, 2008)
8. Marder, *From Dreadnought to Scapa Flow*, volume 2
9. W. Churchill, *The World Crisis*, volume 1 (Thornton Butterworth, 1923)
10. Quoted in, *inter alia*, J. Hattendorf, 'Battenberg', in M. Murfett, *The First Sea Lords from Fisher to Mountbatten* (Praeger Publishers, 1995)

Chapter 20

1. Cradock, signal to Admiralty; The signals between Cradock and the Admiralty are found in, for example, Cabinet papers of 1914 'Admiralty telegrams relating to a concentration of HM ships under Rear Admiral Sir Christopher Cradock, 14 Sept–4 Nov'. The best organisation of them is in Bennett, *Coronel and the Falklands*.
2. *Naval Review* 1917
3. Admiralty signals
4. Churchill, *The World Crisis*
5. I. Nish, 'Admiral Jerram and the German Fleet' in *The Mariner's Mirror*, 1970
6. *Ibid.*
7. Quoted in Bennett, *Coronel and the Falklands*
8. Admiralty signals
9. Cradock to Admiralty
10. Cradock to Admiralty

Chapter 21

1. Bennett, *Coronel and the Falklands*
2. *Navy* Magazine 1917

3. Author's notes, *ipse dixit*
4. Allardyce MSS, SPRI
5. Oldys and Birch, *Miscellaneous Works of Walter Raleigh* (OUP, 1829)
6. H. Hickling, *Sailor at Sea* (Kimber, 1965)
7. Quoted in Bennett, *Coronel and the Falklands*
8. *Ibid.*

Chapter 22

1. Quoted in S. Ross, *Admiral Bridgeman* (Baily's, 1998)
2. *Ibid.*
3. Allardyce MS, SPRI
4. *Ibid.*
5. *Ibid.*
6. *Ibid.*
7. Davidson papers, Houses of Parliament Archives (HOPA) and widely quoted
8. Troubridge Court of Enquiry 1914
9. Quoted in, *inter alia*, Bennett, *Coronel and the Falklands*
10. Quoted in Hickling, *Sailor at Sea*
11. Marder (op. cit.) states that Kit left his medals etc. on Bermuda with Admiral Phipps Hornby. In this he follows P-H's son who wrote to the *Navy* magazine saying he believed this to be the case. I disagree, as we have Backhouse as a first-hand witness, Allardyce burying his papers at the same time, and Kit would never have put himself in a position where he would be inappropriately dressed for any formal occasion.
12. Davidson MSS, Houses of Parliament Archives (HOPA)
13. Hickling, *Sailor at Sea*

Chapter 23

1. C. Gould, *The Last Journey of the Good Hope* (unpublished), JG-B and also quoted in Ross, *Admiral Bridgeman*
2. Quoted in Hickling, *Sailor at Sea*
3. Cradock, signal to Admiralty

4. Quoted in Hickling, *Sailor at Sea*
5. Admiralty signal to Cradock
6. Hickling, *Sailor at Sea*; L. Hirst, *Coronel and After* (Peter Davies, 1934)
7. Quoted in Bennett, *Coronel and the Falklands*
8. Churchill, *The World Crisis*
9. Hickling, *Sailor at Sea*
10. Bennett, *Coronel and the Falklands*
11. Hickling, *Sailor at Sea*
12. Allardyce MS, SPRI
13. Admiralty signals
14. Churchill, *The World Crisis*
15. J. Gray, *Amerika Samoa*, USNI 1960
16. Gould, *Diary*
17. Quoted in Allardyce MS, SPRI
18. Admiralty signal
19. Quoted in Hickling, *Sailor at Sea*
20. Quoted in Hough, *The Great War at Sea*

Chapter 24

1. *Dictionary of National Biography*
2. P. Scott, *50 Years in the Navy* (Murray, 1919)
3. Lowis, *Fabulous Admirals*
4. National Archives, Kew, Cradock service record,

Chapter 25

1. Quoted in, *inter alia*, Bennett, *Naval Battles of the First World War*
2. Cabinet papers 1914
3. J. Spender, *Life of Lord Oxford and Asquith* (Hutchinson, 1932)
4. *Ibid.*
5. Davidson papers, HOPA
6. Churchill, *The World Crisis*
7. *South Pacific Mail*, 5 November 1914
8. Quoted in Hough, *The Great War at Sea*

9. JG-B
10. Cradock signal to Admiralty
11. Cradock signal to Admiralty
12. Admiralty signal to Cradock
13. Quoted in Ross, *Admiral Bridgeman*
14. Keyes, *Adventures Ashore and Afloat*
15. Quoted in Hickling, *Sailor at Sea*
16. *Dictionary of National Biography*

Chapter 26

1. Parish records at North Yorkshire County Records Office, Northallerton
2. See, *inter alia*, C. Bailey, *Black Diamonds* (Penguin, 2008)

Chapter 27

1. Churchill responded to Zetland's comments in a letter to *The Times* of 24 June. In it he implicitly accepts that Cradock did petition him regarding the quality of his ships but then disingenuously states that as he had entirely different ships at Coronel it was irrelevant. This is specious in the extreme. The majority of the 4th Cruiser Squadron when Cradock assumed command comprised county class cruisers of which *Monmouth* was the class leader – just the same ship with a different name. *Otranto* doesn't count and *Good Hope*, an admittedly larger and more heavily armed ship, was nonetheless of an older class and obsolete. Kit's squadron at Coronel was demonstrably worse than the 4th Cruiser Squadron and Churchill was obfuscating the issue!
2. *The Times*, 17 June 1916
3. *Ibid.*
4. JG-B, letter to Gwendoline
5. Letter from the Secretary to the author

Chapter 28

1. *Dundee Advertiser*, 10 April 1923
2. Churchill, *The World Crisis*
3. *Morning Post* and *Daily Telegraph*, 19 April 1923
4. JG-B, collection of press cuttings, April 1923, no mastheads for attribution
5. *Ibid.*
6. *Ibid.*
7. JG-B, Bridgeman and Gould letters
8. *Ibid.*
9. *Yorkshire Post*, 30 April 1923
10. *Morning Post*, 30 April 1923
11. JG-B, *Morning Post*, undated
12. *Ibid.*
13. JG-B, letter to Bridgeman, copied Gwendoline
14. JG-B, letter Carpenter to Gwendoline
15. *National Review*, April 1923

Chapter 29

1. JG-B, letters to and from Monty
2. *Ibid.*
3. JG-B, press cuttings
4. *Ibid.*

Chapter 31

1. Fisher letter to Jellicoe 19 January 1914
2. *Dictionary of National Biography*

Bibliography

These secondary sources were helpful in the writing of this book:

Annan N., *Our Age*, Weidenfeld and Nicolson, 1990.
Bailey, C., *Black Diamonds*, Penguin, 2008.
Bennett, G., *Coronel and the Falklands*, Batsford, 1962.
Bennett, G., *Naval Battles of the First World War*, Batsford, 1968.
Bulwer-Lytton E., *England and the English*, Routledge, 1876.
Churchill, W., *The World Crisis*, Volume I, Thornton Butterworth, 1923.
Cradock, C., *Whispers from the Fleet*, Gieve's, 1907.
Cunningham, A., *A Sailor's Odyssey*, Hutchinson, 1951.
Dundas, C., *An Admiral's Yarns*, Jenkins, 1922.
Fisher, J. A., *Memories*, Hodder and Stoughton, 1919.
Freeman, R., *The Great Edwardian Naval Feud*, Pen and Sword, 2009.
Fromkin, D., *Europe's Last Summer*, Heinemann, 2004.
Girouard, M., *The Return to Camelot*, Yale University Press, 1981.
Goodenough W., *A Rough Record*, Hutchinson, 1943.
Gordon, A., *The Rules of the Game*, John Murray, 1996.
Gray, J., *Amerika Samoa*, USNI, 1960.
Hammerton, J., *The Great War – I Was There!* Amalgamated Press, 1938.
Hattendorf, J., 'Battenberg', in Murfett, M., *The First Sea Lords from Fisher to Mountbatten*, Praeger Publishers, 1995.
Hickling, H., *Sailor at Sea*, Kimber, 1965.
Hirst, L., *Coronel and After*, Peter Davies, 1934.
Hill J., (ed.) *Oxford History of the Royal Navy*, OUP, 1998.
Hough, R., *Admirals in Collision*, Hamish Hamilton, 1959.
Hough, R., *The Great War at Sea*, OUP, 1983.
Jane, Fred T., *Jane's Fighting Ships of World War 1*, Jane's Publishing Company, 1919.

Keyes, R., *Adventures Ashore and Afloat*, Harrap, 1939.

Lambert, A., *Admirals,* Faber and Faber, 2008.

Lowis, G. L., *Fabulous Admirals*, Putnam, 1957.

MacCarthy, F., *William Morris*, Faber and Faber, 2010.

Machiavelli, N., *The Prince*, Antonio Blado d'Asola, 1532.

Marder, A. J., *From Dreadnought to Scapa Flow, Volume II*, OUP, 1965.

Massie, R. K., *Castles of Steel*, Jonathan Cape, 2004.

Massie, R. K., *Dreadnought,* Random House, 1991.

Miller, G., *Superior Force*, Hull University Press, 1996.

Nish, I. H., 'Admiral Jerram and the German Pacific Fleet' in *The Mariner's Mirror* Volume 56, Issue 4, 1970.

Penrose-Fitzgerald, C. C., *From Sail to Steam*, E. Arnold, 1922.

Ross, S., *Admiral Bridgeman*, Baily's, 1998.

Scott, P., *Fifty Years in the Royal Navy*, Murray, 1919.

Sibley D. J., *The Boxer Rebellion*, Hill and Wang, 2012.

Spender, J., *Life of Lord Oxford and Asquith*, Hutchinson, 1932.

Strachan, H, *The First World War, Volume I: To Arms*, OUP, 2003.

Sumida, J. T., *In Defence of Naval Supremacy*, Unwin Hyman, 1989.

Winton, J., *Jellicoe*, Michael Joseph, 1981.

Wragg, D., *Fisher*, History Press, 2009.

I have also found the following primary sources most useful in the writing of this book and acknowledge the help that their records have provided:

The British Library, London, Manuscripts section
North Yorkshire County Records Office, Northallerton
The National Archives, Kew
Parliamentary Archives (HOPA)
Royal Leamington Spa library
Scott Polar Research Institute, Cambridge (SPRI)

The following on-line resources have been helpful (beware, there is much factually incorrect material on-line):

Coronel.org.uk
Ancestry.com

BIBLIOGRAPHY

Wikipedia.com
Dreadnoughtproject.org.uk
Thepeerage.com
Falklands-museum.com

Index

Military ranks are only given where identification is necessary for people otherwise referred to only by surname.

239